INTERNATIONAL ENVIRONMENTAL LAW

IN A NUTSHELL

By

LAKSHMAN D. GURUSWAMY
Professor of Law
Director, National Energy–Environmental Law
and Policy Institute
University of Tulsa, College of Law

BRENT R. HENDRICKS
Visiting Professor of Law
Willamette University College of Law

ST. PAUL, MINN.
WEST PUBLISHING CO.
1997

Nutshell Series, In a Nutshell, the Nutshell Logo and the WP symbol are registered trademarks of West Publishing Co. Registered in the U.S. Patent and Trademark Office.

COPYRIGHT © 1997 By WEST GROUP
  610 Opperman Drive
  P.O. Box 64526
  St. Paul, MN 55164–0526
  1–800–328–9352

ISBN 0–314–21172–1

TEXT IS PRINTED ON 10% POST
CONSUMER RECYCLED PAPER

PREFACE

This Nutshell is a primer on International Environmental Law (IEL)[1] addressed to students, practitioners, teachers, law and policymakers, and inquirers who wish to obtain a functional, as distinct from a theoretical, introduction to the subject. It is also intended to be used by students of IEL in conjunction with other treatises and course books on the subject.

The book commences with an introduction to the relevant concepts of international law. We have assumed no prior knowledge of international law, but do not offer a primer on that subject. Instead, our approach to international law has the more modest objective of promoting a functional awareness and understanding of its more important and germane principles and rules. Our functional approach is noticeable, for example, in the abridged attention we give to the theoretical and doctrinal, as distinct from practical concepts, of international law relating to treaties and custom.

The core of the Nutshell attempts to distill the socio–scientific evidence confronting law-makers,

1. The page constraints of this book, and the changing legal character of the European Union (EU) as it evolves from an international organization into a confederation, restraints us from exploring the substantive corpus of EU environmental laws.

III

along with the resulting corpus of substantive IEL. The principles and rules of international law and the substantive law found in treaties and customary law have been amply addressed and covered by treatises. They have also been dealt with in the problem-oriented course book GURUSWAMY, PALMER & WESTON, INTERNATIONAL ENVIRONMENTAL LAW AND WORLD ORDER (West 1994) in which we have been involved. Unfortunately, the need to recognize and grasp the socio-scientific context of environmental problems has not received the same attention. We have tried to remedy this shortcoming and have provided a more extensive review of relevant socio-scientific findings, and their causal importance to substantive law.

The *raison d'etre* for the creation and development of IEL is the need for a new and identifiable corpus of law that addresses the phenomena of environmental degradation in a way that existing laws are unable to do. In responding to this challenge, negotiators and law-makers in all major treaties have adopted an integrated approach, which assimilates and incorporates the findings of physical, natural, social, and political scientists within an interdisciplinary framework. In contrast, a review of much contemporary theoretical and academic writing addressing the global environment quickly reveals the extent to which different disciplines still remain fragmented in their outlook. Whether emanating from the physical, natural, social or political sciences, or law, the tendency is for writers to address those within their own disciplines. The result is a fractured outlook that contributes little toward the making or implementation of IEL.

In particular, students and practitioners in whose hands the future of IEL lies need to appreciate the interdisciplinary framework of IEL for two connected reasons. The first is pedagogic. An interdisciplinary perspective facilitates a richer appreciation of IEL because it reflects reality rather than an artificially separated legal segment. The second is professional. International environmental lawyers in their law-making or law-applying roles act as the gate keepers of international society, who are constantly confronted with competing theories, ideas, and conclusions that clamor for admission into the law. Lawyers engaged in real life law-making or interpretation do not have the luxury of ignoring the science or the politics surrounding them. They are compelled to make hard decisions about concepts and ideas, and an early introduction to the socio-scientific context equips them to better understand the tasks they will confront.

Our Nutshell attempts to provide such an introduction. We hope it offers those venturing into IEL an enhanced comprehension of this new and diverse field. We also hope, as together we face these challenges, to motivate our readers into approaching

the daunting problems of our global environment
with vision and resolve.

ACKNOWLEDGMENTS

We are deeply indebted to the indefatigable Jason Aamodt, Research Fellow, NELPI, who skillfully accomplished the myriad research, editorial, and computer tasks thrown at him with characteristic grace and charm. We could not have completed this book without his invaluable assistance. We are also indebted to a number of research assistants who in their various ways made willing and significant contributions to this book. They include Kelly Hunter, Anastasia Gogol, Deanna Scott, Connie Page, Mark Whalen, Jason Coatney, and Debra Staudinger. We would like to make special mention of Nancy Von Seggern whose skill, enthusiasm, and unyielding commitment to hard work were outstanding. Sue Lorenz the ever willing Administrative Assistant at NELPI has willingly and cheerfully attended to a host of chores with aptitude, efficiency, and skill. The eclectic and multidisciplinary nature of the readings required special library expertise and this book would not have been possible without the help of the library staff of the Law Library at Tulsa.

We are most grateful to our generous colleagues John Mark Stensvaag, Roy Gardner, Jim Thomas, Bill Hollingsworth, David Caron, Dennis Bires and Bill Rice who despite their strenuous schedules,

ACKNOWLEDGMENTS

found time to read and comment on different parts of this book. We truly appreciate their collegiality and help. Finally, we would like to thank Marty Belsky, Dean of the University of Tulsa College of Law for his enthusiastic support.

OUTLINE

IX

PART II. INTERNATIONAL ENVIRON-
MENTAL PROBLEMS

A. GLOBAL

*

TABLE OF TREATIES

References are to Pages

XXIII

TABLE OF TREATIES

TABLE OF TREATIES

TABLE OF JUDICIAL AND ARBITRAL DECISIONS

References are to Pages

TABLE OF JUDICIAL AND ARBITRAL DECISIONS

INTERNATIONAL ENVIRONMENTAL LAW

IN A NUTSHELL

*

PART I

ANATOMY OF INTERNATIONAL ENVIRONMENTAL LAW

CHAPTER ONE

INTRODUCTION

International Environmental Law (IEL) bears a name that reflects its content. At its substantive core, IEL endeavors to control pollution and the depletion of natural resources within a framework of sustainable development. Although the presence of both "international" and "environmental" in its name suggests parity between national and international laws, IEL is formally a branch of public international law—a body of law created by nation states for nation states, to govern problems that arise between nation states.

IEL possesses some features that distinguish it from traditional international law. First, its creation, and vigorous if uneven growth, owe much to national environmental laws and policies. Nation states frequently have entered into landmark international agreements and practices, driven largely by the momentum of law, regulation, and policies applicable to their own environmental problems, and not necessarily because of the gravity of international problems. Second, the law-making in IEL has been shaped primarily by bio-physical not geo-political forces, and this communal foundation has at times sheltered it from disfiguring political dissension found in other areas of international law. These two factors have inevitably, albeit asymmetrically, infused the objectives of national environmental regulatory laws, and the conceptual frameworks of environmental sciences, into the corpus of IEL.

In the result, IEL, while remaining a division or tributary of international law, possesses its own characteristics and attributes arising as much from its relatively communal subject matter—the environment—as well as the greater influence of domestic law. It is a measure of IEL's stature and recognition that it sits shoulder to shoulder, if uncomfortably, with other principles of public international law developed over the last 50 years, including those controlling the use of force, self-determination, permanent sovereignty over natural resources, and human rights. The present is often illuminated by the past, and landmark developments of IEL from 1972 form a historical continuum that help us better understand the strengths and weaknesses of the subject. We examine these landmarks.

A. THE STOCKHOLM CONFERENCE ON THE HUMAN ENVIRONMENT

The 1972 Stockholm Conference on the Human Environment, (Stockholm Conference), may well have been the chrysalis from which international environmental law emerged as a legal subject in its own right, and it is helpful to recall what was achieved at that great international gathering. Up to about the time of the Stockholm Conference, international environmental problems had been dealt with in a sporadic and ad hoc manner resulting in a few significant treaties. These treaties were isolated events that did not constitute a recognizable corpus of international environmental law. The development of IEL leading into the Stockholm Conference was influenced by the thinking, ideology, and culture of concern about the environment experienced the world over.

The themes articulated in Rachel Carson's book, SILENT SPRING (1962), Barry Commoner's book, THE CLOSING CIRCLE (1971), and Kenneth Boulding's *Spaceship Earth*, [*see generally, The Economics of the Coming Spaceship Earth, in* ENVIRONMENTAL QUALITY IN A GROWING ECONOMY 3 (1966)] resonated from the United States into the thinking of other industrial nations. Many of these themes, and then some, were melded and expressed with crusading cogency within an international context in LIMITS TO GROWTH [MEADOWS, ET AL. (1972)], a computer modeled study sponsored by the Club of Rome, a private group of industrialists and world leaders. The Meadows project team painted an apocalyptic picture of the growth of population, pollution, and exhaustion of natural resources leading to a break down of the carrying capacity of the earth. This book, along with many other phenomena such as acid rain and the poisoning of Japanese fisherman in Minimata bay, led to a realization of the frailty of the planet earth and created a ferment of apprehension among a cross section of common people, influential elites and decision-makers in the developed industrial world.

In the face of these concerns, the United Nations was moved to convene a special international environmental conference to discuss the human environment in 1972, and Sweden, which had begun to experience transboundary acid rain, volunteered to host it in Stockholm. The overall sense of crisis crying out for global action was brilliantly captured in the book by Rene Dubos and Barbara Ward, specially commissioned for the Stockholm Conference. [See generally ONLY ONE EARTH: THE CARE AND MAINTENANCE OF A SMALL PLANET (1972)].

While concern about the environment motivated many rich, developed industrial countries (DCs), the poor, less developed countries (LDCs) did not share the view that environmental degradation was the biggest threat facing the planet. For the LDCs, poverty and the alleviation of misery remained a more poignant and real problem. Also, in the preparatory meetings leading to Stockholm, the LDCs— who called themselves the Group of 77 (their original number)—sharply and forcefully articulated the view that the worst pollution was caused by poverty. LDCs believed that greater development leading to material prosperity far outweighed any damage caused by resource use and pollution. They were particularly scornful of the argument that DCs were genuinely trying to steer them away from pitfalls into which the DCs themselves had fallen. LDCs expressed resentment over the fact that the DCs— whose drive toward wealth had consumed a great part of the earth's resources and had led to devastating pollution—were now asking the LDCs to remain poor and, more gallingly, to pay for the clean up, restoration, and conservation of the earth. Many LDCs feared, moreover, that new environmental standards adopted by DCs would effectively bar the entry of their goods into DC markets.

This ideological impasse presented a formidable challenge to international environmental diplomacy and the question was resolved, as best it might, by way of a compromise. The compromise worked out in a meeting at Founex, near Geneva, Switzerland, held that economic development was not necessarily incompatible with environmental protection, and that development could proceed, provided it avoided damaging the environment. The essence of the understanding was summed up in the Preamble to the Stockholm Declaration of the United Nations Conference on the Environment (Stockholm Declaration), June 16, 1972, 11 I.L.M. 1416. It stated that "[m]ost of the environmental problems of LDCs are caused by under-development" and that LDCs must direct their efforts to development with due regard to the priority to safeguard and improve the environment [*id*. § I, ¶ 4]. Similarly, the industrialized countries were exhorted to make efforts to reduce the gap between themselves and the developing countries. In sum, the LDCs successfully thwarted environmental laws and policies from damaging their efforts to develop and grow economically, whether by industrial progress or trade. They did not, however, obtain substantial bankrolling or pledges to protect the global environment, nor did they meaningfully advance the doctrine of "common but differentiated responsibility" [*See* Chapter Six, Global Climate Change] later accepted at the 1992 Earth Summit [The United Nations Conference on Environment and Development (UNCED), Rio de Janeiro, Brazil].

The Stockholm Conference, under the direction of its dynamic Secretary–General, Maurice Strong, is regarded as perhaps the best documented, best organized United Nations conference of its time. For a number of reasons, it may also be considered the cocoon of IEL. First, the biosphere, or the planet, was identified as an object, and placed on the agenda of national and international policy and law in a way that had never been done before. Second, the conference was widely attended with 114 of the then 131 UN members participating in it. The Soviet bloc abstained from attending, not because it rejected the purpose or mission of the conference, but because of the status accorded to East Germany. Third, the Stockholm Conference resulted in the creation of the United Nations Environment Program (UNEP), (more fully described in Appendix A) the first international organization with an exclusively environmental mandate. UNEP has been instrumental in drafting, facilitating and negotiating a number of environmental treaties. Fourth, it produced a conference declaration of twenty-six principles (Stockholm Declaration) that dealt with the rights and obligations of citizens and governments with regard to the preservation and improvement of the environment. Apart from the Stockholm Declaration, which is generally considered an instrument of IEL in that it either crystallized or generated customary law, the Stockholm Conference also created an action plan containing recommendations for future implementation.

A number of specific principles of the Stockholm Declaration bear mention. Principles 1, 2, and 5, dealing with responsibilities to future generations, were undergirded by an obligation to conserve. Principle 1, albeit counterbalanced by Principle 11, recognized a nascent right to a quality environment. Principle 21 referred to the right of a state to exploit its resources pursuant to their environmental (*not* developmental) policies, and affirmed the obligation not to cause transboundary injury. This was followed by Principle 22, positing that states shall cooperate to develop international law regarding liability and compensation for extra-territorial harm. These Principles have been re-institutionalized in many post-Stockholm agreements. For example, Principle 21 has been incorporated in a wide range of treaties including the Convention on Biological Diversity (Biodiversity Convention), June 5,

1992, 31 I.L.M. 818 (entered into force Dec. 29, 1993), the Vienna Convention for the Protection of the Ozone Layer (Vienna Ozone Convention), Mar. 22, 1985. 26 I.L.M. 1529 (entered into force Sept. 22, 1988), the Convention on Long–Range Transboundary Air Pollution (LRTAP), Nov. 13, 1979, 18 I.L.M. 1442 (entered into force Mar. 16, 1983), and the United Nations Convention on the Law of the Sea (UNCLOS), Dec. 20, 1982, 21 I.L.M. 1261 (entered into force Nov. 16, 1994). Furthermore, the post-Stockholm world has spawned a prolific number of environmental treaties. Over 100 post-Stockholm treaties mirror almost every concern that has been the subject of national laws or regulations including acid rain, hazardous waste, ozone depletion, sea pollution from land and vessels, toxics, resource conservation, and global warming.

B. UNITED NATIONS CONVENTION ON THE LAW OF THE SEA (UNCLOS)

Even before Stockholm, negotiations had commenced concerning the law of the sea and lasted until 1982 when UNCLOS was opened for signature. It finally came into force on November 16, 1994. It is the strongest comprehensive environmental treaty now in existence or likely to emerge for quite some time [Letter of Submittal of the Secretary of State to the President of the United States, 7 Geo. Int'l Envt'l L. Rev. 77 (1994)]. It is in fact a constitution for the oceans, and the character and reach of its 59 provisions obligating environmental protection and conservation, out of 320 provisions in all, possess a fundamental and overarching character. It can be asserted that UNCLOS functions not only as a treaty, but a codification and articulation of the rules applicable to oceans, expressing IEL binding on both signatories and nonsignatories [Jonathan I. Charney, *Entry Into Force of the 1982 Convention on the Law of the Sea,* 35 VA. J. INT'L. L. 381 (1995); LOUIS SOHN & KRISTEN GUSTAFSON, THE LAW OF THE SEA IN A NUTSHELL (1984).

It is worth remembering in this context that the oceans occupy over seventy percent of the landmass of the earth, and are in many ways a proxy for the global environment. Most pollution is deposited into the oceans through direct and indirect pathways, and the control of land-based pollution is clearly directed at environmental controls on land dealing with air, land, and water pollution. Notable areas of oceanic governance such as conservation of wetlands, coastal areas, and biodiversity are of critical significance to international environmental protection in general.

UNCLOS contains at least fifty-nine environmental provisions, ranging from the global to the specific, spread out over several parts of the text including the Territorial Sea and Contiguous Zone (Part II), Exclusive Economic Zone (Part V), High Seas (Part VII), Enclosed or Semi–Enclosed Areas (Part IX), The Area (Part XI), Protection and Preservation of the Marine Environment (Part XII), and Marine Scientific Research (Part XIII). They deal with the conservation and management of living resources, pollution prevention, reduction and control, vessel pollution, and environmental management.

One of the dominant characteristics of UNCLOS is that it is an umbrella convention that brings other international rules, regulations, and implementing bodies within its canopy. At the substantive level of obligation and implementation, many of its provisions are of a constitutional or general character that call to be augmented and supplemented by specific regulations, rules, and implementing procedures formulated by other international agreements and nation states.

C. WORLD COMMISSION ON ENVIRONMENT AND DEVELOPMENT

Despite the uneasy truce at Founex reflected in the Stockholm Declaration, the persistent clash of two cultures, environmental protection *vs.* development, continued to obstruct the progress of IEL. In order to resolve this problem, the World Commission on Environment and Development (WCED or Brundtland Commission) was constituted by the General Assembly of the UN in 1983 and charged with proposing long-term environmental strategies for *sustainable development*. That elusive term was not defined by the UN, and despite the efforts of the Brundtland Commission and the Earth Summit, still eludes satisfactory definition. After four years of deliberation and worldwide consultation, the Brundtland Report, *Our Common Future,* articulated the paradigm on which the Earth Summit, and indeed IEL, has since been based. In essence, it rejected the despairing thesis that environmental problems were past repair, spiraling out of control, and could only be averted by arresting development and economic growth: a policy of no growth. Instead, it argued that economic growth was both desirable and possible within a context of sustainable development [WORLD COMM'N ON ENVIRONMENTAL DEVELOPMENT, OUR COMMON FUTURE (1987)].

Although sustainable development was not clearly defined, some of its key attributes are identifiable. It calls for developmental policies and for economic growth that can relieve the great poverty of the LDCs, while protecting the environment. Such development and growth should be based on policies that sustain and expand the environmental resource base in a manner that meets the needs of the present generation without compromising the ability of future generations to meet their own needs. In order to draw up a global plan for sustainable development, the Brundtland Commission called for an international conference to act as the successor to the Stockholm Conference, and carry forward its legacy.

The UN General Assembly did so, and directed the United Nations Conference on Environment and Development (UNCED or Earth Summit) to take account, *inter alia*, of the Stockholm Declaration and further develop IEL. An ambitious agenda was drawn up for the Earth Summit that included the following three endeavors: 1) an Earth Charter that would be the successor to the Stockholm Declaration; 2) an action plan for the planet called Agenda 21; and 3) the ceremonial signing of two conventions on biodiversity and climate change.

D. UNITED NATIONS CONFERENCE ON ENVIRONMENT AND DEVELOPMENT (UNCED)

The Earth Summit, by which name the UNCED is popularly called, was held in Rio de Janeiro in June, 1992, and attended by over 180 countries and 100 heads of state. It has been heralded as the greatest summit level conference in history. It led to these four institutional results: 1) the *Rio Declaration on Environment and Development* (Rio Declaration); June 13, 1992, 31 I.L.M. 874; 2) *Agenda 21*, U.N. Doc. A/CONF. 151/26 (1992); 3) the *Nonlegally Binding Authoritative Statement of Principles for a Global Consensus on the Management, Conservation and Sustainable Development of All Types of Forests*, U.N. Doc. A/CONF. 151/26, v.3 (1992); and 4) the ceremonial signing of the Climate Change and Biodiversity Conventions.

Initial Earth Summit assessments were for differing reasons generally favorable, while a few were almost unreservedly laudatory, even euphoric. Later, more considered evaluations have begun to cast doubts on these reviews. We do not offer a studied and documented appraisal of that event. Instead, we do very briefly advance some conclusions adverted to in the course of the book.

In our view, the legal results of the Earth Summit were, at best, mottled. Rio undoubtedly offered a great platform for environmental protection, but its contribution to IEL was more apparent than real. While it did draw universal attention to environmental protection and raised many issues onto the global agenda, the legacy of Rio—apart from the Climate Change Convention—remains unimpressive. To begin, the "Rio Declaration on Environment and Development" (Rio Declaration) replaced the intended "Earth Charter," with the former diminishing the environmental resonance of the latter. Second, the tone of the Rio Declaration sets a dubious foundation for IEL and effectively turned the clock back from the Stockholm Convention.

For example, the nascent right to a wholesome environment embodied in the Stockholm Declaration is abandoned in favor of a right to development (Principle 2). Also, the obligation not to cause transfrontier damage contained in Principle 21 of the Stockholm Declaration is weakened in Principle 2 of the Rio Declaration by the addition of crucial language authorizing states "to exploit their own natural resources pursuant to their own environmental and *developmental* policies" (emphasis added). Following a similar theme, the obligation to *conserve* implied by the duty to protect the environment for the benefit of future generations found in the Stockholm Declaration is replaced in the Rio Declaration by a right to *consume* or develop. The Rio

formulation refers to "developmental and environmental needs of present and future generations"
(Principle 3). Disappointingly, this re-formulation
impliedly negates or weakens the obligation to conserve expressed in the Stockholm Declaration. Finally, the Rio Declaration frowns upon action such
as that taken by the United States under the Marine Mammal Protection Act of 1972 [16 U.S.C.A.
§§ 1361–1421 (1994)] to prevent the slaughter of
dolphins by prohibiting imports of tuna caught in
dolphin killing nets. Principle 12 of the Rio Declaration states that "unilateral actions to deal with
environmental challenges outside the jurisdiction of
the importing country should be avoided." While
the substantive shortcomings of the Rio Declaration
do not necessarily restrict the further development
of IEL, the ramifications of the Rio Declaration
need to be addressed and are referred to in Chapter
18.

Major international conferences are epochal
events that shape and sometimes re-direct the living international law of the environment. They
offer an eagle's view of the landscape and frontiers
of IEL. It is to a closer examination of the various
segments of IEL that we now turn.

CHAPTER TWO

SOURCES AND FORMS OF IN-TERNATIONAL ENVIRON-MENTAL LAW

Whether casting a gentle glance or a hard look at IEL, it is difficult to avoid its substantive corpus and powerful presence, or the vigor and fast rate of its expansion. It already has spawned over 300 international agreements and treaties and a host of declarations and UN General Assembly resolutions, some of which express "soft" IEL, while others articulate and re-state existing rules of customary law. Moreover, it boasts a small but growing body of judicial decisions (case law) and general principles of law. A look at the substantial documents supplements to various course books and treatises offers ample evidence of the growing corpus of IEL. *See*, for example, LAKSHMAN GURUSWAMY, ET AL., SUPPLEMENT OF BASIC DOCUMENTS TO INTERNATIONAL ENVIRONMENTAL LAW AND WORLD ORDER (West 1994); BIRNIE AND A. E. BOYLE, BASIC DOCUMENTS ON INTERNATIONAL LAW AND THE ENVIRONMENT (1995); PHILLIPPE SANDS, PRINCIPLES OF INTERNATIONAL ENVIRONMENTAL LAW, V IIA & IIB (1995).

Treaties, customary law, general principles of law and judicial decisions are usually referred to as sources of law. Article 38(1) of the Statute of the International Court of Justice (Statute of the ICJ) confirms that "The Court ... shall apply:

a.   international conventions ...;

b.   international custom, as evidence of a general practice accepted as law;

c.   the general principles of law recognized by civilized nations;

d.   ... judicial decisions and the teachings of the most highly qualified publicists of the various nations, as subsidiary means for the determination of rules of law."

While these are sources of law in one sense, they are also differing forms in which IEL is expressed or cast. For example, the written form of a treaty authoritatively reflects what is agreed upon by its parties. A treaty may, therefore, be considered a source of law because we go to it to find out what the law is. At the same time it is a particular kind of written form, among others, adopted by IEL. Customary law assumes a different form, though it also is a source of law. The form taken by it is usually not a written one; instead, it consists of unwritten, uncodified custom that is established by evidence of practice and *opinio juris*. Even where custom is codified or reduced to writing, for example, by the International Law Commission, there may be doubts as to whether such a restatement is an accurate reflection of customary law. Likewise, as we shall see, general principles of law and judicial decisions are both sources and forms of IEL.

A. TREATIES

While we have just referred to four major sources and forms of IEL, substantive IEL overwhelmingly consists of principles and rules creating preventive, precautionary or remedial norms embodied in treaties. Treaties are written agreements governed by international law, entered into between two or more states, creating or restating legal rights and duties. Treaties are also described as conventions, protocols, covenants, pacts, etc. A question that needs to be answered before we commence our summary of the sources and forms of law is: Why are treaties the primary source of IEL?

The preeminence of treaties is largely attributable to the nature of environmental problems. These problems range over a wide spectrum of factual situations. Moreover, they demand continuous observation and monitoring, as well as quick legal action and implementation in response to ongoing and relatively rapid changes in scientific knowledge and conclusions. The socio-scientific context calls for a substantive IEL that is able to deal with wide and varied kinds of investigations, scientific monitoring, assessments, and findings. The law should be capable of responding to complex international environmental problems with a mix of generality, specificity, and adaptability. None of the four sources of IEL can fulfil all these requirements, although treaties are best able to satisfy at least some of them in a way that other sources are unable to do.

For example, customary law, as we shall see, is made up of state practice and *opinio juris* that usually takes time to crystallize, one issue at time, and is carefully restricted to the specific facts. General principles of law will take even longer to identify and ascertain. Even where customary rules or general principles are clear, these sources do not provide mechanisms for inducing compliance or considering infractions. Treaties, on the other hand, offer a superior framework for dealing with environmental issues. They allow for targeted laws, flexibility of law-making, machinery for inducing compliance, and non-compliance and dispute resolution mechanisms—all of which can be tailored to the problems at hand. Finally, the fact that treaties are authoritatively reduced to writing, and are therefore more accessible and applicable assumes great importance when approaching a subject that requires clarity and certainty of legal response.

The Vienna Convention on the Law of Treaties, May 23, 1969, 1155 U.N.T.S. 331 (1988) deals comprehensively with a number of complex questions about treaties. Of these, we refer only to those of particular importance to IEL. The first concerns the entry into force of a treaty, or the date on which it officially binds the parties. Even though signed, a multilateral treaty typically does not enter into force until it has been ratified, and the deposits of such ratifications reach a minimum number stipulated in the treaty. For example, the Convention on Biological Diversity (Biodiversity Convention), June 5, 1992, 31 I.L.M. 818 (1993) (*see* Chapter Five) requires 30 ratifications [art. 36], and the United Nations Framework Convention on Climate Change (Climate Change Convention), Dec. 31, 1992, 31 I.L.M. 849 (1994) (*see* Chapter Six) requires 50 ratifications [art. 23].

A party to a treaty may enter reservations to the extent that they are not prohibited, and recent environmental conventions such as the Montreal Protocol on Substances that Deplete the Ozone Layer (Montreal Protocol), Sept. 16, 1987, 27 I.L.M. 1550, (1989) (*see* Chapter Seven) the Biodiversity Convention and the Climate Change Convention disallow reservations. Parties have attempted to get around this by making "interpretive declarations" such as those entered by Fiji, Kiribati, Nauru, and Tuvalu to the Climate Change Convention, and those made by the United Kingdom to the Biodiversity Convention, but their legal effect is undetermined.

Treaties may be amended where allowed by their provisions, but an amendment generally will not enter into force unless ratified or accepted by all the parties. This formal, very demanding amendment procedure has proved to be anachronistic, preventing existing treaty regimes from keeping abreast of new developments and technologies or incorporating new and essential scientific findings. In order to overcome this deficiency, a number of environmental treaties are tiered into two or three parts consisting of: 1) a"framework treaty" which usually functions as a constituent instrument containing general principles; 2) "protocols" that supplement or implement the framework treaty; and 3) technical and scientific "annexes" containing details that may need quick alteration according to changing needs. The Vienna Convention for the Protection of the Ozone Layer, for example, has a number of innovative procedures relating to the amendments of its protocols [art. 9] and annexes [art. 10] that do not require unanimous approval.

1. INTERPRETATION OF TREATIES

Not unlike other areas of international law, many principles of IEL embodied in treaties are vague and nebulous for a number of reasons. Among the more important of these reasons is that treaties are drafted, not by gods, but by humans who are unable to anticipate and provide for every factual or legal contingency that might arise in the future. To meet unforeseen contingencies, resort is made to abstractions and concepts of wide scope which almost by definition lack specificity and exactitude, and require interpretation before they can be applied to the facts of a case. When an unpredicted case arises, the extent to which it might be covered by existing provisions through interpretation gives rise to contention.

In addition, there is a tendency for drafting conferences to resort to aspirational and hortatory expression when they cannot agree upon specific obligations. Furthermore, and conversely, when parties to a treaty want to move beyond the aspirational to the obligatory, but are unable to agree on the formulation of such an obligation, they sometimes leave it to be resolved by interpretation on a later occasion.

Treaties are replete with a variety of formulations that do not amount to obligations of effect. These include: aspirational norms; general norms containing inchoate and open-textured obligations; and formulations of rules or principles that codify contentious or competing rules. Illustrations of aspirational and inchoate obligations abound in recent treaties. For example, according to the Climate Change Convention, parties, according to their "common but differentiated responsibilities" (not defined), shall take climate change considerations into account "to the extent feasible" [art. 4(1)(f)]. The Biodiversity Convention is choked by obligations of aspiration, such as "as far as possible and as appropriate," [arts. 5,6,7] and in accordance with a party's "particular conditions and capabilities" [art. 6]. The Basel Convention on the Control of Transboundary Movements of Hazardous Wastes and their Disposal (Basel Convention), March 22, 1989, 28 I.L.M. 657 (1992) (*see* Chapter Nine) requires each party to take "appropriate measures" to minimize the generation of hazardous wastes [art. 4(2)(a)] and also requires that parties manage wastes in an "environmentally sound" manner [art. 4(2)(d)]. The Protocol to the 1979 Convention on Long–Range Transboundary Air Pollution Concerning the Emissions of Nitrogen Oxides or their Transboundary Fluxes, Oct. 31, 1988, 22 I.L.M. 212 (1991) (*see* Chapter Fourteen) requires parties to "act as soon as possible" in article 2(1) and "without undue delay" in article 7.

While the previous citations serve as examples of aspirational norms and inchoate and open-textured obligations, other provisions embody general duties and competing norms that remain undefined, thus creating difficulties of interpretation. A possible conflict in the way general duties and competing norms are resolved may be found in the Biodiversity Convention and UNCLOS. The Biodiversity Convention (*see* Chapter Five) strikes a balance between sovereign rights over natural resources and the duty not to cause transboundary damage in art. 3, but does so somewhat differently to the way the same balance is expressed in article 192 of UNCLOS (*see* Chapter Thirteen). Such a divergence obviously creates interpretive problems in arriving at the general obligation and in reconciling the conflicting norm between respective treaties.

Two interconnected questions concerning treaty interpretation require further attention: (1) Who is empowered to interpret a treaty and (2) how or according to what rules is the law interpreted? Interpretation in IEL operates in a manner similar to national legal systems in which the interpretive task is undertaken by courts and judicial tribunals, as well as administrative agencies charged with implementing the statute in question.

International courts include the International Court of Justice, but the ICJ depends on the acquiescence of the parties for its jurisdiction [Statute of the International Court of Justice, art. 36, June 29, 1945, 59 Stat. 1031 (entered into force Oct. 24, 1945)]. Judicial or arbitral tribunals created by treaties such as UNCLOS or the Climate Change Convention are also empowered to interpret the law. Interpretation may further be rendered by the declarations of Diplomatic Conferences such as the 1972 Stockholm Conference on the Human Environment, the 1992 United Nations Conference on Environment and Development (UNCED), and the General Assembly of the United Nations. Increasingly, interpretation is made by the institutions created by environmental treaties such as the permanent annual conferences of international regimes or even expert organizations, such as those mentioned below.

The Vienna Convention outlines basic rules of treaty interpretation. Article 31 stipulates that a treaty shall be interpreted in good faith in accordance with the ordinary meaning to be given to the terms of a treaty in their context and in the light of its object and purpose. Article 32 allows for supplementary means of interpretation where interpretation according to article 31 leaves the meaning ambiguous or obscure, or leads to a result that is manifestly absurd or unreasonable. While these appear to be reasonably objective rules, they are not self-executing and need to be applied by an interpreter. The process of applying the rules creates an unavoidably subjective human element and can result in demonstrable differences of opinion.

For example, the ICJ in a recent decision [Legality of the use by a State of Nuclear Weapons in Armed Conflict, 1996 I.C.J. 93 (July 8)] denied the World Health Organization (WHO) standing to request an Advisory Opinion on the legality of the threat or use of nuclear weapons. The majority decision of the Court was based on a very narrow and restricted interpretation of the mandate of the WHO, and is dealt with more fully in Chapter Seventeen. On the other hand, as we see below, the Meeting of the Parties under the Montreal Protocol interpreted some of its provisions in an expansive and even non-textual fashion.

2. CONFLICT WITH OTHER TREATIES

Like the body politic of civic society within nation states, the international community is also subject to interest group politics and commits itself through treaties to a variety of competing objectives and goals which are not integrated or even harmonized, and do not operate in unison. The clash of goals and objectives is vividly illustrated by the conflict between environmental protection and free trade (*see* Chapter Eighteen). For instance, a number of environmental treaties such as the Montreal Protocol, the Basel Convention, and the Convention on International Trade in Endangered Species and Wild Fauna and Flora (CITES), Mar. 3, 1973, 993 U.N.T.S. 243 (1975) (*see* Chapter Five) mandate trade restrictions to achieve their environmental goals. It is arguable that many of these trade restrictions could be justified under UNCLOS. Such trade restrictions, however, conflict with the GATT/WTO regime that was restructured in 1994.

The Vienna Convention [art. 30] provides some guidance on how to interpret conflicting treaties dealing with the same "subject-matter." It focuses first on treaties that deal with the same parties and second on treaties which do not deal with the same parties. Where the parties to both treaties are common there are two rules: 1) a treaty that is later in time prevails; however, 2) where a treaty either states that it is subject to, or not incompatible with another treaty, that other treaty prevails. Where there is a conflict between a treaty to which both states are parties and another to which only one state is a party, the treaty to which both are parties will prevail [art. 30(4)(b)].

With regard to the Montreal Protocol, CITES and the Basel Convention, the last in time rule appears to give precedence to GATT/WTO which was adopted more recently, but in the event of a GATT/WTO *vs.* UNCLOS clash, the advantage swings to UNCLOS as it came into force even later, Nov. 16, 1994. A number of questions remain to be answered. For example, does the Basel Convention deal with the same subject matter as the GATT/WTO? If not, will the rule in Vienna Convention article 30(4)(b) apply? Can it be argued that the Basel Convention deals with a specialized area and must obtain precedence over a more general treaty dealing with trade in the round? What if an environmental treaty were to say that its provisions will take priority over other treaties covering the same subject matter? Although one might be tempted to answer these questions in favor of the Basel Convention, there are as yet no conclusive answers to such problems.

B. CUSTOM

Customary law, or custom, refers largely to unwritten law inferred from the conduct of states (*practice*) undertaken in the belief that they were bound to do so by law (*opinio juris*). In the words of the Statute of the ICJ, custom is "evidence of a general practice accepted as law" [art. 38(1)(b)]. Customary international law, therefore, is created by the fusion of an objective element, *practice,* and a subjective element, *opinio juris.*

Practice (the objective element) in IEL takes a number of forms and the evidence necessary to establish it may be gathered, *inter alia,* from the following materials: 1) national legislation; 2) diplomatic notes; 3) statements and votes by governments in international organizations and forums of varying kinds; 4) ratification of treaties containing the obligations in question; 5) opinions of legal advisers; and 6) restatements of the law by scholars and jurists like the International Law Commission. Evidence gathered from these sources will testify to what states actually do, and how they react when faced with a particular problem. Suppose it is asserted that customary law establishes the right to take countermeasures in respect of an environmentally wrongful act, the evidence must prove that nations have resorted to such countermeasures following a pattern of conduct that is consistent, extensive, uniform, and general.

The next question is whether the practice of states was undertaken in the belief that what they were doing was compelled or mandated by law (the subjective element). If a practice is regarded as discretionary, or simply convenient or self-serving rather than obligatory, it is an example of usage that does not possess the critical element of *opinio juris*. In modern times, the *opinio juris* of states has been gathered from their declarations or admissions in international forums like the International Law Commission and the General Assembly of the UN, in addition to the other more traditional sources listed above.

The unwritten, uncodified form of custom is one of its chief weaknesses, and one way to remedy this shortcoming is to codify or restate customary law— thus making it known and accessible. Restatements of customary law are undertaken by the International Law Commission, other scholars and jurists, courts, legal tribunals, conference declarations, and by treaties. A restatement or codification by scholars and jurists serves the important purpose of reducing the law's uncertainty, but leaves open the extent to which it is accepted as accurate. Questions may arise as to whether the codification of a particular rule is a faithful and true reflection of the customary law, and as to the degree of consensus surrounding its codification. Such doubts weaken the authority of any restatement of customary law.

If the codification occurs during a law-making conference, it may take the form of a draft treaty which if accepted becomes binding as a treaty. As we have noted (Chapter One, Introduction) it is possible to assert that the 15–year process of negotiating UNCLOS led to the crystallization of customary IEL, and that Part XII, relating to the protection of the marine environment is a codification of existing customary rules of law. In such a situation a written form (the text of a treaty) expresses both treaty and custom, and the text of UNCLOS assumes a dual jural status. It is activated as a treaty when signed and ratified, but it possesses the authority of customary law only if it is accepted as law by the community of nations. Important duties under customary IEL have been codified or restated in treaties and conference declarations as "principles" rather than "rules." In ordinary legal analysis, rules typically embody standards that are definitively applied to a specifically described state of affairs, and the application of such a rule frequently determines a particular controversy. Principles on the other hand are more abstract general norms from which specific rules or standards are derived, and embody reasons that argue for moving in a particular direction, rather than arriving at a specified result. Consequently, principles—unlike rules—do not themselves postulate obligations of result. Instead, principles are the foundations upon which rules incorporating obligations of result are built. One principle may be offset by another, and principles may therefore be seen as only one among a number of considerations to be taken into account in reaching a decision [RONALD DWORKIN, TAKING RIGHTS SERIOUSLY 24–26 (1978)].

While many principles and rules have been espoused, only a few have been accepted into the corpus of customary IEL. The biggest impediment to the formation of customary law lies in the element of generality which requires that the practice be widespread among at least a majority of states. This is difficult to establish in a world divided along cultural, economic, social, and religious lines. There are a number of principles that aspire to the status of customary law, but have not as yet attained that designation. They include the principle of common but differentiated responsibility, the polluter pays principle, the preventive and precautionary principles, and various principles of good neighborliness and cooperation. They are found in a treaties, conference declarations, General Assembly resolutions, and the documents of various other international organizations and fora. These instruments of *soft*, embryonic customary law play an important part in the development of IEL. They may not amount to customary law *per se*, but they do constitute a presence and a backcloth that facilitates the creation and interpretation of IEL in general. The more important of them are referred to in Chapter Eighteen, The Future of IEL.

In addressing the limited corpus of "hard" customary IEL, we first turn to the prohibition against transboundary harm. The obligation prohibiting transboundary harm is perhaps the most established of customary IEL obligations and creates an obligation of effect—or a rule—premised on the broader principle of *sic utere tuo ut alienum non laedus* (use your own property in such a manner as not to injure that of another). It has been supported by the practice and *opinio juris* of states.

Nonetheless, it has generally been described as a principle, not a rule. This obligation is codified in Principle 21 of Stockholm, and is now entrenched in numerous provisions of treaties and declarations. It has been included as a "principle" in the Biodiversity Convention according to which: "States have . . . the sovereign right to exploit their own resources pursuant to their own environmental policies, and the responsibility to ensure that activities within their jurisdiction or control do not cause damage to the environment of other States or areas beyond the limits of national jurisdiction" [Biodiversity Convention, art. 3]. A variation of it is also articulated as a principle in the Rio Declaration [Principle 2].

UNCLOS expresses the general duty, under customary international law, to preserve and protect the marine environment and its natural resources—including the obligation to prevent, reduce and control pollution of the marine environment [UNCLOS arts.192–196]. This set of obligations meshes with others dealing with state responsibility. In the result, "[s]tates are responsible for the fulfilment of their international obligations concerning the protection and preservation of the marine environment" [UNCLOS art. 235].

It could also be argued that there is a customary law principle of notification and consultation before embarking on potentially damaging environmental activities (*see* Chapter Fifteen, Transboundary Water Pollution). Finally, the principles of sustainable development and conservation (*see* Chapter One, Introduction) lie at the foundations of modern IEL. These principles are more fully dealt with in Chapter Eighteen, The Future of IEL.

C. GENERAL PRINCIPLES OF LAW

We might expect article 38(1)(c) of the Statute of the ICJ dealing with sources of international law to be interpreted in accordance with its ordinary or plain meaning, in context, and in light of its object and purpose [*see* Vienna Convention, art. 31]. When so interpreted, "the general principles of law recognized by civilized nations" enjoy a parity of status with treaties and custom. Such a view is reinforced by its context in which a contrasting source of law, "judicial decisions," are relegated to the status of "subsidiary" sources [Statute of the ICJ, art. 38(1)(d)]. A persuasive case can, therefore, be made out that the courts, not states, now possess the power and discretion to enunciate relevant general principles of law by induction. [ANTONIO CASSESE, INTERNATIONAL LAW IN A DIVIDED WORLD 170–172 (1986)].

The inductive task of ascertaining general principles from legal systems around the world falls to the comparative lawyer, and involves the gargantuan task of studying all major legal systems to discover and distill general principles of law. (Note that the search is all-inclusive and not limited to "civilized nations"—an embarrassingly anachronistic phrase of the 1940s). The systematic study of all legal systems has been fitfully attempted, and is by no means complete, though it is possible to garner general principles from some areas of national law such as contract, criminal, and environmental law. However, international courts have not yet acknowledged that general principles of national law constitute a significant source of law that should be incorporated into international law. On the contrary, general principles have never been considered a major source of law, and have only been used in an interstitial manner to fill in very small gaps in procedural—not substantive—law.

The ICJ and other judicial bodies appear to have reasoned that general principles of domestic or "municipal" jurisprudence should be followed only so far as they are specifically applicable to relations between states [IAN BROWNLIE, PRINCIPLES OF PUBLIC INTERNATIONAL LAW 16 (4th ed. 1990)]. National, or domestic laws which on the whole are applicable to jural parties within a state, as distinct from interstate relations, have fallen short of this standard and have largely been ignored.

General principles have the potential for assuming a new role under IEL. In Chapter Eighteen, "The Future of IEL," we envision IEL's merger with national environmental laws to become part of the Common Law of Humankind (CLH). A successful merging of IEL and national environmental laws which creates a CLH demands that general principles of national environmental law be recognized as such and be woven into the fabric of international law.

D. JUDICIAL DECISIONS

As we have noted, the Statute of the ICJ diminishes the role of judicial decisions to a "[s]ubsidiary means for the determination of rules of law" [art. 38(1)(d)]. One reason is that judicial decisions, including those of the ICJ, have no binding force "[e]xcept between the parties and in respect of that particular case" [art. 59]. In national common law systems, the best known of which developed in England, the common law is the customary law that is developed, modified, and sometimes fundamentally redirected by the judges, the legal profession, and the courts. The common law system grew through judicial decisions recorded by lawyers. Judicial decisions form the foundations of law and theoretically constitute the background against which statutes are introduced. Even civil law systems that repudiate the common law method of judge-made law possess hierarchical legal systems in which judicial decisions play a part and possess value because they contain principles of law that may be binding on subsequent courts.

It is evident that the international legal process lacks a hierarchical system of courts or a machinery of justice and cannot, therefore, adopt a strict doctrine of binding precedent. Judicial decisions are binding only on the parties. But it is also clear that judicial decisions play an important role in any system of customary law by restating, codifying, and clarifying the often uncertain and usually unwritten customary law. In a judicial decision we find an analysis of the evidence supporting the law, an articulation or declaration of what the law is, and a demonstration of how law should be applied to the facts. In so doing, a court or tribunal performs the difficult and valuable duty of collecting, examining, and assessing the evidence and arguments, deducing rules from amorphous general concepts, reducing them into written form and arriving at conclusions derived from the application of law to facts. The art of judging is a strenuous, costly, challenging, and time-consuming job, requiring training, discipline, diligence, and expertise.

Where a court exercises its responsibilities and decides a case, it is a perfectly natural tendency to learn from what has been achieved and to avoid duplication. Moreover, it is foolish, for example, to embark upon repeated investigations to rediscover the wheel whenever we need to use one. The judicial use of precedents by international tribunals, therefore, reflects a practical habit of mind that avoids duplication and looks to past history for guidance. Not surprisingly, subsequent international courts and tribunals have given earlier decisions a persuasive authority that shades into a form of precedent, albeit not of the strictly binding kind.

Judicial decisions have become part of the substantive corpus of IEL. They include the Trail Smelter Arbitration, (U.S. v. Can.), 3 R.I.A.A. 1938 (1949) (*see* Chapter Fourteen, Transboundary Air Pollution); Corfu Channel Case (U.K. v. Alb.), 1949 I.C.J. 4; Case Relating to the Territorial Jurisdiction of the International Commission of the River Oder (Czech., Den., Fr., Ger., Swed., U.K., Pol.), 1929 P.C.I.J. (ser. A) No. 23, at 5; Lake Lanoux Arbitration (Spain v. Fr.), 12 R.I.A.A. 281 (1957) (*see* Chapter Fifteen, Transboundary Water Pollution); and Nuclear Test Cases (I) (N.Z. v. Fr.), 1974 I.C.J. 253 (*see* Chapter Seventeen, Nuclear Pollution).

In 1993, the ICJ created a new chamber for environmental law and a cluster of IEL cases have since come before the ICJ. In 1993, Nauru took Australia to court for environmental damage caused by land degradation consequent upon Australian mining in Nauru when Australia governed that island. [Certain Phosphate Lands in Nauru (Nauru v. Australia), 1993 I.C.J. 316 (June 25)]. The case was settled and removed from the docket of the court. The court has yet to determine two other environmental cases. The Case Concerning the Gabcikovo–Nagymaros Project [Gabcikovo–Nagymaros Project (Hungary/Slovakia), 1994 I.C.J. 151 (Dec. 20)] concerns the Gabcikovo–Nagymaros Project between Hungary and the Slovak Republic and involves the use of water resources and their environmental implications. The Fisheries Jurisdiction Case [Fisheries Jurisdiction Case (Spain v. Canada),

1995 I.C.J. 87 (May 2)] arose out of action taken by Canada under legislation adopted by it to halt the destruction of fish stocks by prohibiting all fishing of straddling stocks off its coasts and in the adjacent high seas. Canada seized a Spanish ship believed to be fishing illegally in the high seas and this resulted *inter alia* in the Application filed by Spain instituting proceedings in the ICJ against Canada. Canada denies the jurisdiction of the ICJ and, despite extra-judicial diplomatic actions to settle this case, it still remains on the docket of the ICJ.

Additionally, three recent decisions of the court have thrust the ICJ into the throes of IEL: 1) the Request for an Examination of Situation in Accordance with Paragraph 63 of the Court's Judgment of 20 December 1974 in Nuclear Tests (N.Z. v. Fr.), 1995 I.C.J. 288 (Sept. 22) (Nuclear Test Cases (II)); 2) the Legality of the Use by a State of Nuclear Weapons in Armed Conflict, 1993 I.C.J. 467 (Request for an Advisory Opinion by the WHO of Sept. 13); and 3) The Legality of the Threat or Use of Nuclear Weapons, 1995 I.C.J. 3 (Request for an Advisory Opinion by the UN General Assembly of Feb. 1); The Legality of the Use by a State of Nuclear Weapons in Armed Conflict, 1996 I.C.J. 93 (July 8). It is not clear from its decisions in Nuclear Test Cases (II) and the WHO Advisory Opinion (*see* Chapter Seventeen) as to whether the ICJ is willing to play an active role in the development of IEL.

E. OTHER SOURCES OF LAW

Other subsidiary sources of law include the writings of "the most highly qualified publicists" or scholars, again "as subsidiary means for the determination of rules of law" [Statute of the ICJ, art. 38(1)(d)]. The most influential example of this source would be the work of the International Law Commission (ILC), empowered by Article 13 of the UN Charter to "initiate studies and make recommendations for the purpose of encouraging the progressive development of international law and its codification."

Further sources include, resolutions, declarations, action plans, and agendas of the United Nations and other inter-governmental organizations, such as the Stockholm Conference and UNCED. We have already adverted to the way in which international organizations can interpret the law. In addition, it is possible for governments to create customary law by how they vote within international organizations. Where, for example, a nation votes in favor of a resolution affirming that it is illegal to build a nuclear reactor without consulting those who might be affected by an accident, that nation's supporting vote may demonstrate both practice and *opinio juris*. This would show *opinio juris* if the vote for the resolution was premised upon the assumption that there was no option but to vote for it because it embodies established law, or because the state now accepts that it is the law.

The possibility exists for such resolutions to assume a quasi-legal or "soft law" character in which the evidence surrounding a resolution does not give birth to law as of its passing, but takes the law into a grey zone between gestation and labor. It must be stressed that the law-making character of such actions depends on the internal quality of the text adopted, as well as the surrounding circumstances. A text that purports to create, declare, codify, or restate law carries more weight than one that does not. External factors that strengthen the legal as distinct from the political quality of the instruments include statements affirming, not qualifying or diminishing the legal character of an instrument, the consistency of the affirming majority, and the support of major world powers.

CHAPTER THREE

IMPLEMENTATION

International environmental problems first arise within nation states, and often cause territorial harm to the peoples and communities of those states before creating extraterritorial damage. These environmental problems demand national legislative, administrative, and judicial measures. Any international action taken to abate extraterritorial harm must necessarily address the roots of the problem located within nation states. Most international treaties demand to be implemented within individual nation states. The various problems discussed in Part II of this Nutshell illustrate the extent to which national problems have become international ones and demonstrate why international answers cannot be separated from national responses.

Implementation of treaty obligations, however, is hampered by the fact that the vertical command and control power structure governing domestic politics within nations is conspicuously absent within the international legal order. In international society, power or authority rests on a horizontal base made up of co-equal sovereign states, and can be built into a pyramidal structure only if these nations consent to and join in such an endeavor. While piecemeal building upon the base has resulted in the substantial corpus of IEL noted in Chapter Two, there is no overarching pyramid of authority consisting of law-making, law-interpreting, law-implementing, or law-enforcing institutions. The absence of institutions cloning those within nation states does not signify a complete void in international implementing institutions. On the contrary, what we have are international implementing agencies and mechanisms correlated to the international society in which we live. They merit examination, and we begin with the many international organizations that facilitate the implementation of IEL, and follow this by examining compliance mechanisms, diplomatic avenues and judicial remedies as methods of implementation.

A. INSTITUTIONS AND ORGANIZATIONS

Despite the impressive growth of IEL and its expanding domain, there is still no single institution or organization that serves environmental protection in the way that the World Trade Organization (WTO) advances, interprets, implements, and enforces the concept of free trade. General Agreement on Tarrifs and Trade, Final Act Embodying the Results of the Uruguay Round of Multinational Trade Negotiations, Apr. 15, 1994, LEGAL INSTRU-MENTS—RESULTS OF THE URUGUAY ROUND vol. 1, 33 I.L.M. 1125 (Hereinafter GATT 1994). The institutions and organizations enlisted to advance IEL are fractured, fragmented, and divided along functional, regional, bureaucratic, and geo-political lines. It is useful to take note of the more important of these entities, and a fuller description of them is found in Appendix A, *infra*. They are classified as Global Organizations, Regional Organizations, Treaty Specific Organizations and Non–Governmental Organizations.

1. GLOBAL ORGANIZATIONS

The United Nations was founded in 1947 before the dawning of environmental awareness, and its Charter creates seven principal organs including the General Assembly, the Security Council, the Economic and Social Council (ECOSOC), and the International Court of Justice (ICJ) [Charter of the United Nations (UN Charter), art. 7, Oct. 24, 1945, 1 U.N.T.S. xvi]. The UN Charter neither creates an environmental organ nor specifically mandates the protection of the environment.

A number of international organizations created by treaty or agreement have been brought into a familial relationship with the UN pursuant to charter provisions, and are known as Specialized Agencies of the UN. They enjoy juridical personality and may exercise rights and duties as subjects of international law. A number of them have broadly interpreted their constituent treaties to adopt an environmental competence. Those presently assuming environmental responsibilities include the Food and Agricultural Organization (FAO), the International

Labor Organization (ILO), the World Health Organization (WHO), the World Meteorological Organization (WMO), the International Maritime Organization (IMO), the UN Educational, Scientific, and Cultural Organization (UNESCO), and the International Atomic Energy Agency (IAEA).

While the IAEA does not possess Specialized Agency status as such, it plays a role in advancing environmental protection along with other semi-autonomous UN bodies such as the UN Development Program (UNDP), the United Nations Institute for Training and Research (UNITAR), and the United Nations Conference on Trade and Development (UNCTAD). After UNCED, the General Assembly of the UN created the Commission on Sustainable Development (CSD) as a functional commission of ECOSOC. Perhaps the most important of the UN Organizations, the UN Environment Program (UNEP) was created by a General Assembly resolution, not by treaty or agreement.

UNEP was established to act as a focal point for environmental action and coordination, but possesses no executive power. All UNEP programs are financed directly by member states. Consequently, its mission is to persuade and convince states of the need for environmental action, provide information, expertise and advice, and sponsor treaties. It has accomplished these limited objectives credibly.

Increasingly, incentives, financial mechanisms, and technology transfers have become part of the architecture of IEL, and it is necessary to take note of the more important of the institutions involved. The World Bank group consists of the International Bank for Reconstruction and Development (IBRD), the International Development Bank (IDA), and the International Finance Corporation (IFC). The World Bank has developed a bad record by encouraging environmentally damaging developments, but appears to be mending its ways. The Global Environment Facility (GEF) was established in 1990 on an experimental basis to provide financial and technical assistance to developing countries to promote environmental protection. It was restructured permanently in 1994 and is a potential source of green funds for *Agenda 21*, U.N. Doc. A/CONF. 151/26 (1992), the United Nations Framework Convention on Climate Change (Climate Change Convention), May 22, 1992, 31 I.L.M. 849 (entered into force Mar. 21, 1994), and the Convention on Biological Diversity (Biodiversity Convention), June 5, 1992, 31 I.L.M. 818 (entered into force Dec. 29, 1993).

A review of global environmental institutions would not be complete without a reference to two legal institutions: 1) the International Court of Justice (ICJ), and 2) the International Law Commission (ILC). The ICJ is the principal judicial organ of the UN system, and exercises jurisdiction by consent. It has now set up an environmental chamber and recently demonstrated in the Advisory Opinion on the Threat or Use of Nuclear Weapons that it possesses the authority to address vexing environmental issues and apply the law to changing situations [Legality of the use by a State of Nuclear

Weapons in Armed Conflict, 1996 I.C.J. 93 (July 8)]. The ILC was created by the UN General Assembly to work toward the codification and development of international law, and it has reported on subjects of great importance to IEL such as state responsibility and international watercourses.

2. REGIONAL ORGANIZATIONS

A number of regional organizations are playing an important role in developing IEL. The most important of these is the European Union (EU), formerly known as the European Community (EC) and the European Economic Community (EEC). The EU is the most advanced form of international organization in the world and is evolving into a confederation. It possesses three key attributes lacking in other international organizations: 1) law-making agencies; 2) law-interpreting and enforcing agencies; and 3) a court with compulsory jurisdiction. Clothed with explicit environmental jurisdiction, the EU has enacted a large number of environmental laws over a wide range of subject areas. The extent of its corpus of environmental law, and the changing jurisprudential character of EU, deters us from dealing with EU law in this volume. Other regional bodies of note are the Council of Europe, the Organization for Economic Cooperation and Development (OECD), the Organization of American States (OAS), and the South Pacific Regional Organization.

3. SPECIFIC TREATY ORGANIZATIONS

Many treaties set up institutional arrangements (or rudimentary international organizations) for their implementation. They range from *ad hoc* conferences to more permanent institutional structures. A number of them are called conferences of the parties, which include a permanent secretariat and a budget, and in some cases, special science advisory bodies. Representative examples include the sporadic conference of the parties under the Vienna Convention for the Protection of the Ozone Layer (Vienna Convention on Ozone), March 22, 1985, 26 I.L.M. 1529 (1988) and regular meetings of the parties under the Montreal Protocol on Substances that Deplete the Ozone Layer (Montreal Protocol), Sept. 16, 1987, 26 I.L.M. 1550 (1989) (*see* Chapter Seven). Additionally, the Climate Change Convention (*see* Chapter Six) institutes an annual conference of the parties, and the Biodiversity Convention (*see* Chapter Five) provides for a conference of the parties on regular intervals. Finally, the Paris Convention for the Prevention of Marine Pollution from Land–Based Sources (1974 Paris Convention), June 4, 1974, 13 I.L.M. 352 (1978) (*see* Chapter Thirteen) requires regular meetings of the Paris Commission, while the Convention on International Trade in Endangered Species of Wild Fauna and Flora (CITES), Mar. 3, 1973, 12 I.L.M. 1085 (1975) (*see* Chapter Five, Biodiversity) sets up a conference of the parties that meets at least every two years.

4. NON–GOVERNMENTAL ORGANIZATIONS (NGOS)

Global NGOs are playing an increasingly important role in IEL. We mention three out of hundreds to illustrate their diversity and spread. The World Conservation Union (IUCN) is a unique hybrid comprised of non-governmental conservation groups, states, and public law entities such as universities and research institutes. The World Wildlife Fund (WWF) is a non-governmental conservation group whose goals parallel those of IUCN. WWF finances conservation strategies throughout the world. A third is the Earth Council endorsed by the Earth Summit which assists grassroots organizations pressing for the implementation of sustainable development (*see* Appendix A).

NGOs have become established actors in the implementation of environmental law for a number of reasons. To begin, they are closer to the people affected by environmental degradation, and represent them more faithfully and diligently than their governments. Second, having played a major role in organizing the once invisible colleges of scientists to study the effects and impacts of various environmental problems, and having participated in the making of treaties, they have a legitimate and well-founded interest in the implementation of IEL. Third, the international character of these organizations embraces the concept of global as distinct from national environmental protection, and their large numbers have given them an undeniable international political standing.

As such, NGOs exert pressure on nations and international organizations to comply with IEL, but they have not yet attained the status of States as subjects of international law. There are fundamental conceptual problems in their achieving theoretical parity with States within a legal system comprised of sovereign states alone. However, on a functional level there ought not to be objections to states or international organizations allowing NGOs to perform the role of private attorneys general empowered to protect the international environment. Some treaties point the way in this direction.

For example, the IAEA has granted consultative status to NGOs having special competence in the nuclear field [Rules on Consultative Status of NGOs with the Agency, IAEA Doc. INFCIRC/14, (1959)]. The Convention on the Protection of the Environment Between Denmark, Finland, Norway and Sweden (Nordic Treaty), art. 2, Feb. 9, 1974, 1092 U.N.T.S. 279 (entered into force Oct. 5, 1976) goes further and grants all legal persons, including individuals, and non-governmental organizations the right to protest and vindicate environmental rights and duties in the legal systems of the parties. So, too, does the European Union [see Treaty Establishing the European Community, Mar. 25, 1957, art 173 (as amended), reprinted in BASIC COMMUNITY LAWS 130 (Bernard Rudden & Derrick Wyatt eds., 1993); see also Case t–585/93, Stichting Greenpeace, et al. v. Commission, 695 B.O. 219 (Ct. First Instance 1995)]. The Convention for the Protection of the Marine Environment of the North–East Atlantic (OSPAR Convention) [1992 WL 675186], goes even further by granting NGOs observer status—a role which entitles them to participate in the meetings of the parties, and to submit reports, but not to vote [arts. 11(1) & (2)].

Formal treaty provisions are not the only means of obtaining NGO input. For example, the Commission on Sustainable Development is mandated to receive input from NGOs relating to the implementation of Agenda 21 [UNGA Res. 47/91, ¶ 3 (h) (1992)]. Even more striking, the Inspection Panel of the World Bank was created to provide an independent forum for private citizens who believe that they or their interests have been or could be directly harmed by a project financed by the World Bank. In a number of cases the World Bank has taken action pursuant to the claims and reports of the Inspection Panel. [Report of the Inspection Panel, 1994–1996,].

B. COMPLIANCE MECHANISMS

The international organizations we have noted are not possessed of the power and authority of legislative, executive, and judicial bodies that supervise and enforce the implementation of national laws. It is important, therefore, that the substantive rules of international law should first possess an internal force or dynamic that makes sense to the parties and invokes an attitude of compliance rather than non-compliance. Treaty negotiators try to formulate and endow substantive rules with some compliance generating character that induces implementation without the need for supervision. Second, conventions or treaties also create institutions and techniques that induce compliance and confer power on appropriate authorities to deal with non-compliance. In order to secure compliance, treaties have instituted various processes, procedures and techniques. As we have seen, some set up their own institutions, while others delegate power to existing international organizations such as those mentioned above. Individual treaties contain varying baskets of measures addressing such tasks, and provide *inter alia* for the following: interpretation, research, information and data collection and/or dissemination, monitoring, reporting, reviews of performance, rule-making by experts subject to differing types of confirmation, and management by international organizations. These compliance mechanisms call for further description.

To begin, we have referred to the importance of interpretation, *supra* in Chapter 2 § C, as a method of implementing a treaty. The interpretation and implementation of the Montreal Protocol provides illustrations—more adventerous than others—of how interpretation and other processes are used as compliance techniques [*see* T. Ghering, *International Environment Regimes: Dynamic Legal* Systems, 1 Y.B. Int'l Envt'l L. 35, 47–54 (1990)]. The First Meeting of the Parties under the Montreal Protocol clarified and interpreted various treaty obligations, including those in Annex A which expressly stated that the Ozone Depletion Potential (ODP) figure for one of the halons was "to be determined." Inserting an ODP figure technically required amending the Annex of the Protocol, and involved a circuitous procedure, plus ratification by two thirds of the parties. Instead, the parties inserted an ODP figure into the Annex of the Protocol by way of interpretation, thereby circumventing the more cumbersome and demanding amendment procedures.

The Second Meeting continued further along these lines, and states adopted a comprehensive "Amendment" to the Montreal Protocol that came into force upon ratification by one third of the parties, even though the explicit language of the Protocol itself required amendments to be ratified by two thirds of the parties. They also established an Interim Multilateral Fund to support ozone friendly technology in developing countries even though there was no provision either in the framework convention or the Protocol that authorized such a step. The Second Meeting of the Parties also adopted a "non-compliance procedure" not provided for in the Protocol, that allowed for the amicable resolution of disputes to be finally determined not by a judicial body but by a decision of the Meeting of the Parties. Finally, the "noncompliance procedure" adopted by the Second Meeting of the Parties sets up an "Implementation Committee" which deals with non-compliance and reports to the Meeting of the Parties.

In addition to implementation, research to ascertain the true environmental impacts and effects of any activities identified in a treaty is of crucial importance. This is particularly the case when dealing with a framework treaty that requires later protocols to deal with unfolding facts. Treaties are replete with references to research. For example, the parties to the Vienna Convention on Ozone (*see* Chapter Seven) undertake to carry out research and scientific assessments on a variety of activities that may affect the ozone layer. These assessments include research into the physics and chemistry of the atmosphere, health and biological effects, and effects on climate of a variety of chemicals that might have a potentially deleterious effect on the ozone layer [arts. 2 & 3 & annex 1]. The Climate Change Convention (*see* Chapter Six) calls for research on the causes, effects, magnitude, and timing of climate change, and the economic and social consequences of various response strategies [arts. 4(g) & 5], and sets up a subsidiary body for scientific and technological advice [art. 9]. The Biodiversity Convention (*see* Chapter Five) seeks to promote research that, *inter alia*, contributes to the conservation and sustainable use of biological diversity [art. 12] and sets up a subsidiary body on Scientific, Technical, and Technological Advice [art. 25].

The three treaties mentioned above also call for data collection and the dissemination of research and data. The purpose of the dissemination of research and data is to facilitate compliance. Reporting requirements may include the information obtained from research and data collection, and can take the form of reports by a particular international treaty organization to the parties, or more often, reports by the parties to the international organization or the other parties. The objective of reporting is to bring compliance into the sunlight of scrutiny by other parties and the treaty machinery. The importance of reporting as a technique to secure compliance is illustrated in the Climate Change Convention. All parties are obliged to communicate to the Conference of the Parties a general description of steps taken to implement the Convention, including a detailed description of anthropogenic emissions by sources and removal by sinks [arts. 4(1)(a) & (j); 12(1)(a) & (b)]. The reporting responsibilities of developed countries is even more onerous [art. 12(2)].

Assessments and reviews of performance are tied to reporting. On the basis of the reports and research made available, the parties or a specific treaty organization may assess the extent of implementation, and the progress made towards objectives. The Climate Change Convention entrusts this responsibility to the Conference of the Parties [art. 7(e)], while the Montreal Protocol requires assessment and review of control measures based on the reports submitted by a panel of experts at least every four years [art. 6].

Where a framework treaty institutes an objective, or final goal, the task of approaching it is usually undertaken in steps and requires interim measures. The task of making these rules and drawing up other measures, or recommending what they should be, is sometimes delegated to a group of scientific experts. We have seen that panels of experts have been set up under the Montreal Protocol, while the Climate Change Convention and the Biodiversity Convention have each created special scientific bodies. In our discussion on the amendment of treaties (*see* Chapter Two), we noticed how the use of protocols and scientific annexes is directed at avoiding the tortuous process of treaty amendment. We have also noted above how annexes under the Montreal Protocol are amended. In addition, Chapter Eight on Antarctica offers examples of how the Commission under the Convention on the Conservation of Antarctic Marine Living Resources (CCAMLR) is possessed of management powers that will help nations comply with that treaty regime.

International treaty rules inhabit a consensual legal order and the implications of non-compliance with such rules stand in sharp relief to the comparable non-implementation of statutory rules within national legal systems. In the absence of bodies empowered to enforce compliance, the pressing goal of the parties to a treaty is to persuade the defaulter to comply. A medley of diplomatic and administrative measures are employed to secure such compliance. Judicial supervision leading to court-type decisions are available but are resorted to only in rare instances, and many environmental treaties provide for negotiation, conciliation, and arbitration as alternatives or preconditions to court litigation.

C. DIPLOMATIC AVENUES

Many environmental treaties require that parties resort to diplomatic and other means of settling their differences before resorting to judicial or quasi-judicial settlement of disputes. They include: CITES [art. XVIII]; the International Convention for the Prevention of Pollution from Ships (MARPOL), Nov. 2, 1973, art. 10, 12 I.L.M. 1319; the Convention on International Liability for Damage Caused by Space Objects (Space Liability Convention), Mar. 29, 1972, art. IX, 961 U.N.T.S. 187; the Vienna Convention on Ozone [art. 11(1)], the Climate Change Convention [art. 14]; and the Biodiversity Convention [art. 27(1)]. These provisions signal the importance of diplomatic means for securing treaty compliance, and a number of treaties in fact institutionalize consultation between parties: the 1974 Paris Convention [art. 9(1)]; the Nordic Convention [art. 11]; and the Convention on Long–Range Transboundary Air Pollution (LRTAP), Nov. 13, 1979, (art. 5, 18 I.L.M. 1442 (1983)). Thus, diplomatic pressures and consultations are part of the implementing architecture of IEL.

D. JUDICIAL REMEDIES

Apart from regulatory regimes supervised by or through agencies established by treaty, judicial enforcement provides another avenue for securing compliance with the law. Judicial remedies could be used to obtain specific acts of compliance and can act as deterrents by bringing embarrassment, perhaps ignominy, to bear on wrongdoing states. In a community of nations where good standing and reputation are important, judicial remedies may have some use even though they lack mechanisms for enforcement.

It is necessary, at the outset, to point out that the arrangements in a few environmental treaties allow private individuals to prosecute claims for breaches of a treaty within national courts—even though this practice is highly unusual in most areas of international law. *See*, for example, the Nordic Convention, art. 3, the Convention on Third Party Liability in the Field of Nuclear Energy (Paris Nuclear Liability Convention), July 29, 1960, art. 3, 956 U.N.T.S. 251 (entered into force Apr. 1, 1968), the Vienna Convention on Civil Liability for Nuclear damage (Vienna Nuclear Liability Convention), May 21, 1963, art. II, 7 I.L.M 727 (entered into force, Nov. 12, 1977) and the International Convention on Civil Liability for Oil Pollution Damage, art. III, Nov. 29, 1969, 9 I.L.M. 45 (entered into force June 19, 1975). In Chapter Eighteen, The Future of IEL, we refer to the potential for developing national remedies for implementing international treaties.

Much more commonly, judicial or quasi-judicial remedies within IEL are invoked through inter-state litigation, and are based on the grievance remedial principles of "state responsibility" or international tort law that enables one state to demand *ex-post* compensation and other relief for harm caused to it by another state. Typically, adjudication arising under international laws governing such questions is handled by international courts, tribunals, and arbiters, and not national courts or institutions. Despite ongoing efforts to enlarge the domain of public international law by giving standing to injured persons other than states, such as NGOs and even private citizens, the actors in public IEL remain confined almost exclusively to state parties.

If a state decides to take the traditional grievance-remedial judicial route, it can demand compensation from the wrongdoing state, and ask for a termination of the specific harmful conduct. However, this kind of *ex post* judicial remedy is a flawed way of dealing with an endemic problem for a number of reasons. First, judicial remedies can only be granted by a judicial forum and international judicial bodies suffer from an underlying constitutional infirmity: lack of jurisdiction. The lack of jurisdiction becomes evident when dealing with the more serious problems of the global commons like climate change, ozone depletion, or biological diversity. These problems require concerted and coordinated action by all relevant state actors, and judicial supervision must extend to all affected parties. Unfortunately, some states will not consent to being brought within the compulsory and binding jurisdiction of courts or tribunals established under the treaties addressing these problems.

1. JURISDICTION

For example, the settlement of disputes by way of compulsory and binding judicial proceedings is optional under the Climate Change Convention [art. 14(2)], the Biodiversity Convention [art. 26(3)], and the Vienna Convention on Ozone [art. 11(3)]. UNC-LOS, on the other hand, does establish a system of compulsory dispute settlement and it remains to be seen how vigorously it will be used. The ICJ also possesses some level of compulsory jurisdiction, but as of 1996 only 60 states had signed the so called "optional clause" [art. 36(2)], giving the court general jurisdiction. Even where they have signed the "optional clause," 75% of those doing so have entered reservations, some of the self-judging type, that allow a state to decline jurisdiction where it determines that a case involves questions of domestic jurisdiction or national defense.

Jurisdiction can prove to be a difficult obstacle. In the recent case of The Legality of the Use by a State of Nuclear Weapons in Armed Conflict, 1996 I.C.J. 93 (July 8), the ICJ defined the concept to include legal capacity or status, and held that it lacked jurisdiction because the World Health Organization (WHO) was unable to demonstrate legal capacity. In this case, the WHO, a specialized agency of the UN, sought an Advisory Opinion from the ICJ. The Constitution of the WHO commits it to the attainment by all peoples of the highest possible level of health [art. 1], and it is required to take all necessary action to attain this objective [art. 2(v)]. The question posed to the Court was: "In view of the health and environmental effects, would the use of nuclear weapons by a State in war or other armed conflict be a breach of its obligations under international law including the WHO Constitution?"

In its majority opinion, the Court admitted that the WHO's Constitution authorized the WHO to deal with the effects of the use of nuclear weapons, or any other hazardous activity, and to take preventive measures aimed at protecting the health of populations in the event of such weapons being used [¶ 21]. Despite this, the ICJ determined that preventive action, including asking the Court for the present Advisory Opinion, was not of the kind that fell within the scope of the WHO's activity [¶ 22]. Furthermore, the authority to take preventive actions did not confer upon it "[a] competence to address the legality of the use of nuclear weapons . . . or to ask the Court about them" [¶ 21].

According to the Court, questions affecting the legality of nuclear weapons are matters of arms control and disarmament and they are not the concern of a "specialized agency" such as the WHO whose authority is restricted to the sphere of public health. Questions of arms control and disarmament are matters for the UN itself, not the specialized agencies [¶ 26]. Because the question posed to the Court was not one that fell within the scope of the WHO, the Court declared that it lacked jurisdiction to entertain the case [¶ 31].

This decision highlights a number of more general defects concerning the concept of jurisdiction which enables judicial forums to widen or narrow access to justice. The granting of an Advisory Opinion is a discretionary remedy [art. 65], and the ICJ could have assumed jurisdiction and declined to grant an opinion because, for example, the petitioning party lacked standing, status, capacity, or authority. Instead, it broadened the concept of jurisdiction to include questions of standing, status, or authority of a party to bring an action, and thereby widened the opportunities for denying jurisdiction and restricting access to the Court.

Apart from jurisdiction, judicial remedies addressing non-compliance suffer from other defects. Judicial remedies are confined to the facts of a specific dispute, and cannot deal with the whole or part of a broader environmental problem. Furthermore, there is no mechanism for enforcing or systematically monitoring the implementation of the order of an international court. This is particularly unsatisfactory because most environmental problems occur on a continuous and recurrent basis. Finally, typical judicial decisions are restricted to containing damage after the fact rather than preventing it from happening in the first place.

Despite these defects, judicial remedies can prove to be an effective way of implementing the law if they are administered by a tribunal having compulsory and binding jurisdiction like the UNCLOS tribunals, and if the tribunals assume a more activist role in interpreting and applying the substantive law. Such tribunals ought not to model themselves on the ICJ. The WHO case gave the ICJ an admirable opportunity to demonstrate its willingness to grapple with difficult issues of IEL. Instead, as

Judge Weeramantry pointed out in his powerful separate opinion, the Court took a peculiarly obtuse view of the scope of the WHO, and in so doing signaled its unwillingness to play a more vigilant role within IEL to those who might invoke its intervention.

2. STATE RESPONSIBILITY

When one nation brings another to court it relies on a form of international tort law called "state responsibility" (SR). Before examining the main features of SR, it is relevant to note that the considerable theoretical attention given to the concept stands in stark contrast to its conspicuous absence in environmental treaties. The stubborn fact is that questions of how to claim compensation for the breach of international environmental obligations, either in national or international forums, have been deliberately neglected or omitted. The examples of IEL that were referred to above are the exceptions, not the rule, and the absence of a willingness among states to develop principles of SR is yet another reason why judicial enforcement can prove elusive.

The foundational principle of SR, as of tort law, is the concept of a wrongful act. A state commits an internationally wrongful act if it violates or breaches an international obligation, as found in treaty or customary law. We begin to see, therefore, that all obligations contained in treaties as well as in customary law have the potential to give rise to SR.

Thus, an obligation could be very general, like that which places responsibility on states to ensure that activities within their jurisdiction or control do not cause damage to the environment of other states or to areas beyond their jurisdiction. On the other hand, very specific obligations such as those relating to timetables for reduction of ozone damaging chemicals, monitoring or reporting could give rise to state responsibility [*International Law Comm'n Draft Articles on State Responsibility*, Adopted by the International Law Comm'n at its 1642nd Meeting, arts. 20 & 21, U.N. Doc. A/35/10 (1981) (ILC Draft Articles on State Responsibility)].

There are numerous conceptual difficulties about the nature of a *wrongful* act that need to be noted [Ricardo Pisillo Mazzeschi, *Forms of International Responsibility for Environmental Harm, in* INTERNATIONAL RESPONSIBILITY FOR ENVIRONMENTAL HARM 15 (Francioni & Scovazzi, eds. 1991)]. The first set of difficulties surround the question as to whether fault (wrongful intention or negligence) is a necessary ingredient of a wrongful act that is prohibited by international law. It can be argued that a requirement of fault must be implied in all primary obligations because there could be no wrong (state responsibility *stricto sensu*) without fault. Impelled by the theoretical cogency of this doctrinal thesis, the ILC accepted the need for fault in its Draft Articles on State Responsibility. At the same time, it appreciated the practical need to deal with the reality of environmental harm caused without *fault* and attempted to establish a parallel basis for reparation in circumstances where there was no wrongful intention or negligence. In effect, the ILC attempted to create a form of strict liability for harmful acts under a less detractive name, which we have called the *liability principle* [*International Law Commission Draft Articles on International Liability for Injurious Consequences Arising Out of Acts Not Prohibited by International Law*, Report of the International Law Commission on the Work of its Forty-first Session, arts. 1 & 9, U.N. GOAR, 44th Sess., Supp. No. 10 (1989)].

This attempt of the ILC which articulates an alternative jurisprudential basis for accommodating strict or absolute liability for lawful activities which cause environmental harm without fault or negligence has been criticized [*see, e.g.*, Alan E. Boyle, *State Responsibility and International Liability for Injurious Consequences Not Prohibited by International Law: A Necessary Distinction?* 39 INT'L & COMP. L.Q. 1, (1990)]. Without getting into the details of this rather academic debate, an approach based on general principles of law suggests that we should look at the primary obligation to determine if fault is an ingredient or element of the breach giving rise to a wrong. If fault is an element of breach in the primary obligation, then it is a requirement. If not, there should be other reasons for so implying. If, for example, the obligation we are examining is the one presented in Principle 21 of the Stockholm Declaration, the fact that it does not state that the transboundary harm should be caused intentionally or negligently would suggest that fault is not a requirement. But does this mean that Principle 21 imposes strict or even absolute liability? The reluctance of some commentators and of the ILC in its own work on transboundary water pollution to answer this question in the affirmative triggers a second cluster of difficulties that encompasses strict liability (*see* Chapter Fifteen, Transboundary Water Pollution).

An affirmative answer posits that no-fault *liability* supercedes fault-based *responsibility* for all practical purposes. The idea of affirming state liability, therefore, without the need to establish even a duty of care based on a due diligence standard, remains untenable to some scholars [*see* BRIAN D. SMITH, STATE RESPONSIBILITY AND THE MARINE ENVIRONMENT: THE RULES OF DECISION 34–43 (1988), BOYLE, *infra*]. Such critics would rather stay with a graduated concept of *responsibility* based on differentiated standards ranging from due diligence to strict and absolute responsibility.

In the main, the concepts of strict and absolute liability have not been authoritatively defined, but standards of strict liability are less rigorous than absolute liability, and may constitute no more than a reversal of the burden of proof, allowing a defending State to establish circumstances precluding wrongfulness or liability. Absolute or objective liability on the other hand is more conclusive and prohibits, or very severely limits, evidence of circumstances preventing liability.

A number of conventions on nuclear liability implement regimes of absolute civil liability. They only admit of very limited exceptions based on armed conflict and civil war [see Chapter Seventeen, Nuclear Damage]. The distinction between fault, strict and absolute liability are common to state responsibility (stricto sensu) and to civil liability. The examples cited below are drawn from the spheres of state responsibility as well as civil liability. While illustrative of these distinctions, they do not remove all of the doubts still surrounding them.

The Oil Pollution Convention illustrates strict liability. It places liability on the owner of the ship subject to exceptions such as war, hostilities, certain kinds of natural phenomena and acts of a third party [art. III(2)(7)(d)]. The Space Liability Convention illustrates absolute liability. Where damage is caused to the surface of the earth or to aircraft in flight, it asserts that, "A launching State shall be absolutely liable to pay compensation for damage caused by its space object ..." [art. II]. In addition, the Space Liability Convention draws a further distinction between absolute liability [art. II] and fault liability [art. III]. While absolute liability is imposed for damage to the surface of the earth [art. II], damage resulting elsewhere can result in liability only where fault is established [art. III].

Apart from proving the breach of an obligation, with or without fault, a wrongful act must be attributed to a state. In environmental wrongs, the acts resulting from the wrong must be laid at the feet of the state or an agency of the state. Because transboundary environmental wrongs are often committed by private parties, it is necessary to attribute the wrong to the agency or government department that authorized, mandated or failed to prevent the wrongful action [ILC Draft on State Responsibility arts. 5–10].

In addition, a claimant for judicial remedies has to prove damage and causation. This can prove difficult, particularly where there is more than one source of the impugned pollutant as illustrated by the case of acid rain. Sweden, for instance, had to resort to very elaborate monitoring and measuring devices to trace the source of acid rain to the particular suspect countries of the United Kingdom and Germany.

Finally, the remedies sought attempt to restore the injured party to the position prior to the wrong. The judicial tribunal can regulate future actions and order compensation as happened in the Trail Smelter Case (see Chapter Fourteen), or it can declare the rights of parties and order interim measures as was done in the Nuclear Test Cases I (see Chapter Seventeen).

E. THE EFFECTIVENESS OF INTERNATIONAL ENVI-RONMENTAL LAW

Hundreds of treaties establish scores of rules, along with the institutional machinery for securing compliance, and supervising non-compliance. Sometimes, as we have seen, the treaties also provide judicial remedies. Do all these legal measures make a difference to the way nations, corporations, and individuals behave? Much legal analysis centers around the jural nature of treaties, their interpretation and implementation, making the *a priori* assumption that treaties do shape and change the behavior of the relevant parties.

There is, however, a substantial body of *realist* thinking, subscribed to by some of the worlds most eminent states-persons, that defines international behavior and practice in terms of geo-political power rather than law. According to the realists, who base themselves on the writings of Hans Morgantheau, nations agree to treaties and the rules therein embodied because they codify the existing or intended behavior or practice of the parties [*see* POLITICS AMONG NATIONS: THE STRUGGLE FOR POWER AND PEACE (Kenneth Thompson ed., 1993)]. Parties conform their behavior to treaty provisions because it is in their self-interest to do so, and not because they are obliged to by law. The realists argue that it would be a mistake to equate this spurious correlation with true causation, as international lawyers tend to do. [*see* RONALD B. MITCHELL, INTENTIONAL OIL POLLUTION AT SEA 28–29 (1994)] Despite the strenuous exhortations and exertions of many international lawyers, the core of realist thinking, now backed by the critical legal studies (CLS) adherents popularly known as *crits*, is alive and well [Philip Trimble, *International Law*, *World Order*, *and Critical Legal Studies*, 42 STAN. L. REV. 811, 833–34 (1990)].

For the crits, or "new stream" of international scholars, the distinction between law and politics exists as an illusion [see David Kennedy, *A New Stream of International Law and Politics*, 7 Wis. Int'l. L. J. 1 (1988)]. Legal language—whether embodied in rules, treaties or aspirational principles—like all language, simply operates in the service of persuasion towards some practical end. As Martii Koskenniemi has suggested, international law is the "*practice* of attempting to reach the most acceptable solution in the particular circumstances of the case. It is not the application of ready-made, general rules or principles but a conversation about what to do, here and now" [Martii Koskenniemi, From Apology to Utopia 486 (1989)].

It may be reassuring for some students and practitioners to learn that empirical studies have attempted to repudiate the alleged cynicism of the realists and the crits. In one well known study, a political scientist evaluated the evidence drawn from the control of intentional oil pollution, and concluded that the empirical evidence "unequivocally demonstrates that governments and private corporations have undertaken a variety of actions involving compliance, monitoring, and enforcement that they would not have taken in the absence of relevant treaty provisions." [Ronald Mitchell, Intentional Oil Pollution at Sea, 299, 1994]. In response, a "new stream" proponent would argue that the "relevant treaty provisions" simply exist as a political arrangement—and that whatever "compliance, monitoring and enforcement" results from such an arrangement, does so out of further political expediency.

Finally, though debate continues as to causal impetus, it is worth reiterating that international law is a social force that commands respect in the form of compliance. Despite its renowned asymmetry with domestic law, and its publicized defects in lacking a law-making and law-enforcing sovereign, international law does invoke compliance because it governs a law-abiding community of very politically minded states—not a gang of bandits or bank robbers [see ROGER FISHER, IMPROVING COMPLIANCE WITH INTERNATIONAL LAW 16 (1981)].

PART II

INTERNATIONAL ENVIRONMENTAL PROBLEMS

A. GLOBAL

CHAPTER FOUR

POPULATION

A. NATURE OF POPULATION GROWTH

The population of the world which stood at 500 million in 1690 grew to approximately 2.5 billion by 1950 [DENNIS MEADOWS, ET. AL., LIMITS TO GROWTH 34 (1973)]. Today, approximately 5.7 billion people inhabit the world [WORLD RESOURCES INSTITUTE, WORLD RESOURCES; A GUIDE TO THE GLOBAL ENVIRONMENT 27–42 (1994) (hereinafter WRI 1994)]. Although the global population growth rate slowed to 1.8 percent per year in 1990 from the peak of 2.1 percent in the 1960's, the world's population continues to increase by about 90 million people per year, with more than 85 percent of the increase occurring in developing countries. The current population growth rate is expected to continue to decline to 1 percent by the year 2025, but the world's population could reach 8.5 billion by then, and possibly 10 billion by 2050. A pessimistic view is that the world's population will rise to 12.5 billion by 2050 [WRI 1994, at 27].

B. DECREASING RESOURCES

Economic and industrial growth has kept pace with population increases, but as national populations and economies expand, basic resources are dwindling [WRI 1994, at 27, 255–257]. Any environmental assessment of population growth must evaluate the extent to which larger numbers of people consuming larger quantities of resources cause damaging environmental impacts, leading to the depletion, even exhaustion, of scarce natural resources. While resources can be grouped in different ways, the classification of resources as non-renewable versus renewable enables us to understand that resources are exhaustible, and that unlimited growth cannot be supported perpetually.

It is abundantly clear that richer people consume more natural resources than poorer ones. In fact, one study found that the environmental impact of a United States citizen was many times that of a citizen of India [WRI 1994, at 17]. For example, an average United States citizen consumes 43 times as much petroleum as an average citizen of India, 386 times as much pulpwood (used in paper production), and 11 times as much beef. The United States consumes 25 percent of the world's energy but accounts for less than 5 percent of the world's people. The United States also is responsible for 25 percent of the world's greenhouse gases, which contribute to global warming.

At the same time, one cannot dismiss the actual impact of rapidly increasing numbers of human beings in developing countries. Larger numbers of people consuming larger quantities of resources leads to damaging environmental impacts and to the over-utilization of natural resources. The countries with the greatest population increases are India (17 million people per year) and China (16 million people per year) [WRI 1994, at 268–269]. When growth is measured as percentage increase, the mid-eastern countries Jordan and Yemen are growing at the highest rates of 3.4 percent and 3.5 percent per year, respectively. In contrast, African countries are growing at a mean average of 2.9 percent, compared with India at 1.9 percent and China at 1.4 percent. By any measure, such population increases will have adverse environmental consequences.

In a seminal examination of natural resource policy, MEADOWS, ET AL., LIMITS TO GROWTH (1973), researchers from Massachusetts Institute of Technology found that at least nineteen important natural resources were seriously depleted and would be exhausted in the foreseeable future. Though wrong about some conclusions, their original thesis about the finite nature of resources is buttressed by the fact that the physical environment itself is a resource. Global warming, loss of biodiversity, and depletion of the ozone layer are all related to growing populations whose demands for material needs are supplied by industry; industry in turn uses natural resources and causes pollution in a way that endangers the planet itself. Thus, the kernel of the *Limits to Growth*, if not the whole thesis, remains true even today.

C. ENVIRONMENTAL IMPACTS

The environmental impacts of population growth are ubiquitous and universal. Our examples illustrate only part of the problem. Population growth, for instance, has a direct impact on agricultural resources. The demand for food created from population growth has necessitated an increase in required crop-land area at the expense of natural ecosystems such as forests, grasslands, and wetlands. To increase agricultural productivity, scientists have developed "high-yield" varieties of crops, but have typically ignored genetic diversity. The use of irrigation and chemical pesticides and fertilizers has increased production, but has contributed to the depletion of arable land suitable for cultivation [*see* Laura Jackson, *Agricultural Industrialization and the Loss of Biodiversity, in* PROTECTION OF GLOBAL BIODIVERSITY: CONVERGING INTERDISCIPLINARY STRATEGIES (Lakshman Guruswamy & Jeffrey McNeely, eds. forthcoming 1997); Robert Horsch & Robert Fraley, *Biotechnology Can Help Reduce the Loss of Biodiversity, in* PROTECTION OF GLOBAL BIODIVERSITY:

CONVERGING INTERDISCIPLINARY STRATEGIES (Lakshman Guruswamy & Jeffrey McNeely, eds. forthcoming 1997)]. The use of harmful pesticides and fertilizers has also poisoned soil and water resources, while vermin have become resistant to chemical pesticides. Overuse of irrigation has resulted in salinization of the soil (buildup of salts and minerals) and waterlogging. The International Soil Reference and Information Center, for example, has determined that improper agricultural practices have moderately degraded 1.2 billion hectares of arable land world wide (10 percent of the Earth's surface), while all higher life-forms have been eliminated on about 9 million hectares of once arable land (an area about the size of the states of Vermont and Connecticut combined)[WORLD RESOURCES INSTITUTE, WORLD RESOURCES; A GUIDE TO THE GLOBAL ENVIRONMENT 233 (1996) (hereinafter WRI 1996)].

Many countries with a shortage of arable land also have a shortage of fresh water. Almost 75 percent of the world's fresh water now flows into irrigation, but diverting water for agricultural, domestic and industrial use usually means less water for aquatic environments like wetlands, lakes and rivers. While the oceans are vast, and contain 97 percent of the Earth's water, ocean water is not potable. Two of the remaining three percent of fresh water is trapped in the polar ice caps, leaving less than 0.008 percent of the remaining available for drinking. Compounding the problem, the use of fresh water has quadrupled between 1940 and 1990 [WRI 1994, at 181–2].

As a whole, the quality of the earth's environment has rapidly degraded over the last 40 to 50 years. While some experts believe that population growth is the major cause of such environmental deterioration [PAUL EHRLICH & ANNE EHRLICH, THE POPULATION EXPLOSION, (1990); PAUL EHRLICH & ANNE EHRLICH, EXTINCTION, THE CAUSES AND CONSEQUENCES OF THE DISAPPEARANCE OF SPECIES 74 (1981)], others believe that the most powerful factor in determining environmental quality is the technology used to produce goods and services, and that any chosen technology may cause either environmental degradation or improvement [Barry Commoner, *Rapid Population Growth and Environmental Stress*, 21 INT'L J. HEALTH SERVICES 199 (1991)]. It is difficult to deny, however, that population growth, even if not the single most important factor, does have a dramatic impact on the environment [PARTHA DASGUPTA, AN INQUIRY INTO WELL BEING AND DESTITUTION 269–96 (1995)].

D. REMEDIAL OBJECTIVES

1. THEORIES ON POPULATION GROWTH

Experts disagree on how to balance population growth and economic growth, but almost all agree that the current use of essential resources, that the current rates of environmental degradation are not infinitely sustainable, and that continued population growth will eventually exceed the earth's carrying capacity (the maximum number that can be sustained by the Earth's natural resources year after year without diminution of the quality of life or diminution of the resources). The differing theories fall into three categories.

Theories in the first category predict disaster if population growth is not drastically reduced, but also predict a technically and economically sustainable society if the rate of population growth is significantly reduced [DAVID PEARCE & R. KERRY TURNER, ECONOMICS OF NATURAL RESOURCES AND THE ENVIRONMENT 6 (1990)]. These predictions are premised upon the Neo–Malthusian theory that population growth will exceed the food supply because a finite availability of farmland sets a limit to agricultural expansion. These experts believe that even technologies providing unlimited resources and reduced pollution would be insufficient to counteract the effects of land overuse leading to decreased food production and shortages [ROBERT CASSEN, ET AL., POPULATION AND DEVELOPMENT: OLD DEBATES, NEW CONCLUSIONS (1994)].

The second and third category of theories are more optimistic and reject what they consider the alarmism and panic sown by the first category. The fact of continuing increases in the amount of food production and output throughout the undeveloped world, they point out, flies in the face of Neo–Malthusian predictions of famine [Amartya Sen, *Fertility and Coercion*, 63 U. CHI. L. REV. 1035, 1050 (1996)]. The second category of "developmentalists" believes that economic and social development, technical innovation, better management of resources, and market substitutes can overcome the limits of natural resources and allow continued population growth [DAVID PEARCE & R. KERRY TURNER, ECONOMICS OF NATURAL RESOURCES AND THE ENVIRONMENT 43–53 (1990)]. They reject the position that economic development resulting in improved living standards causes rapid population growth *per se*. Instead, they subscribe to a theory of two-stage demographic transition. In stage one, improved living standards reduce the death rate without creating sufficient economic security. A second stage follows in which the birth rate falls because of education, delayed marriage, and cultural changes. Some of these theorists point to prices of resources as indicators of scarcity, arguing that when prices become too high because of scarcity, a technology-driven market substitutes an equivalent but cheaper resource. This theory, that prices will guide the market adjustment, depends on resources being owned, while the fact is that many resources such as water and the atmosphere are a "common pool" and are not owned. Consequently, others reject such price theories, and argue that there are often no incentives to conserve or to protect such resources.

The third category of "redistributionists" blame the problems associated with unsustainable growth and environmental depletion on inequities of consumption, and the unequal distribution of rights among the nations and peoples of the world [ROBERT CASSEN, ET AL., POPULATION AND DEVELOPMENT: OLD DEBATES, NEW CONCLUSIONS (1994)]. This group also believes in sustainable development, but maintains that the major cause of environmental depletion lies in a consumption explosion by the industrialized world, rather than a population explosion in the Third World. This, they claim, is illustrated by the fact that 15 percent of the world's population enjoys 80 percent of the world's income.

To them the problem is poverty, rather than scarcity, and the solution is economic development that goes beyond providing technology. This third group claims that resources must be distributed more fairly between industrialized countries and developing countries. They emphasize that the population problem is not about an increase in the number of humans, but in a lack of human rights that includes the right to a decent standard of living and the right of women to control their own reproduction.

2. THE WAY FORWARD

These theories and corresponding practical problems jostle for recognition within the new international framework of sustainable development. One approach, fostered and proclaimed at the "Earth Summit," the 1992 United Nations Conference on Environment and Development (UNCED), hopes to integrate development and production with resource conservation and enhancement to provide an adequate livelihood and equitable access to resources for all people in the present, without compromising the ability to meet those needs in the future. In a related approach, experts, governments, non-governmental organizations and international agencies have worked for three years negotiating and revising a program to stabilize world population. Adopted, after some modification in Cairo, Egypt at the 1994 United Nations International Conference on Population and Development (1994 Population Conference), the result is a comprehensive plan that incorporates ideas from many theories [the Programme of Action of the International Conference on Population and Development, U.N. Conference on Population and Development, U.N. Doc. A/CONF. 171/13/Annex (1994)(hereinafter Program of Action)][*Focus on Population and Development: Follow-up on Cairo Conference*, U.S. DEPT. OF STATE DISPATCH, Jan. 2, 1995, *available in* DIALOG, 1995 WL 8643457]. The Programme of Action includes extending family planning facilities, improving women's education, health, and social status, encouraging sustainable economic development, and reducing the impact of population on the environment.

E. LEGAL RESPONSE

The above Program of Action was adopted at the 1994 Population Conference by consensus amidst controversy, and this dissension raises substantial doubts as to whether the Program of Action can become the *fons et origio* (source and origin) of a new international regime for population. Indeed, the legal response to population growth cannot be found in a discrete body of law dealing with population *per se*. Instead, it resides uneasily at the intersection of the laws dealing *inter alia* with sustainable development, social development, economic development, environmental protection, gender equity, health, education, and child welfare.

The 1994 Population Conference attempted to merge all these strands of law into a comprehensive whole in its Program of Action. A handful of Islamic nations, however, were so opposed to it that they withdrew in protest, while parts of this document were strenuously opposed by a number of nations led by the Vatican [Report of the International Conference on Population and Development, at 146–149, U.N. Doc. A/Conf.171/13(1994)]. The whole Program of Action, therefore, cannot be seen as a crystallization of customary international law, and may possess dubious value even as soft law.

The lack of agreement over population growth may seem surprising. All nations of the world, joined by the Catholic Church, recognize the environmental dangers of burgeoning populations, even though the Catholic Church advocates population control through "natural family planning" [Gregory M. Saylin, *The United Nations International Conference on Population and Development: Religion, Tradition and Law in Latin America*, 28 VAND. J. TRANSNAT'L L. 1245, 1270 (1995)]. Moreover, there is international consensus, falling short of unanimity, that coercion be eschewed as a method of family planning [Program of Action, para. 7(3)]. Closer examination, however, reveals that a number of entrenched reasons block the creation of an international population regime.

The first of these arises from differing perceptions of the population question. As we have noted, Neo–Malthusians fear that increasing population will inexorably lead to shortages of food and natural resources, and a failure of the carrying capacity of the planet. They demand immediate government intervention to defuse this time bomb in the form of family planning programs. This view is countered by "developmentalists" and "redistributionists" of varying stripes. In general, developmentalists see overpopulation as a symptom of underdevelopment, while the "redistributionists" argue there is sufficient food and resources to feed increasing populations if there were better distribution, more international equity, and less profligate consumption by the developed world.

Second, there are deep divisions separating the developmentalists and redistributionists. It is true they agree that the Neo–Malthusians, ignoring strong evidence to the contrary, continue to sow panic. They also agree on the need for economic development and international equity. On social development, they agree on gender equity, and the need for women to have improved health care. But agreement stops there.

Developmentalists and redistributionists disagree fundamentally on well-established tenets of western feminism such as the empowerment of women through accessibility to abortion, contraception and education, and the assertion that "women are crippled by unbridled fertility" [Draft Program of Action, *supra*]. The empowerment of women became a driving force at the 1994 Population Conference, and western feminists along with most developed countries saw this as a critical step in the move toward population control. For western feminists and developed countries, it is absolutely essential to give women reproductive freedom, emancipate them from anachronistic customs that bind women to the home, deny them an education, force unwanted children upon them, and then commit them to a lifetime of unrelenting labor of caring for those children.

For many religious traditionalists, whether Roman Catholic or Islamic, such a view insults the dignity of women. Religious traditionalists argue that western feminism seeks to limit a woman's freedom to bear children, denigrates motherhood, propagates immorality, promotes abortions, and assails the concept of a nurturing family: the very foundation of society.

While such doctrinal differences stand in the way of a legal regime controlling population growth, a third political reason militates against a legal regime instituting population control. In brief, such a regime may be seen as violating national sovereignty—encroaching on cherished notions of individual state control. And fourth, the Program of Action appears to have institutionalized, rather than resolved, deep controversies between feminist organizations, conservatives, environmentalists, religious traditionalists, and family planners [Bolan, *supra*, at 42].

Despite these problems, it is possible to point to some features of the sixteen-chapter Program of Action that may amount to a crystallization of customary law. For example, the sixth principle set out in chapter II of the Program of Action, which was accepted by the religious traditionalists, endorses the concept of sustainable development and requires that:

> [S]tates should reduce and eliminate unsustainable patterns of production and consumption and promote appropriate policies, including population-related policies, in order to meet the needs of current generations without compromising the ability of future generations to meet their own needs.

This may be viewed as a restriction on unfettered consumption by the developed countries, which according to some commentators significantly contributes to the population problem [Judith E. Jacobson, *Population, Consumption, and Environmental Degradation; Problems and Solutions*, 6 COLO. J. INT'L ENVT'L. L. & POL'Y 255 (1995)].

Furthermore, even though the community of nations may disagree as to the means, a consensus exists that population growth should be controlled. The next population conference, the first in the 21st century, may see greater agreement on the concrete steps necessary to achieve this objective. In the meantime, the implementation of policies aimed at sustainable development, gender equity, education, and health may all work in concert to reduce population growth.

CHAPTER FIVE

BIODIVERSITY

A. NATURE OF THE PROBLEM

Life on earth is supported by communities of plants, animals, and microorganisms interacting with each other within ecosystems, and with the physical environment [BIODIVERSITY 21 (E. O. Wilson ed., 1988)]. Biodiversity encompasses three concepts: the genetic diversity within each species, the diversity of species, and the diversity of ecosystems within a region. Biodiversity sustains life on earth by maintaining atmospheric quality, regulating local climates, absorbing pollutants, protecting watersheds, and generating and maintaining soils. The greater an ecosystem's diversity, the greater its capacity to support life and adapt to changing conditions.

Our anxiety over the loss of biodiversity may be based on the "use-value" of species and ecosystems, within economic, ecological, and aesthetic frameworks. Our concern may also be premised on ethical values, which are different than use-values and arise from a belief in the intrinsic worth of a species.

Within the use-value nexus, biological resources have economic value as food, medicines, chemicals, fibers, structural materials, fuel, and for other purposes. A benefit-cost figure can be calculated for preserving species with known economic values, and can even be estimated for those with unknown economic value; if a species is lost, the possibility of deriving use from it is also lost [BRYAN G. NORTON, WHY PRESERVE NATURAL VARIETY? 27 (1987)].

On the other hand, the ecological services provided by ecosystems are so diffuse and untraceable that actual economic value for those services cannot be estimated for individual species. Each species contributes to, and is interrelated and interdependent upon other species in the ecosystem. The ecological value of preserving biodiversity is based on the incalculable value of the essential services provided, for example by ecosystems, such as forests removing carbon dioxide from the atmosphere.

It should also be remembered that an ecosystem is vulnerable to the weaknesses of its species. For example, loss of genetic diversity within plant and animal species leads to uniformity that makes species more susceptible to diseases and pests. This weakness renders them less able to adapt to a changing physical environment, and in turn makes the ecosystem less stable [PAUL EHRLICH & ANNE EHRLICH, EXTINCTION, THE CAUSES AND CONSEQUENCES OF THE DISAPPEARANCE OF SPECIES 74 (1981)].

Biological resources also have aesthetic value as sources of recreation and beauty. Like economic and ecological values, aesthetic values are based on the uses provided by species and ecosystems. The value of nature is difficult to quantify, but can be assigned based on the value of a similar experience, such as the ability to visit a pristine North Slope in Alaska, or a preserved tropical rain forest, or what a person would be willing to pay for the experience, or be willing to accept for not having the opportunity. Even the aesthetic value of nature's spiritual effect on humans may depend on the "use-value" of nature.

In contrast, preserving nature for its own sake, as distinct from its use, depends on the intrinsic value of a species in its own right, independent of its value to any other. Ethical reasons for preserving biodiversity are based, quite simply, on the right of species and ecosystems to exist. Arguably, their enduring existence denotes the right to continued existence, which in turn carries responsibilities for humans. As the dominant species on earth, humans have a moral responsibility as caretakers or trustees to preserve other species.

B. ENVIRONMENTAL IMPACTS

The richest remaining areas of biodiversity are rain forests, coral reefs, and wetlands. Tropical forests contain 50 to 90 percent of the approximately 10 million species that live on earth. These ecosystems are threatened with rapid destruction as a result of pressure from growing local populations for agricultural land and fuel wood supplies, coupled with world markets for tropical hardwoods and animal products [NATIONAL ACADEMY OF SCIENCES, ONE

EARTH, ONE FUTURE (1990)]. The annual rate of tropical deforestation in the 1980s averaged 0.8 percent, with the greatest losses in Latin America, West Africa, and Southeast Asia. At this rate, scientists estimate that 5 to 10 percent of tropical forest species (hundreds of thousands) may face extinction by the year 2020.

Tropical deforestation to clear agricultural land is often accomplished by a *slash and burn* method which releases carbon dioxide and other gases that contribute to global warming and depletion of the ozone layer. Tropical deforestation may also lead to degradation of soil fertility and changes in regional hydrology, as watersheds are destroyed, and precipitation patterns change. However, the most serious long-term impact of tropical deforestation may be the loss of plant and animal species.

Coral reefs cover only 0.17 percent of the sea floor, yet they contain 25 percent of all known marine species. Coral reefs are created in tropical saltwater by animals called stony-coral polyps. With the aid of symbiotic algae living within the corals' tissues, the corals secrete the limestone reefs over thousands of years. The fragile coral reef ecosystems are vulnerable to both natural environmental threats such as disease and predation, and human activities that pollute or physically destroy the reefs.

Coastal wetlands which provide vital breeding, nursery, and feeding areas for marine species are threatened primarily by pollution, development pressures from expanding human populations (six out of ten people live within 40 miles of the coast), and rising sea levels predicted to result from climate changes and subsidence [WALTER V. REID & MARK C. TREXLER, DROWNING THE NATIONAL HERITAGE: CLIMATE CHANGE AND U.S. COASTAL BIODIVERSITY 8 (1991)]. For example, over half of the wetlands in the contiguous United States have been dredged or developed, destroying ecosystems valuable not only for fish, waterfowl, and endangered species habitat, but also for natural water purification and flood prevention systems.

C. CAUSES

The primary cause of the loss of biodiversity is habitat destruction resulting from the expansion of human populations and activities. Among terrestrial ecosystems, the expansion of agriculture and commercial harvesting has led to the destruction of forests, while overgrazing and conversion to agricultural crop land has significantly altered natural habitat. In aquatic ecosystems, dams have destroyed large sections of freshwater habitat, while coastal development is responsible for destroying reefs and near-shore marine habitat.

Other direct causes include invasion by introduced species, over-exploitation of biological resources, industrial agriculture and forestry, pollution, and potentially, global climate change. Clearly the introduction of predators, competitors, and pathogens into isolated ecosystems poses a serious threat to the survival of native species. Just as clearly, forest, marine, and wildlife resources have been over-exploited—sometimes to the point of extinction—not only for food but also for commodities such as elephant ivory and ceremonial objects such as tiger bones. In a related vein, industrial agriculture and forestry techniques use fewer varieties of plants to increase productivity; the result is a loss of biodiversity, and an increased susceptibility to pests. In addition, pollution of the air, soil, and water has led to the reduction, and even extinction, of some sensitive species which can, in turn, lead to the destruction of entire ecosystems. Finally, many species and ecosystems may not successfully adapt to predicted global climate changes brought on by air pollution.

D. REMEDIAL OBJECTIVES

The goal of species biodiversity conservation is to meet people's needs for biological resources while ensuring that those resources last indefinitely. As we shall see, remedial actions need to be based within global frameworks of equity and justice as well as sustainable development. Earlier treaty regimes attempted to deal with biodiversity as a self-contained problem, but subsequent geo-political developments demanded a different approach governed by two systemic principles that have become a foundational part of modern international environmental law. The two contrast starkly with environmental protection simpliciter.

The first principle is international equity or justice. It demands that the endemic problems of global poverty must constitute the bedrock of any discussion of other global predicaments such as environmental protection. The second principle is sustainable development. This is a new paradigm endorsed by the Earth Summit that generally allows for the use and exploitation of resources subject to environmental restraints (*See* Chapter Eighteen).

Consistent with a pattern established during the negotiations at the Stockholm Conference on the Human Environment (1972), the protection of biodiversity has become part of the North–South debate on equity and sustainable development, traversing the issues of development (economic growth) and global poverty. The experience of the Convention on Biological Diversity (CBD), June 5, 1992, 31 I.L.M. 818 (entered into force Dec. 29, 1993) signed at Rio in 1992, has demonstrated the near impossibility of segregating or surgically isolating the environmental or scientific problems of biodiversity from its socio-political milieu.

E.   LEGAL RESPONSE

1.   THE CONVENTION ON BIOLOGICAL DIVERSITY (CBD)

In 1987 the UNEP Governing Council asked an ad hoc working group to "explore the desirability and possible form of an umbrella convention to rationalize current activities" in this area. By umbrella convention, the Governing Council meant a treaty that would consolidate the existing treaties into a workable whole, eliminating jurisdictional overlap and filling perceived gaps. As this proved politically unattainable, the international community settled for the current CBD—a framework treaty which possesses only the power to seek "appropriate forms of cooperation" with the executive bodies of other biodiversity conventions [arts. 22(1), 23(4)(h)].

As a framework treaty, the CBD contains primarily aspirational provisions, with matters of substance left to future development by its own Conference of the Parties (COP). In fact, the CBD has received a great deal of criticism for its lack of substantive provisions, and because its most general obligations contain heavily qualified language. Others have defended the CBD by noting its resolution of long-standing problems such as access to biological resources—while reminding detractors of the forward-looking nature of the framework approach in setting the stage for future solutions among political difficulties.

In summarizing the provisions of this framework convention, for analytical purposes we have returned to the two overriding principles of (1) Equity and Resource Transfers, and (2) Sustainable Development (Conservation and Sustainable Use). Of course, the two principles are conceptually bound together, and one way that the CBD approaches that connection is by applying an underlying, if not expressly articulated, third principle known as Common But Differentiated Responsibility (CBDR).

CBDR links equity and sustainable development together by contemplating resource transfers such that "developed countries acknowledge the responsibility that they bear in the international pursuit of sustainable development in view of the pressures their societies place on the global environment and of the technologies and financial resources they command" [Principle 7, Rio Declaration]. In our analysis, we have located the specific commitments—including those based on CBDR—within a general discussion of the issues.

(a) Principles of Equity and Resource Transfers

In reviewing the outcome of equity issues in the CBD, we have noticed the differences in the background positions of the richer countries of the developed world, the North, and the poorer countries of the developing world, the South (*see* Chapter One, Introduction). As most of the biological diversity in the world exists in the South, the South understandingly felt, and continues to feel, possessive of those resources. While accepting the importance of preserving biodiversity, they perceived outside attempts to curtail internal development as a threat to sovereignty; in addition, as these nations experience conditions of real poverty, the cordoning off of large tracts of land from development loomed as an impediment to alleviating deprivation through economic progress. Should the North—which has already consumed a substantial degree of its own biodiversity—now want the South to curtail its development in the name of biodiversity, the latter would exact a price. The South would embrace sustainable development only if the North would assume the costs, and only through projects that would not compromise a growing sense of sovereignty over natural resources.

On the other hand, the North viewed the protection of biological diversity less from the point of past sins, and more as a present global problem which entailed shared sacrifice. Thus, as the North had generally placed restrictions on development in its own countries—creating a series of protected areas such as parks, preserves and wilderness areas—it tended to believe that the South should do the same. Although the North recognized that the South should receive some financial help in its efforts to protect biological diversity, the North saw that protection as an outright obligation of each member of the global community, an obligation independent of financial transfer and ability to pay. Furthermore, in transferring financial resources to the developing countries, the developed countries wanted to retain control over exactly where that money would go; in other words, they wanted targeted and efficient use of their contributions.

i. Common Concern of Humankind

One outcome of the conflict between the developed and developing countries is expressed in the preamble of the CBD, which affirms that "the conservation of biological diversity is a common concern of humankind." Early in the negotiating process the parties dropped the phrase "common heritage" from consideration because of its connotation of community access to, and the sharing of proceeds from, the development of those resources. They rejected the formulation of the Food and Agricultural Organization of the United Nations (FAO), which had earlier confirmed that "plant genetic resources are a heritage of mankind ... [which] consequently should be available without restriction" [International Undertaking on Plant Genetic Resources, art. 1 (1983) (HEREINAFTER the Undertaking)]. Previously, both the Law of the Sea and the Outer Space Treaty employed the common heritage language calling for the sharing of proceeds from resources lying outside the area of national jurisdiction. These agreements were concluded, however, at a time when developing countries would benefit from such a concept. By contrast, in the case of biological diversity developing countries were dealing with resources within their own borders—resources to which they were reluctant to surrender sovereignty. Needless to say, due to its linguistic history the "common heritage" term did not gain favor. Even so, the "common concern" formulation—though less broad in scope—does recognize the loss of biodiversity as a major problem which the international community must attend to on a global basis.

ii. Access to Genetic Resources

The CBD therefore discards the principle of "free access" to genetic resources, a principle which maintained the right of a developed country to obtain and freely use the genetic material of a developing country. Though later annexes to the FAO Undertaking, referred to above, make clear that free access does not mean "free of charge," only with the CBD did the international community make a clean break from the original concept of free access. Under article 15(1) of the CBD, "the authority to determine access to genetic resources rests with the national governments and is subject to national legislation." The CBD adopts the principle of Prior Informed Consent, now a standard concept with regard to North–South environmental transactions [art. 15(5)], and developing country parties can negotiate with private companies or other parties on the "mutually agreed" price of access to genetic material [art. 15(4); *see* Chapter Nine, Toxic and Hazardous Substances for a discussion of Prior Informed Consent concerning hazardous waste transfers].

On a related issue, genetic resources taken from the country of origin before the CBD's entry into force—such as those now held in gene banks throughout the world—are excluded from the present access provisions. The COP will soon take up the question of such resources, deciding what benefit, if any, developing countries will receive from genetic material previously removed from the country of origin.

iii. Biotechnology

Biotechnology, as considered in the CBD, "means any technological application that uses biological systems, living organisms, or derivatives thereof, to make or modify products or processes for specific use" [art. 2]. This ranges from the ancient practice of the selective breeding of animals and plants, to sophisticated DNA technology and genetic engineering. The CBD covers two important and controversial areas with regard to biotechnology.

Transfer of Technology

The CBD makes explicitly clear that "technology includes biotechnology" [art. 2], so that any reference to the transfer of technology also includes the transfer of biotechnology. The issue of access to and transfer of technology is dealt with in article 16—a convoluted article with a number of overlapping and cross-referenced provisions. As a first requirement, the article mandates that all parties, developed and developing countries, must "provide and/or facilitate" the access to and transfer of biotechnology [art. 16(1)]. The transfer of technology to developing countries must be made on "fair and favorable terms, including concessional and preferential terms where mutually agreed," and such transfer can occur by way of the financial mechanism [art. 16(2)]. Making the transfer available through the financial mechanism means that technology transfer qualifies as a fundable enterprise under the CBD. Finally, article 16(2) also provides that technology protected by an intellectual property right (IPR) in a developed country, if transferred, must receive "the adequate and effective protection" of that right in the developing country.

The controversy involving transfer of biotechnology again reflects fundamental differences of opinion between the North and the South. First, most biotechnology remains in the hands of private corporations in developed countries, and as market players within market economies, these corporations demand some remuneration for their investment. Second, biotechnology generally exists under IPR protection in developed countries, and corporations insist on similar protection in the developing countries. Without such protection, even payment for the technology will not suffice as the technology might be copied and pirated in the developing country.

In contrast, developing countries see the transfer of biotechnology as a main incentive for participation in the CBD. With transfer, over time they might develop their own biotechnology industries, developing the wealth of their own biodiversity. In addition, the South views IPRs as an impediment to technology transfer, as IPRs make the protected technology more expensive and thus more restrictive. They maintain that the level of IPR protection should be commensurate with an individual country's level of economic development, and thus a matter for national determination.

Resolution of the impasse concerning IPRs now rests with the new Trade–Related Aspects of Intellectual Property Rights (TRIPS) of the World Trade Organization. In effect, under this agreement developing countries must generally respect IPRs, but have a number of years in which to implement protective legislation. As for the channeling of resources to developing countries (who then might remunerate corporations involved in the transfer), article 16(2) makes clear that such projects are fundable by the financial mechanism—either for the cost itself and/or for the cost of the IPR protection foregone [*see* art.19]. In fact, the first COP listed the matter as a program priority for the financial mechanism to consider, giving emphasis "[i]n accordance with article 16 of the Convention ... [to] projects which promote access to, transfer of and cooperation in joint development of technology" [*Decisions Adopted by the First meeting of the Conference of the Parties*, annex I(III)(4)(f), U.N. Doc. UNEP/CBD/1/17 (1994)].

Transfer of the Benefits of Biotechnology

As previously mentioned, the CBD provides for negotiations between developed country entities (usually corporations) and developing country parties concerning the price of access to genetic resources [art. 15(4) & 15(7)]. In this way, the CBD foresees a mechanism by which the developing countries might: (1) negotiate the acquisition of biotechnology developed from genetic resources [art. 16(3)]; (2) participate in research projects connected to genetic resources [art. 19(1)]; and (3) gain priority access to the results and benefits (such as royalties) arising from biotechnologies based upon genetic resources [art. 19(2)]. The governments of developed countries must facilitate the above outcomes, but on the whole negotiations will take place between private corporations and developing countries. Again, article 15(7) makes allowance for use of the financial mechanism to fund projects which share the research, development and benefits of genetic resources.

iv. Financial Transfers

Under the CBD, developed countries must pay "to enable developing country Parties to meet the agreed full incremental costs to them of implementing measures which fulfill the obligations of this Convention" [Art. 20(2)]. Again, as stated above, this provision enshrines the principle of Common But Differentiated Responsibility (CBDR) as noted in Principle 7 of the 1992 Rio Declaration, in which developed countries acknowledge their greater financial responsibility in addressing global environmental degradation. Developed Countries, listed in an annex adopted at the first meeting of the COP, will channel their contributions through the newly restructured interim financial mechanism, the Global Environment Facility (GEF) [see Appendix A]. Following the Programme Priorities laid down by the COP, the GEF will then fund individual projects put forth by the developing countries—the "incremental cost" to be determined by individual negotiations between the GEF and the respective applicant. Also, developed countries may bypass the

GEF through regional, bilateral and multilateral channels under article 20(3), but the extent to which such funding might meet a developing country's financial obligations under the CBD remains an open question for the COP.

(b) Principles of Sustainable Development (Conservation and Sustainable Use)

As our second operating principle, sustainable development functions as a prevailing force within, and ultimate objective of, the CBD. Reference to sustainable development is only made once in the treaty, but it is repeatedly inscribed within two common terms of the CBD: "conservation" and "sustainable use." These might be seen as the twin poles of sustainable development. On the one hand, sustainable use acknowledges the necessity of utilizing biological resources:

> "sustainable use" means the use of components of biological diversity in a way, and at a rate that does not lead to the long-term decline of biological diversity, thereby maintaining its potential to meet the needs and aspirations of present and future generations.

[art. 2]. On the other hand "conservation" is not defined in the treaty, but its usage clearly speaks to the preservation of biological diversity. For example, the treaty does define *in-situ* conservation as "the conservation of ecosystems and natural habitats and the maintenance and recovery of viable populations of species in their natural surroundings ..." [art. 2]. Thus, in combining the development connotation of "sustainable use" with the preservation connotation of "conservation," the CBD strikes the balance of sustainable development.

The treaty imposes various obligations with regard to sustainable development, weaving these through a myriad of overlapping provisions. In summarizing these commitments, however, one is immediately confronted with the qualifying language, "as far as possible" and "as appropriate," that accompanies nearly every obligation. These qualifications severely limit the strength of very important provisions, and create the perception of the CBD as an empty treaty. Particularly with regard to the obligations of developing countries, these qualifications greatly reduce their respective commitments—and, as most of the remaining biodiversity lies within their borders, significantly diminishes the worldwide effort to save biodiversity. On the other hand, no treaty can go beyond the political realities of the time, and at least the framework approach to international law-making provides a flexible method to institute stronger measures.

i. All Parties (Including Developing Countries)

In implementing sustainable development under the CBD, the focus is on national action. In general, all parties must develop "national strategies, plans or programmes for the conservation and sustainable use of biodiversity" [art. 6(a)], and then must integrate these approaches into other relevant national programs such as forestry and agricultural planning [art. 6(b)]. As part of this process each country must also conduct studies to identify the components of biodiversity [art. 7(a)], and then must monitor those components most in need of conservation as well as those "which offer the greatest potential for sustainable use" [art. 7(b)].

More specifically, with respect to the conservation of *in situ* biodiversity—that is, biodiversity in its natural setting—the CBD in article 8 makes a number of important mandates, including the establishment of protected areas, the management of biological resources within and without such protected areas, the protection of ecosystems, and the maintenance of viable species populations. Responding to articles 19(3) and 8(g), the parties at COP II also committed themselves to the development of a Protocol on Bio-safety, recognizing that the advent of biotechnology may have adverse environmental impacts on the conservation and sustainable use of biodiversity [Report of the Open Ended Ad Hoc Group on Bio–Safety, UNEP/CBD/COP/2/7]. And, though the CBD stresses *in situ* conservation as the primary means of protecting biodiversity, a number of *ex situ* provisions also exist. *Ex situ* conservation includes gene banks, captive breeding programs and zoos. Under article 9, parties must adopt measures to promote *ex situ* conservation through the establishment of appropriate facilities and through the development of appropriate species rehabilitation programs.

Parties must also incorporate a consideration of sustainable development into their national decision-making, protect traditional cultural uses of biological resources, and encourage cooperation between the public and private sectors [*see* art. 10]. On a related issue, parties must also consider the implementation of environmental impact assessment (EIA) procedures for proposed projects that are likely to have significant adverse impacts on biological diversity—clearly a step forward in achieving the overall goal of sustainable development [art. 14].

Again, all of these critical provisions remain qualified with the phrase "as far as possible and as appropriate," except for the simple duty to create "national strategies, plans or programmes" which receives the arguably less evasive escape clause "in accordance with its [a specific nation's] particular conditions and capabilities." In overseeing the implementation of all these requirements, such as they are, the COP will receive reports from each party concerning its fulfillment of the provisions and objectives of the convention [art. 26]. The first national reports are due by the fourth COP in 1997, and will focus on the general measures for conservation and sustainable use under article 6.

ii. Developed Countries

Following the concept of Common But Differentiated Responsibility (CBDR)—which as stated earlier links together the two principles of equity and sustainable development—the CBD creates additional commitments for developed countries. These primarily involve obligations of funding and technology transfer, outlined above, which developed country parties must discharge in furtherance of sustainable development. In fact, as stated clearly in article 20(4), the obligations of developing countries to fulfill their obligations depends on the "effective implementation of developed country Parties of their commitments under the Convention related to financial resources and transfer of technology." In other words, one might see the qualifying language of developing country commitments, such as "as far as possible and as appropriate," as contingent on the contributions of developed countries. In this way the North, in effect, controls just how "qualified" these "qualified" commitments are. If the North wants real action by the South on sustainable use and the conservation of biodiversity, it need only contribute a commensurate amount.

Of further note, the CBD also distinguishes between Organization for Economic Co-operation and Development (OECD) members and former Soviet bloc nations. The latter, those "countries undergoing the process of transition to a market economy," can voluntarily assume the obligations of developing countries over time [art. 20(2)].

(c) Institutions

The CBD offers the typical institutional arrangements of a framework treaty. The COP acts as the "all-powerful" legislative organ which makes decisions on a range of substantive, administrative and procedural matters. The COP, which meets annually, also votes on amendments, protocols and amendments to protocols. The method for adopting informal or "everyday" decisions—whether administrative or substantive—remains to be decided. Procedural questions are resolved by a simple majority vote. Amendments to the convention or to protocols are by at least a two-thirds majority of parties present and voting [art. 29].

The Secretariat functions as the administrative arm of the COP, working year round to coordinate action with other international bodies and preparing reports and material for the next meeting of the parties. The Subsidiary Body on Scientific, Technical and Technological Advice (SBSTTA) provides expertise to the COP, creating scientific and technical assessments of both the status of biodiversity and the effects of measures taken to implement the CBD [art. 25]. Significantly, the first meeting of the COP also established a Clearing–House Mechanism for Technical and Scientific Cooperation, an institution that will act as a catalyst for collaborative research and joint projects under the CBD [art. 18(3)]. The pilot phase of the clearing-house mechanism was commenced for the years 1996–1997.

(d) Relationship to Other Conventions

As we shall see, the nations of the world have already created a number of international as well as regional treaties on specific subjects concerning biological diversity. Significantly however, the CBD would trump all other treaties, including the WTO (formerly GATT), where the exercise of rights and obligations under those treaties "would cause serious damage or a threat to biological diversity" [art.

22(1)]. The one exception to this is in regard to the marine environment, in which the rights and obligations of the CBD may not conflict with those created by the United Nations Convention on the Law of the Sea (UNCLOS), Dec. 10, 1982, art. 22(2), 21 I.L.M. 1261 [entered into force (Nov. 16, 1994)]. Thus, in effect we now have two dominant environmental treaties dealing with biological diversity: the CBD for terrestrial biodiversity and UNCLOS for marine biodiversity.

As the preeminent treaty with respect to terrestrial biodiversity, the CBD directs the Secretariat to seek "appropriate forms of cooperation" with the executive bodies of other biodiversity treaties. The goal is to (a) facilitate the exchange of information, (b) harmonize reporting procedures, (c) coordinate respective programs of work, and (d) consult on how such conventions can contribute to the implementation of the CBD (UNEP/CBD/COP/3/29). To this end, the CBD Secretariat has entered into Memoranda of Cooperation with a number of executive bodies of other treaties, including the Ramsar Convention, CITES, and the Bonn Convention (see below). Over time, the CBD may in this way function as a type of "umbrella" convention—the proverbial "gleam in the eye" of the UNEP Governing Council back in 1987—eliminating inefficient jurisdictional overlap and filling perceived gaps [see Brent Hendricks, *Postmodern Possibility and the Convention on Biological Diversity*, 5 N.Y.U.ENV. L.J. 1 (1996)].

2. INTERNATIONAL TREATIES RELATED TO BIOLOGICAL DIVERSITY

(a) The 1973 Convention on International Trade in Endangered Species of Fauna and Flora (CITES)

The CITES convention, an early international treaty pertaining to the environment, attempts to protect endangered plant and animal species through restrictions on international trade [Mar. 3, 1973, 12 I.L.M. 1085 (entered into force July 1, 1975)]. Such trade has contributed greatly to the decline of those wild species who possess some commercial viability, including the high profile mammals of Africa. Ratified by most countries involved in this type of commerce, CITES creates a number of bureaucratic hurdles that prevent particularly harmful exchanges. In effect, CITES establishes a paper trail for all allowable trade in protected species, and any trade without proper documentation is considered illegal under the treaty.

To date, CITES protects literally thousands of species, with a large number coming from the developing countries of the South. To keep track of such a high volume of trade, the COP has established both a Plants Committee and an Animals Committee—recently reconfiguring the membership in these to allow for greater representation by developing or "producer" countries. In addition to protecting both plant and animal specimens, either alive or dead, the treaty also covers "any recognizable part or derivative thereof" [art. I(b)]. This latter provision restricts legal trade in coveted items such as rhino horns and elephant tusks, though a great deal of illegal traffic still occurs in by-products as well as in whole specimens.

i. Commitments

The treaty actually creates only a few substantive duties for the parties. To begin, each party must establish both a "Management Authority" and a "Scientific Authority"—whose collective job it is to administer the permit system as detailed below. Each party must also submit annual reports to the Secretariat of the convention documenting the number and types of permits granted, and biennial reports on the legislative, regulatory and administrative measures taken to enforce the convention [art. VIII]. Finally, each party must follow the procedures of documentation regarding the three appendices of protected species.

Appendix I "includes all species threatened with extinction which are or may be threatened by trade" [art. II(1)]. To engage in commerce involving an Appendix I species, a trader must obtain both an export and import permit. An importing state will grant an import permit only after its Scientific Authority advises that the import will not be "detrimental to the survival of the species involved" and that the recipient can suitably care for the specimen, if living [art. III(3)]. In addition, the importing nation's Management Authority must confirm that the proposed use of the specimen is not "for primarily commercial purposes" [art. III(3)].

Similarly, the exporting state may grant an export permit only after its Scientific Authority finds the exchange non-threatening to the survival of that species [art. III(2)]. Furthermore, its Management Authority must (1) discover no violation of its own species protection laws, (2) believe that the transfer will minimize the risk of injury, damage to health or cruel treatment, and (3) confirm the previous granting of an import permit [art. III(2)]. Thus, the CITES regime disallows most harmful trade in Appendix I species, and for permissible exchanges generates an intricate paper trail.

Appendix II of the convention includes species which may become threatened in the future without trade controls [art. II(2)]. For this category CITES requires only an export permit and not the additional burden of an import permit. Following the exact model for Appendix I, the exporting party may grant the permit only after its Scientific Authority deems the exchange non-threatening to the survival of the species, and after its Management Authority finds the specimen both legally obtained and safely transferable [art. IV(2)]. Therefore, though less involved for the parties than Appendix I exchanges, the treaty still generates a considerable paper trail for all legal trade in Appendix II species.

Appendix III includes those species "which any Party identifies as being subject to regulation within its jurisdiction for the purpose of preventing or restricting exportation" [art. II(3)]. To trade in a species on this list, one must obtain an export permit (if from a country listing such species in Appendix III) and a Certificate of Origin. The export permit in this case dispenses with the need for any determination by the exporting country's Scientific Authority, requiring only satisfaction by the Management Authority that no domestic laws were violated in the taking of the specimen and that the transfer would not involve undue harm [art. V(2)]. The convention, however, does require a Certificate of Origin for all trade in Appendix III species, even if the transaction does not involve a party having placed the species on the list [art. V(3)].

To amend either Appendix I or II requires a two-thirds majority of parties present and voting at a meeting of the COP [art. XV]. This includes transfers of a species from one appendix to another, as occurred with the "uplisting" of the African Elephant from Appendix II to Appendix I in 1989. In practice, this super-majority voting procedure provides the COP with a dynamic tool, allowing it to alter the protections of the regime as circumstances change. An amendment to Appendix III occurs simply by the communication of any party that it wishes to designate a species as such [art. XVI].

ii. Continued Trade in Listed Species

Despite the commitments cited above, legal trade under the treaty—not to mention illegal trade outside the treaty—still takes place in several different ways. A major loophole of the CITES regime lies in the ability of parties to file reservations against the listing of a species in Appendix I, II, or III—or in any parts and derivatives of Appendix III species [art. XXIII]. A reservation avoids the permit system with regard to that species, in effect placing the objecting party in the position of a non-party who can freely trade with other non-parties.

A second problem involves such non-parties (or an objecting party for a particular species), with whom parties may still engage in trade. Parties may do so, however, only when the non-party issues "comparable" documentation which "substantially conforms" to CITES permits and certificates—a practice which remains open to fraud by traders and non-parties [art. X].

The treaty also authorizes certain exemptions for listed species. Specimens, for example, acquired within an owner's usual state of residence and deemed "personal or household effects" generally are not covered by the treaty [art. VII(3)]. The convention also exempts specimens documented by an exporting state's Management Authority as acquired before that particular species became listed [art. VII(2)]. Of greatest significance, CITES also excuses from its restrictions species "bred in captivity" if the trader obtains a certificate of captive breeding from the state of export [art. VII(5)]. To prevent fraud in this exemption, the COP oversees a register of all operations that breed Appendix I species worldwide, and has successfully urged Parties not to receive certificates of captive breeding from unregistered facilities.

The COP also allocates quotas for range states for certain species—including Appendix I species such as the leopard, various crocodilians, and the cheetah—when it determines that trade within set limits will not be detrimental to the survival of that species [see Res. 9.21, Ninth Meeting (1994)]. Recently, the COP has recommended that range states with a population of African elephants establish quotas for the export of raw ivory [id., Res. 9.16]. This reinstitutes the quota system for raw ivory that was discontinued when the African elephant was "uplisted" to Appendix I in 1989. Again, the quotas should function so as to manage the resident population and not to the detriment of the species as a whole. In this way the CITES regime has acted to promote the principle of sustainable development—in effect rewarding those parties and local communities which have successfully protected their herds—by endorsing a managed and limited cull.

Overall, the CITES regime has performed well given its limited resources and broad scope. As the COP acknowledges, however, illegal trade in the most sought after species still continues at an alarming rate. Whether the treaty proves ultimately successful will depend on the North's greater financial commitment in promoting diligent enforcement in the South.

(b) The 1972 UNESCO Convention Concerning the Protection of The World Cultural and Natural Heritage (World Heritage Convention)

Another early environmental treaty, the World Heritage Convention plays a small but important role in the conservation of biological diversity [Nov. 16, 1972, 1037 U.N.T.S. 151]. The convention recognizes and protects examples of "cultural" and "natural" heritage, and as of January 1996 the parties have listed 102 "natural" and 17 "mixed" cultural/natural sites. For inclusion on the World Heritage List, a qualifying example of "natural heritage" must fit within one of the following categories specified in article 2:

> natural features consisting of physical and biological formations or groups of such formations, which are of outstanding universal value from the aesthetic or scientific point of view; geological or physiographical formations and precisely delineated areas which constitute the habitat of threatened species of animals and plants of outstanding universal value from the point of view of science or conservation; natural sites or precisely delineated areas of outstanding universal value from the point of view of science, conservation or natural beauty.

As defined, "natural heritage" typically includes the habitat of endangered species, and most sites on the World Heritage List are national parks.

To obtain a listing, individual countries nominate a domestic site for the World Heritage List, and the World Heritage Committee (an elected group of 21 parties) then judges the request with the help and expertise of the World Conservation Union (IUCN). The Committee also administers a "List of World Heritage in Danger," which consists of sites "threatened by serious and specific dangers, such as the threat of disappearance caused by accelerated deterioration ..." [art. 11(4)]. Not only are developing country sites represented, but recently the Committee has included on this list both the Everglades and Yellowstone National Parks of the United States. The Convention additionally creates a World Heritage Fund which helps developing countries in the establishment and maintenance of sites on the two lists [arts. 15–26].

Commitments

As a matter of international law, the convention creates obligations both at the national and international levels. Domestically, the convention recognizes a duty for each party—"to the utmost of its own resources and where appropriate"—to identify, conserve, protect and transfer to future generations the natural heritage located within its jurisdiction [art. 4]. As this provision suggests, a party must fulfill this duty for every site it designates as natural heritage—regardless whether the site actually makes it onto the World Heritage List. Furthermore, each party must undertake specific actions to meet this obligation, such as legal and administrative reforms [art. 5]. The parties must also submit reports on the efforts that they have expended to comply with the convention [art. 29].

At the international level, while reaffirming territorial sovereignty the treaty recognizes that natural heritage "constitutes a world heritage for whose protection it is the duty of the international community as a whole to co-operate" [art. 6(1)]. This is an early example of the "common heritage" concept, which was downgraded in the CBD to "the common concern of humankind" [*see supra* E. 1. (a)]. In addition, the World Heritage Convention imposes a collective obligation on the parties to assist poorer countries, at the latter's request, in their efforts to fulfill the substantive obligations of the treaty [art. 6(2)].

Though the effectiveness of the World Heritage Convention remains limited by the narrow definition of "natural heritage"—in practice constraining its application to the establishment and protection of national parks—it has proven a helpful tool in the global effort to conserve biological diversity. To multiply its effect in the future, the treaty administration must closely coordinate its activities with the CBD. As of this writing, a Memorandum of Understanding between the two conventions remains at the discussion stage.

(c) The 1971 Convention on Wetlands of International Importance, Especially as Waterfowl Habitat (Ramsar Convention)

The Ramsar Convention, signed at Ramsar, Iran in 1971, is the oldest international treaty created solely for the protection of ecosystems [Feb. 2, 1971, 1976 U.N.T.S. 245]. The treaty specifically attempts to safeguard wetlands, with an emphasis in protecting those areas of "international importance to waterfowl" [art. 2(2)]. Like the World Heritage Convention, the Ramsar Convention establishes a list of protected sites called the List of Wetlands of International Importance (the List). Presently, the List contains over 700 entries. The COP has also created a Record of Ramsar Sites (again, one can analogize to the List of World Heritage in Danger), which includes List sites most in need of conservation.

For inclusion on the List of Wetlands of International Importance parties designate sites, and the COP thereafter votes for approval (and removal) of such sites [art. 6(2)(b)]. To become a full party to the convention, each contracting party must designate at least one wetland for the List [art. 2(4)]. This latter requirement actually has proved an impediment to the accession of developing countries, which often cannot meet the expense of creating a reserve. To assist developing countries in the creation of reserves, the convention established the Ramsar Wetland Conservation Fund in 1990. This move has attracted new parties from the developing world and total membership now exceeds eighty parties.

Conservation

In addition to designating at least one wetland for inclusion on the List [art. 2(4)], the Parties in general must promote the conservation of wetlands by establishing and maintaining nature reserves, whether included on the List or not [art. 4(1)]. The parties shall also "endeavor through management to increase waterfowl populations on appropriate wetlands" [art. 4(4)]. Concerning listed sites, the parties must inform the managing "Bureau" of any change in ecological character [art. 3(2)], and should a particular party delete or restrict the boundaries of a designated site, it should compensate for any net loss through the creation of additional reserves [art. 4(2)]. Finally, by recommendation of the COP each party must inventory and monitor its national wetlands.

Wise Use

In potential conflict with the obligation to conserve, the Ramsar Convention also mandates that parties "formulate and implement their planning so as to promote ... as far as possible the wise use of wetlands in their territories" [art. 3(1)]. In juxtaposing conservation and wise use, the treaty offers an early example of the protection/development schism found in the CBD. In 1987 the COP defined "wise use" in terms of "sustainable utilization," and since has promulgated a number of requirements toward this end. Most notably, parties should adopt and apply the COP's Guidelines for Implementation of the Wise Use Concept, including the establishment of National Wetlands Policies. Additionally, each party must develop management plans for each Ramsar site, and recent monitoring procedures require parties to file annual reports concerning the health of threatened areas on the Record of Ramsar Sites. The COP has also instituted the rule of environmental impact assessment prior to any proposed development of national wetlands.

Consultations

The convention further mandates that the parties "consult with each other about implementing obligations arising from the Convention"—especially emphasizing this requirement with regard to transboundary wetlands [art. 5]. The preamble also makes the general point "that the conservation of wetlands and their flora and fauna can be ensured by combining far-sighted national policies with coordinated international action."

Though wetlands continue to deteriorate worldwide due to development and population pressures, the Ramsar Convention has achieved a significant amount given its limited budget and its only recent growth in developing country membership. With greater resources channeled to developing country parties—and with increased coordination of its efforts with other treaty regimes such as the CBD— the convention can undoubtedly increase its contribution to the global effort of protecting wetland biodiversity.

(d) The 1979 Convention on the Conservation of Migratory Species of Wild Animals (Bonn Convention)

The Convention on the Conservation of Migratory Species of Wild Animals, known as the Bonn Convention after its signing at Bonn, Germany, covers the entire spectrum of animal species including birds, mammals, reptiles and fish [June 23., 1979, 1980 MISC 11, *available in Westlaw* 1979 WL 37754]. After a slow start, the convention has recently made considerable strides in effecting range state cooperation to protect migratory species. It now has nearly 50 parties, though the bulk of its parties are still European. Many nations have not signed the treaty because they presumably consider migratory species sufficiently protected under other conventions, often bilateral in nature. Neither Canada nor the U.S. is a party, for example, because their own bilateral treaty (now including Mexico) arguably defends the flyways of most ducks and geese. Such a stance, however, does little to protect the numerous other species listed in the Bonn Convention's annexes and fails to recognize the continued threat to all migratory species. Despite this unequal participation, the treaty continues to gain adherents in the effort to protect migratory species.

Commitments

The Bonn Convention adopts an interesting wrinkle to the usual framework approach to international law-making. Rather than relying on the adoption of protocols, the treaty facilitates the creation of cooperative arrangements among range states. This strategy is employed for species listed in Annex II and is described more fully below. At a more general level, the convention contains perhaps the most evocative plea for inter-generational equity in international law, proclaiming "that each generation of man holds the resources of the earth for future generations and has an obligation to ensure that this legacy is conserved and, where utilized, is used wisely" [pmbl.]. The treaty then leaves its specific requirements for actions undertaken with regard to the two annexes.

Appendix I lists endangered species, creating broad duties for range states whose territory comprises any part of a listed species' range, or whose flag-ships hunt the species extra-territorially [art. I(1)(h)]. "Endangered" under the convention "means that the migratory species is in danger of extinction throughout all or a significant portion of its range" [art. I(1)(e)]. For Appendix I species, range states must endeavor to conserve and restore habitats; to minimize the adverse effects of activities or obstacles impeding migration; and to reduce or control further endangerment [art. III(4)]. Range states must also prohibit takings of Appendix I species except in exceptional circumstances [art. III(5)]. To monitor progress in protecting both Appendix I and Appendix II species, the treaty requires each party to submit reports on measures taken to implement the commitments [art. VI(3)].

Appendix II contains those species with an "unfavorable conservation status," a broad term which suggests all threatened migratory species (*see* arts. I(1)(c) & (d)). Rather than general protection duties, however, the convention requires that range states strive to enter into cooperative Agreements with other range states to promote conservation and restoration of selected species [*see* arts. IV & V]. Any Agreement should attempt to cover the entire migratory route of the species, and should remain open to accession by all range states, including those not party to the convention [art. V(2)]. To date, the parties have concluded four such Agreements, including three Agreements that entered into force in 1994: the Conservation of Bats in Europe, the Conservation of Small Cetaceans (whales and dolphins) of the Baltic and North Seas, and the Conservation of Seals in the Wadden Sea. These three Agreements have successfully attracted a significant number of range states as parties. The newest and most ambitious of these Agreements deals with the Conservation of African–Eurasian Migratory Waterbirds which collected 54 range states—some non-parties to the Bonn Convention— as signatories to the final text in 1995.

One criticism of the Bonn Convention is that it has not fostered more of the Agreements required for Appendix II species. At least part of the problem rests with the formal quality of such arrangements. As structured under the convention, Agreements for the protection of Appendix II species are themselves binding legal instruments, necessitating long, and often politically exhausting periods of negotiation and ratification. In lieu of such formal agreements, the COP has recommended that range states first develop informal Memoranda of Understanding (MOUs), a practice which might allow substantial cooperation until more formal arrangements come into being. To this end, the parties (and non-parties) have developed two recent Memoranda of Understanding: the MOU Concerning the Conservation of the Siberian Crane and the MOU Concerning the Slender-billed Curlew.

The Bonn Convention therefore has dramatically improved its record over the last five years, with a number of additional Agreements and MOUs in the development stage. The convention has also created a strong working relationship with the CBD, the Ramsar Convention and CITES. With increased party recruitment, especially in the Americas and Asia, it can continue to enhance its performance.

3. REGIONAL TREATIES AND AGREEMENTS RELATED TO BIODIVERSITY

In addition to the above international treaties, a number of regional agreements have emerged over the years. These include the Convention on Nature Protection and Wildlife Conservation in the Western Hemisphere, Oct. 12, 1940, 1953 U.N.T.S. 194; the African Convention for the Conservation of Nature and Natural Resources, Sept. 15, 1968, 1976 U.N.T.S. 4; the Convention on Conservation of European Wildlife and Natural Habitats, Sept. 19, 1979, E.T.S. 104, *available in Westlaw* 1979 WL 42275 (the Berne Convention); and the 1985 Agreement on the Conservation of Nature and Natural Resources adopted by the Association of South East Asian Nations (the 1985 ASEAN Convention), July 9, 1985 E.P.L. 64. Members of the European Union also remain bound by Council Directive 92/43 on the Conservation of Natural Habitats and of Wild Fauna and Flora [1992 O.J. (L 206/7 1)], as well as the more specific Council Directive 79/409 on the Conservation of Wild Birds [1979 O.J. (L 103) 1].

This proliferation of agreements, some effective and some not, has compounded the need for coordination and cooperation among these various entities. As stated above, the CBD was originally intended to be an umbrella treaty—one which would consolidate the present cacophony of treaties into a workable whole. Hopefully the existing CBD, though lacking any direct power over the other conventions, can still play a significant part in coordinating the diverse activities within the field.

CHAPTER SIX

GLOBAL CLIMATE CHANGE

A. NATURE AND CAUSES OF THE PROBLEM

Enormous quantities of heat trapping, or infrared trapping gases know as greenhouse gases (GHGs) are emitted into the atmosphere today, creating a need for global action. In the right quantities, GHGs help support life and ecosystems on earth by maintaining a relatively constant surface temperature that averages nearly 60°F. Where they are not present, as on Mars, the average surface temperature falls to a low 39°F and where GHGs are present in excess, as on Venus, that average rises to a high 810°F.

The earth must radiate energy away in an amount equal to that absorbed from the sun, if surface temperature is to remain in balance. GHGs, at their natural level, maintain such a heat balance. They enable the earth to trap infrared radiation which warms surface temperature while at the same time permitting excess heat to escape. A build-up of GHGs upsets this important equilibrium, with trapped infrared radiation causing a rise in surface temperature [JOSEPH DRAGAN & STEFAN AIRINEI, GEO-CLIMATE AND HISTORY 44–52 (1989)]. Unfortunately, each year human activities discharge six billion tons of carbon dioxide (CO_2) and significant quantities of other GHGs such as methane and nitrous oxides, altering the natural distribution of atmospheric gases that blanket the earth. [JOHN FIROR, THE CHANGING ATMOSPHERE: A GLOBAL CHALLENGE 51 (1990)].

To some extent, debate continues as to the significance of global warming. Scientists using mathematical models forecast an abnormal degree of climate change as a result of increased levels of CO_2 and other GHGs. Other scientists challenge this assessment claiming actual data, such as surface temperature measurement, does not support this conclusion. These skeptics argue that theories of global warming remain predicated on unreliable mathematical models. [Patrick J. Michaels & David E. Stooksbury, *The Failure of the Popular Vision of Global Warming,* 9 ARIZ. J. INT'L & COMP. L. 53–82 (1992)].

Despite the fact that the awesome complexity of atmospheric mechanisms cannot be fully replicated by mathematical models, the overwhelming majority of the scientific community agree that global climate change will negatively impact earth's environment. Indeed, a strong general consensus exists among the international scientific community that some action should be taken now to limit or reduce atmospheric GHGs on a global basis, because corrective actions will be ineffective after climate change has gained momentum. [INTERGOVERNMENTAL PANEL ON CLIMATE CHANGE, CLIMATE CHANGE 1995 CONTRIBUTIONS OF WORKING GROUPS I, II & III (1995)].

Since the 1950s, when the global monitoring of climate began, data has been collected in strategically located measuring stations that gauge many parameters of climate. To obtain information prior to the 1950s necessitates different techniques. For example, polar ice caps trap CO_2 present in the historical atmosphere, and these ice layers are tested at various depths to determine concentrations at the time of deposition. Scientists then interpret this data using computer models in an effort to predict the amount of GHGs worldwide on that date, and to correlate atmospheric concentrations with climate change.

We know for sure that carbon dioxide is the most abundant GHG. Other GHGs include methane (CH_4), nitrous oxide (N_2O), ozone (O_3) and halocarbons (human-made compounds that contain chlorine or bromine and carbon atoms) [INVENTORY OF U.S. GREENHOUSE GAS EMISSIONS AND SINKS: 1990–1994, USEPA ES2–4 (1995)]. Since the beginning of the industrial revolution, or about 1800, atmospheric CO_2 concentrations have increased about 25%. Atmospheric methane (CH_4) has more than doubled, but it may be stabilizing. Also human-made halocarbons, because of reduction activities spurred by the Montreal Protocol, appear to have stabilized. Atmospheric nitrous oxide (N_2O) has increased about 12%. Ambient ozone, on the other hand, has actually been decreasing, perhaps due to its destruction by atmospheric chlorine.

A growing scientific consensus holds that atmospheric CO_2 levels will increase between seventy-five and two hundred percent by 2100 if no changes are made to current policy and practice. This could correspond to a mean global temperature increase from 1.5°C to 4.5°C, with a best estimate placing the increase near 2.5°C [INTERGOVERNMENTAL PANEL ON CLIMATE CHANGE, CLIMATE CHANGE 1994: RADIATIVE FORCING OF CLIMATE CHANGE AND AN EVALUATION OF THE IPCC IS92 EMISSION SCENARIOS, 16 (1995) [hereinafter IPCC EVALUATION]]. Over the past century, data reveals a 0.5°C increase in average global temperature, a change that has yet to make a discernible difference to the earth's environment. However, larger temperature increases such as those now predicted to occur over the next century may cause a different result.

Many naturally existing processes keep the CO_2 level in check by providing "sinks" that mitigate the effects of accumulated GHGs. The workhorse of these processes is common photosynthesis. In this way forest vegetation converts CO_2 to oxygen (O_2) in the presence of sunlight during photosynthesis. Another photosynthetic contributor is ocean phytoplankton. Scientific theory suggests that rising levels of CO_2 actually stimulate the production of photoplankton to compensate for additional CO_2 [IPCC EVALUATION, at 163–199; Jane S. Shaw and Richard L. Stroup, *Getting Warmer? Planning for Global Warming*, NAT'L REV., July 14, 1989 at 26].

B. THE IMPACTS

In 1988, the Intergovernmental Panel of Climate Change (IPCC) was formed jointly by the World

Meteorological Organization (WMO) (*see* Appendix A § W) and the United Nations Environment Programme (UNEP) (*see* Appendix A § R) to evaluate the scientific phenomenon of global warming and its effects on earth's community. Several hundred working scientists participated in three individual IPCC working groups named "Working Group I: Scientific Assessment", "Working Group II: Impacts, Adaptation and Mitigation" and "Working Group III: Socio-economic and Cross-cutting Issues" which assess, respectively, scientific information, response strategies and socio-economic impacts. The working groups reports were published in 1990, and updated in 1992, 1994 and 1996.

The IPCC concluded in its original report that global climate change might have its greatest impact in the polar regions, melting polar ice caps and causing a rise in sea-level of about 1 meter by 2100 and a rise in temperature of the surface ocean layer of between 0.2°C and 2.5°C [INTERGOVERNMENTAL PANEL ON CLIMATE CHANGE, CLIMATE CHANGE: THE INTERGOVERNMENTAL PANEL ON CLIMATE CHANGE IMPACTS ASSESSMENT 1–1 (1990)]. They predicted that climate changes will affect agriculture, forestry, natural terrestrial ecosystems, hydrology, water resources, human settlements, oceans and coastal zones, seasonal snow cover, permafrost, and ice. Specific predictions were difficult on a regional scale since climate varies regionally. The IPCC supplements confirmed the original findings and provided additional supporting data and a refinement of specific predictions.

According to the IPCC evaluations, the most pronounced impacts will relate to water resources. Rising global temperatures will change existing patterns of precipitation, which in turn will cause meteorological shifts affecting seasonal snow patterns. Additionally, melting polar ice caps are expected to cause a rise in sea level which will directly impact commercial marine industries like shipping and fishing. Sea level rises will also severely challenge coastal land use. Agriculture will follow precipitation and temperature, and entire species will either adapt to the new habitats, shift locations, or face localized and potentially widespread extinction.

Human settlements will also change, due to the proximity of world population and trading centers to coastal areas. Developing countries and areas with significant lowlands may suffer extreme health impacts because of changing water and food supplies. Finally, human migration may disrupt settlement patterns and cause social instability.

C. REMEDIAL OBJECTIVES

The objective of any regime controlling climate change must be to arrest the increase of GHG's. Doing so requires a comprehensive package of measures involving modifications of present and projected demands for energy, as well as the enlargement of carbon sinks. They include, energy conservation and efficiency measures that reduce our energy consumption along with transportation remedies addressing improved fuel efficiency and the development and use of more efficient transportation systems. In addition, significant research and development should explore the feasibility and viability of GHG-free alternatives such as nuclear power, renewables such as solar and wind power, geothermal energy sources and alternative fuels such as hydrogen. [Lakshman Guruswamy, *Integrated Environmental Control: The Expanding Matrix*, 22 ENVTL L. 77 (1992)].

Furthermore, it is important to enlarge the capacity of carbon "sinks" by the growth of forests and phytoplankton in the oceans. Scientists who hope to use this phenomena to curb global climate change are, at the time of this writing, experimenting with different techniques that will fertilize phytoplankton, causing them to grow in profusion and absorb more CO_2 from the air [William Broad, *Debating the use of Iron as a Curb of Climate*, N.Y. Times, Nov. 12, 1996, at B5]. In addition to the reduction of CO_2, remedial measures should also include the reduction of nitrous oxide (N_2O), methane (CH_4), and the other GHGs as part of a comprehensive agenda dealing with global warming.

Historically, contributions to atmospheric GHGs have been made by the industrialized countries, led in volume by the United States. Unfortunately, forecasts for the next century show significant increases in emissions from developing nations, presenting a major diplomatic challenge. Current efforts include crafting treaties and abatement agreements among nations that work to curb emissions and stabilize the climate. Factors inhibiting diplomatic progress include geographical differences in the impact of global warming effects and the remote manifestation of actual changes to the ecosystem. The challenge is to elicit cooperation among members of the global community to curb this global environmental phenomenon.

D. LEGAL RESPONSE

The whole of the international law response to the threat of global warming revolves around the United Nations Framework Convention on Climate Change (Climate Change Convention), May 29, 1992, 31 I.L.M. 849 (entered into force Mar. 21, 1994). Unlike some areas of international environmental law, such as the conservation of biological diversity, there are no prior bilateral or regional treaties to consider. Accordingly, our analysis in this section will focus exclusively on the international law implications of the Climate Change Convention.

1. SUBSTANTIVE LAW

(a) History and Overview of the Climate Change Convention

Completed at the Earth Summit in 1992, the Climate Change Convention came into existence after an accelerated process of negotiation. As scientific concern increased over the prospects of global warming, international attention focused rapidly on the issue in the late 1980s. Then in 1990 the UN

General Assembly created the Intergovernmental Negotiating Committee (INC), calling for the adoption of a global convention on climate change at UNCED in 1992. Though there was a substantial political base which desired long-term quantitative emission limits, eventually a "go-slow" approach prevailed. The short negotiating period, combined both with the enormous economic stakes and a substantial amount of scientific uncertainty, resulted in the adoption of only cautious controls in the final version of the treaty.

The Climate Change Convention, however, is not an empty framework treaty whose substantive details entirely await further elaboration. Instead, it is a framework convention with a number of built-in requirements. First, developed countries must strive to reduce their overall emissions of greenhouse gases to 1990 levels by the year 2000. As of this writing, by virtue of the Berlin Mandate [United Nations Framework Convention on Climate Change Conference of the Parties: Decisions Adopted by the First Session (Berlin), 34 I.L.M. 1671 (1995)] adopted at the Conference of the Parties (COP I), the parties are presently negotiating a protocol that strengthens this requirement—setting binding controls for developed countries beyond the year 2000. Second, developed countries have a general commitment to make financial and technological transfers to developing countries. Third, all parties—both developed and developing countries—must create inventories of GHGs, as well as national mitigation and adaptation programs. The Climate

Change Convention, however, provides different timetables and requirements for developed and developing countries with regard to inventories and other programs, and the COP has established different guidelines for the national reports communicating such programs to the COP.

In mandating different requirements for developed and developing countries, as well as making further delineations within those groups, the Climate Change Convention in contrast to the CBD, explicitly embraces the concept of "common but differentiated responsibility" (CBDR) [pmbl. para. 6]. This principle recognizes that only international cooperation will help to resolve a problem of the magnitude of global warming, but that in responding to the problem different states have different social and economic conditions that affect their response capabilities. CBDR also incorporates the equitable notion that developed countries, which have the largest share of historical and current emissions of GHGs, should take the first painful actions to ameliorate the problem. As we shall see, however, the exact application of CBDR remains controversial.

In negotiating the appropriate response to be taken by developed countries, the parties struggled with a number of possible strategies. One such point of contention involved the Comprehensive Approach to GHG emissions, a discussion of which we have included here to show both the complexity of the problem and the difficulty of available solutions.

(b) The Comprehensive Approach

In the original push toward creation of the Climate Change Convention, the international community generally limited its focus to the reduction of carbon dioxide emissions. As we have seen, CO_2 is the primary GHG, and because its sources and sinks were better understood than those of most other GHGs, controlling CO_2 seemed the prudent place to start. Late in the negotiating game, however, the United States presented a different approach: parties could choose any mix of GHG reductions and removals by sinks—not just CO_2 reductions—in meeting their respective commitment to reduce their overall contribution to global warming. By this strategy, each GHG receives a scientifically based value, known as its global warming potential (GWP), which measures that GHG's contribution to global warming relative to other GHGs. In order to calculate the total emissions of any particular GHG, a party need only multiply the GWP by the volume emitted for each gas. In this way, a party can arrive at its total emissions of all GHGs by adding up the respective contributions of each individual GHG. Thus, to reduce its net contribution to global warming under the Comprehensive Approach, a party could then choose any combination of GHG reductions and/or removals by sinks.

Proponents of the Comprehensive Approach argued that the method makes both economic and environmental sense. In the economic argument, supporters persuasively pointed out that a party could choose the most efficient (and thus the cheapest) combination of measures for its particular situation. Obviously, it may be cheaper for some countries to reduce emissions of methane rather than carbon dioxide, for example. Simultaneously, proponents argued for the environmental benefits of the Comprehensive Approach—the strategy would prevent countries simply switching from one controlled harmful emission (carbon dioxide) to another uncontrolled harmful emission (such as sulphur dioxide). Opponents have acknowledged the theoretical benefits of the Comprehensive Approach, but have argued that too little knowledge exists concerning the respective sources and sinks of GHGs other than carbon dioxide. Therefore, because developing accurate counting methods for each GHG would require more time and effort, they saw the approach as simply another call for research, another prescription for delay on the part of some developed countries, particularly the United States [Lakshman Guruswamy, *Energy and the Environment: A True Comprehensive Approach*, 9 Ariz. J. Int'l & Comp. L. 115 (1992)].

In the end, on the emissions side of the equation, the Climate Change Convention adopted language which ultimately approves of the Comprehensive Approach. At two junctures, articles 4(2)(a) & (b), the treaty refers to the reduction of "anthropogenic emissions of carbon dioxide and other greenhouse gases"—which, though singling out carbon dioxide, also includes the full panoply of GHGs. The ambiguity of this language actually provides the COP under article 4(2)(d) (as well as the negotiating committee for a new protocol) with real latitude in attempting to develop quantifiable emissions limits in the future. One possibility remains the "phased-in" Comprehensive Approach—which might specifically require carbon dioxide reductions in the near term, while allowing a flexible mix of other GHGs over time. Meanwhile, concerning the present requirement that developed country parties strive to reduce the level of GHGs to a 1990 standard, parties are free to employ the Comprehensive Approach to meet this commitment. In an oversight role, the Secretariat and nominated experts will conduct in-depth review reports, in which they will critically evaluate the scientific validity of the chosen mix.

As to the inclusion of sinks in the equation, again the phrasing of the Climate Change Convention endorses the Comprehensive Approach in articles 4(2)(a), (b) & (c). Thus, a party is free to subtract appropriate sinks in its calculation of total emissions of GHGs, and the COP has developed methodologies that developed countries should follow in making this important calculation.

(c) Commitments

In implementing the concept of CBDR, the Climate Change Convention creates several classes of parties through annexes. Annex I includes the wealthier Organization for Economic Cooperation and Development (OECD) countries, as well as the former Eastern Bloc countries "undergoing the process of transition to a market economy." Annex II includes only the OECD countries. By omission, therefore, all remaining parties not included in Annex I or II are developing countries. At several junctures, which will be noted below, the Climate Change Convention makes further special provision for "least developed countries" and "small island states."

i. All Parties (Developed and Developing Countries)

All countries, including developing countries, have a number of general commitments under the Climate Change Convention. These include a duty to "promote and cooperate in the conservation and enhancement, as appropriate, of sinks and reservoirs of all greenhouse gases" [art. 4(1)(d)]. Significantly, this commitment omits any special protection for forests—the most important GHG sink—due to the concern of developing countries that the treaty not impinge on their freedom to develop that resource. The parties must also cooperate in preparing for adaptation to the impacts of global warming [art. 4(1)(e)], and must promote and cooperate in research and development [art. 4(1)(g)], exchange of information [art. 4(1)(h)] and education, training and public awareness [art. 4(1)(i)]. To the extent feasible, each party must also take climate change considerations into account in domestic policies and actions, employing appropriate methods of environmental impact assessment [art. 4(1)(f)]. Furthermore, each party must create national programs to mitigate climate change by addressing GHG emissions, which would also contain measures to "facilitate adequate adaptation to climate change" [art. 4(1)(b)].

More specifically under the Climate Change Convention, all parties must undertake certain reporting requirements. To begin, all parties must "[d]evelop, periodically update, publish and make available ... national inventories of anthropogenic emissions by sources and removals by sinks of all greenhouses gases" [art. 4(1)(a)], and communicate these to the COP [art. 12(1)(a)]. In the creation of inventories, the treaty lightens the burden on developing countries, qualifying the requirement by the article 12(1)(a) phrase "to the extent [their] capacities permit." In these national communications, the parties must also include a general description of steps taken or envisioned so as to implement the convention, such as progress on the creation of national mitigation and adaptation programs [art. 12(1)(b)]. In addition, as stated above, the COP has established different guidelines for developed and developing countries in making the required national communications, and most developing countries are given until 1997 to meet this requirement (assuming that developed countries provide the necessary financial resources to create such reports), while "least developed countries" may submit their first reports "at their discretion" [art. 12(5)].

ii. Annex I Parties (OECD and Former Eastern Bloc Parties)

Targets and Timetables

For Annex I parties the Climate Change Convention stipulates limited targets and timetables, requiring that all such parties "aim" to return to 1990 emissions levels for all GHGs by the year 2000 [art. 4(2)(b), art. 4(2)(a)]. The obligation—qualified as it is by the word "aim" rather than "must"—has created some confusion as to its binding quality. In fact, at the time of the treaty's creation a domestic policy advisor under former President Bush questioned the nature of the requirement, stating that "there is nothing in any of the language which constitutes a commitment to any specific level of emissions at any time" [Michael Weisskopf, *Bush to Attend Rio Earth Summit in June,* Washington Post, May 13, 1992, at A3.]. Regardless, a number of developed countries, including the United States, have admitted that they will not meet the proposed target by the end of the century. There has also been some confusion as to what happens after the year 2000—must Annex I parties "stabilize" their emissions by that year or are they allowed to increase overall emissions after that date?

The COP, rather than clarifying these details, instead chose a forward-looking approach—adopting the Berlin Mandate at its first meeting in 1995. The Berlin Mandate commits the parties to the development of a protocol that sets "quantified limitation and reduction objectives within specified time-frames, such as 2005, 2010 and 2020" for Annex I countries [United Nations Framework Convention on Climate Change Conference of the Parties: Decisions Adopted by the First Session (Berlin), [34 I.L.M. 1671, 1678 (1995)]. At COP II in 1996, following the dramatic Second Assessment Report of the IPCC calling for urgent action to control global warming [INTERGOVERNMENTAL PANEL ON CLIMATE CHANGE, CLIMATE CHANGE 1995: CONTRIBUTIONS OF WORKING GROUPS I, II, AND III (separate volumes)] (1995)], the ministerial declaration at Geneva upgraded these negotiations to that of a "legally-binding protocol" with "quantified legally-binding objectives of emission limitations and significant overall reductions" within the same specified time-frames [Geneva Declaration, U.N. Doc. FCCC/CP/ l.17 (1996)]. The parties are to complete negotiations on this protocol for submission to COP III in 1997.

Joint Implementation

Perhaps the most controversial of issues that remains unresolved in the Climate Change Convention is that of joint implementation. Joint implementation simply means that states can work together to fulfill their commitments under the treaty. A number of very difficult questions lurk within this apparently benign concept. To begin, can developed countries only work with other developed countries, or can they also work with developing nations? In either case, how should the

Climate Change Convention award credits for such action?

Let us first imagine an actual joint implementation scenario between two developed countries. Suppose that developed country A (which is already very energy efficient) can only return to 1990 levels of GHGs at a steep price, and suppose that developed country B (an energy inefficient state just "undergoing the process of transition to a market economy") can do so much more cheaply. Proponents of joint implementation argue that for reasons of economic efficiency, country A should be able to help pay for country B's movement toward energy efficiency, and that the two parties should share a negotiated percentage of the reduced GHG emissions as a result of the project. In effect, both countries would benefit: country A could apply the credit to the GHG reductions of its target, and country B could do so also, and receive financial assistance it would not otherwise obtain. The most cogent argument against an arrangement such as this is that states should first make adjustments at home before attempting to "buy" their way out of their obligations under the Climate Change Convention. In reality, however, not a great deal of political resistance exists to joint implementation projects between developed countries, though the question of credits does remain problematic and unsettled.

On the other hand, dramatic controversy surrounds joint implementation projects between developed and developing countries—if the developed country seeks a credit for the project against its present commitments under the Climate Change Convention. Proponents foresee a global system of tradeable emission rights, while opponents remain staunchly against such a proposal. Let us suppose for example that developed country A above enters into a project with country C, a developing country, in which country A offers to pay country C not to develop a tract of pristine rainforest. In this scenario, proponents of joint implementation again point to the economic benefit to both sides, reminding those opposed of the inherent economic efficiency of the arrangement. Country C can reduce global warming more cheaply than country A by preserving the rainforest as a "sink," country C is willing to negotiate as to the price of foregoing development, and country A remains willing to pay an appropriate price to offset its extremely expensive obligations under the Climate Change Convention. The percentage credit gained by country A would most likely be set by the appropriate authorities under the Climate Change Convention.

Rather than an efficient economic arrangement between equal bargainers, the developing countries see this second example in a much different light. First, the developed countries have created the problem of global warming and, developing countries contend, they should not try to escape from the moral commitment to curb their profligate GHG-generating lifestyles. Thus, developed countries must begin by attending to the source of the problem at home, and should not attempt to soften the economic blow to their own constituencies by creating obligations for developing countries. Second, developing countries fear that joint implementation of this kind will stifle their future economic progress. Projects which force maintenance of "sinks"—and thereby prevent development—especially are perceived as continuing the neo-colonial dynamic which prevents developing countries from catching up economically. Third, if developing countries eventually have future net emissions targets under the treaty, developing countries fear that the developed countries would have already appropriated the cheapest and most cost-effective projects for mitigation. Finally, and at the most general level, the poorer nations perceive joint implementation projects as a threat to sovereignty—simply another case of developed countries telling developing countries what to do on their own soil.

The Climate Change Convention itself endorses the notion of joint implementation, but again the exact application of that endorsement remains a future question for the COP. In the Climate Change Convention, both articles 4(2)(a) & (b) make reference to the possibility that parties may "jointly" arrive at their obligations, with the inference that joint implementation potentially is appropriate between all parties and not just developed country parties. At the first meeting of the COP, the parties could not resolve the most difficult issues concerning the concept, but did decide on a program of pilot joint implementation projects whose effectiveness would be reviewed at the end of 1999. Participants in the projects would receive no credits during this trial phase. As for future credits, as well as the broader notion of north-south joint implementation projects after the year 2000, nothing has yet been decided. One possible compromise is to discount the credits received in a north-south transaction, so that wealthy countries would only pursue such projects when dramatically cheaper than projects at home. Perhaps the proposed legally-binding protocol will further clarify the role joint implementation will play in the global effort to stabilize and reduce GHG emissions.

Financial and Technological Transfers

According to article 4(3), Annex II parties (OECD members only) must pay for all the reporting requirements undertaken by developing countries. This includes the developing countries' obligation to create national inventories of GHGs under article 4(1) and to communicate such information to the COP under article 12. In addition to the full costs of reporting, the Annex II parties must pay for the full incremental costs of projects undertaken by developing countries to fulfill the latter's general commitments pursuant to article 4(1). However, these projects—such as designating and maintaining a sustainable rainforest preserve—must be approved by the financial mechanism as outlined below [*see infra* § 2(e)].

Concerning adaptation costs—the costs involved in dealing with the effects of higher seas and higher temperatures—Annex II parties have a fairly vague financial responsibility to developing countries. Article 4(4) merely states that Annex II parties "shall also assist the developing country Parties that are particularly vulnerable to the adverse effects of climate change in meeting costs of adaptation to those adverse effects." Coupled with article 4(8), this commitment could require Annex II countries to pay for a number of adaptation measures, such as the construction of sea walls for small island countries. With adaptation costs presumably several decades away, however, the full weight of this provision awaits development by future Conferences of the Parties.

With regard to technology transfer, the developing countries settled for a rather weak commitment in article 4(5), which stipulates that developed countries "shall take all practicable steps to promote, facilitate and finance, as appropriate, the transfer of ... environmentally sound technologies." The Climate Change Convention, therefore, contains a greater emphasis on financial costs than on the transfer of technology. Some transfer of technology is expected though, and it will either take place through joint implementation projects or through the financial mechanism itself. All Annex II parties must include measures taken for the transfer of technology in their national communications to the COP.

2. INSTITUTIONS AND IMPLEMENTATION

(a) Conference of the Parties (COP)

As is the general case with framework conventions, the COP functions as "the supreme body" of the treaty. In effect, it possesses the legislative power to create additional protocols and amendments to the convention, as well as the authority to make any other "decisions necessary to promote the effective implementation of the Convention" [art. 7(2)]. This last mandate, though not rising to the formal character of amendments and protocols, allows the COP broad authority to interpret or clarify vague treaty provisions without embroiling itself in the complicated political process of formal law-making. It also provides the COP with implied power to make any other "necessary" decisions, even if such decisions are not specifically delegated to the COP by the convention. This ongoing process of informal law-making—when coupled with the majority voting procedures outlined below—exists as a dynamic tool of the framework convention. For a general discussion of the dynamic quality of the framework convention, see Brent Hendricks, *Postmodern Possibility and the Convention on Biological Diversity*, 5 N.Y.U. ENVTL. L. J. 1 (1996).

Regarding protocols, the voting procedure for adoption remains unstated in the Climate Change Convention, but the practice is that they be adopted by consensus—though only parties who actually sign on to the instrument are bound by its provisions. As for amendments, the Climate Change Convention requires the agreement of a three-fourths (3/4) majority of parties "present and voting at the meeting" [art. 15(3)], and again only those parties who sign will be bound. Annexes, limited to "lists, forms and any other material of a descriptive nature that is of a scientific, technical, procedural or administrative character," require a similar three-fourths majority as amendments. In a burden-shifting move, however, even opposing parties are presumed bound by annexes unless they file a "notification of non-acceptance" [art. 16 (b)]. With respect to the informal decision-making process noted above, the Climate Change Convention states that the COP "shall, at its first session, adopt its own rules of procedure ... which ... may include specified majorities" [art. 7(3)]. Nonetheless, the COP failed to do so at both its first and second meetings, and the majority voting procedures concerning such matters remain unsettled. In general, parties who fear the tyranny of the majority—who perceive themselves as having the most to lose if the Climate Change Convention imposes strict emissions limits or substantial financial transfers—have attempted to block the implementation of majority voting. Until the COP reaches agreement on the subject, it will continue to employ the consensus approach regarding such informal decision-making.

The Climate Change Convention also provides several noteworthy and specific requirements for the COP. First, the COP must help "facilitate" the development of joint implementation projects between parties [art. 7(2)(c)]. Second, the COP must continue to monitor the individual obligations of the parties and to assess the cumulative effect of their implementation [*see generally* art. 7(2)(a) & (b), and art. 12]. Third, where appropriate the COP must seek the help of competent international organizations and non-governmental organizations (NGOs) [art. 7(2)(l)]. In fact, this last requirement finds more specific expression in article 7(6), which mandates that qualified NGOs have access to the meetings of the COP "unless at least one-third of the Parties present object." Such participation by NGOs is generally the rule for framework conventions, and although NGOs have no voting rights, they typically do have the right to speak and to distribute literature.

(b) Secretariat

The Secretariat of the Climate Change Convention serves as the administrative arm of the COP [art. 8]. It works to organize new meetings of the COP, to compile and transmit reports submitted by the Parties and to help find assistance for developing countries in compiling their respective reports. In addition, the Secretariat undertakes any further tasks as designated by the COP in the future. The executive secretary of the convention is the United Nations Development Program (UNDP), which operates the convention Secretariat with the institutional assistance of the UN as a whole.

(c) Subsidiary Body for Scientific and Technological Advice

The Climate Change Convention creates a Subsidiary Body for Scientific and Technological Advice (SBSTA), whose primary function is to advise the COP on technical matters [art. 9]. Given the high degree of scientific complexity regarding climate change, the SBSTA plays an important informational role. It must continually assess the state of scientific knowledge concerning climate change, as well as assess the effects of measures taken to curb climate change under the convention. Its mandate is to draw "upon existing competent international bodies"—ranging from the IPCC to qualified NGOs such as IUCN—in summarizing, compiling and synthesizing information for the COP [art. 9(2)].

(d) Subsidiary Body for Implementation

An innovative body created by the Climate Change Convention, the Subsidiary Body for Implementation (SBI) assists the COP in evaluating the implementation of the convention [art. 10]. In particular, the SBI considers the in-depth review reports of the national communications submitted by the parties under article 12, and makes broad assessments and recommendations concerning the overall aggregated effects of the steps taken by the parties. In effect, the SBI does not evaluate the individual efforts of parties—instead, it looks at the total picture of compliance in making suggestions to the COP. In developing the in-depth review reports, however, the Secretariat and nominated experts may critically evaluate an individual country's performance.

(e) Financial Mechanism

The Climate Change Convention names the Global Environment Facility (GEF) as the "interim" financial mechanism [art. 21(3)]—a status extended by the first meeting of the COP and to be reevaluated in 1999 [See the general discussion of the GEF in Appendix A, § D]. The present "restructured" GEF meets the criteria of article 11(2) that the financial mechanism have an "equitable and balanced representation of all Parties within a transparent system of governance." To summarize, the restructured GEF, the entity now has both a Council and an independent Secretariat. The Council employs a voting method known as "the double-weighted majority," in which affirmative decisions require a 60 percent majority of the total number of participants as well as a 60 percent majority of the total contributions. The Secretariat (under the authority of the World Bank) approves individual projects, submits them to the Council, and the projects become final unless four Council members wish to put the project before a full vote of the Council. In effect, the Council only possesses a veto power over individual projects.

As for the relationship between the GEF and the Climate Change Convention, the GEF functions "under the guidance of and [is] accountable to the Conference of the Parties" [art. 11(1)]. Significantly however, the COP cannot recommend individual projects to the GEF, but only specifies "policies, programme priorities and eligibility criteria" [art. 11(1)]. Nevertheless, as the 1996 Memorandum of Understanding between the COP and GEF makes clear, the COP does retain the power to have a specific project reconsidered for funding under article 11(3)(b). At the first meeting of the COP, the parties adopted initial guidance procedures for the GEF—entrusting it with the task of meeting "the agreed full costs of relevant adaptation activities" undertaken in formulating national communications. These may include "studies of the possible impacts of climate change, identification of options for implementing the adaptation provisions . . ., and relevant capacity building." Thus the GEF will continue to work closely with the COP in channeling necessary resources to developing countries.

CHAPTER SEVEN

OZONE DEPLETION

A. NATURE OF THE PROBLEM

While tropospheric ozone can be a harmful pollutant, stratospheric ozone—found in a layer 12 to 20 miles in altitude—functions as a beneficial, even vital shield. Atmospheric ozone absorbs harmful ultraviolet radiation emitted from the sun; in particular it absorbs ultraviolet radiation, which has wavelengths between 280 & 320 nanometers. Composed of three loosely bonded oxygen atoms, ozone is both formed and destroyed in the stratosphere through photochemical reactions with ultraviolet radiation [HOWARD BRIDGMAN, GLOBAL AIR POLLUTION: PROBLEMS FOR THE 1990S 45 (1990)].

Ozone is formed when ultraviolet radiation splits diatomic oxygen molecules into free oxygen atoms that bond with other diatomic oxygen molecules. It is destroyed when ultraviolet radiation splits ozone molecules into free oxygen atoms and diatomic oxygen molecules. The process continues in "equilibrium," a balance of formation and destruction of stratospheric ozone that results in the absorption of harmful ultraviolet radiation. The equilibrium of formation and destruction of stratospheric ozone, and the absorption of harmful ultraviolet radiation that is a part of that balance, is upset by the introduction of gases emitted from human activities and natural sources.

B. CAUSES OF THE PROBLEM

Chlorofluorocarbons (CFCs) were initially discovered in the 1930's. In the four decades after their discovery millions of tons of CFCs had been produced, primarily for use as refrigeration coolants, aerosol propellants, and blowing agents. Concern about the ozone-depleting effect of CFC's began in the early 1970s when scientists theorized that chlorine atoms released from the CFCs were depleting stratospheric ozone by attracting the loosely bonded oxygen atom from the ozone molecule.

In 1985, British scientists published findings on what has been called the "Antarctic ozone hole." Ozone concentrations fluctuate naturally by season, latitude, and altitude, and the British data showed that ozone levels over the Antarctic between September and November (springtime in the Antarctic) had fallen 50 percent compared with 1960s levels, and that this "ozone hole" covered an area larger than the United States. The theory was confirmed by NASA in 1994. CFCs and hydrogen and fluorine gases, which are released along with chlorine when CFCs break down, were detected in the stratosphere by NASA's Upper Atmosphere Research Satellite (UARS). Scientists now believe that data from the UARS provides "conclusive evidence" that chlorine from human activities is responsible for the Antarctic ozone hole and refutes the theory that chlorine from volcanic eruptions, ocean spray, biomass burning, or other natural sources is responsible for the depletion of ozone measured over Antarctica. Based on the amount of hydrogen and fluorine gas detected, NASA researchers calculated that only 17 percent of the chlorine could come from natural sources [*NASA Reveals New Evidence for Chemical Cause of Ozone Depletion*, Global Env't Change Report, Dec. 23, 1994, *available in* DIALOG, File No. 1994 WL 2513797].

Ozone depletion is a global problem, not confined to Antarctica. In the Northern Hemisphere, the depletion of ozone over the Arctic was not severe enough during the winter of 1994–95 to be considered an "ozone hole," but the depletion was significant and was attributed to chemical pollutants. Over Siberia, the ozone concentration was 35 percent less than 1979. In 1991, the ozone layer above northern Britain and southern Spain had decreased by approximately 8 percent between 1981 and 1991, twice the rate for previous decades. The EPA announced that ozone levels during late fall to early spring over the United States had decreased 4.5 percent to 5 percent over the past decade. During the 1994–95 winter, concentrations of ozone over the United States were down 15 percent to 20 percent and those in Europe had decreased over 10 percent, compared with 1979. These decreases were attributed to a combination of chemical pollutants and unusual weather patterns involving record low temperatures and less circulation in the strato-

sphere, reducing the flow of ozone into the mid-
latitudes [*see generally*, S. WILLIAMS, *A Historical
Background on the Chlorofluorocarbon Ozone Depletion Theory and its Legal Implications, in* TRANS-
BOUNDARY AIR POLLUTION (C. Flinterman et al. eds.
1986); WILLIAM H. RODGERS, JR., 1 ENVIRONMENTAL LAW
§ 3.1C (West Supp.1995)].

C. OZONE DEPLETING CHEMICALS

The most destructive of the ozone-depleting
chemicals are chlorofluorocarbons (CFCs) and halons (containing bromine). Other major ozone-depleting chemicals of lesser threat are carbon tetrachloride, methyl bromide, methyl chloroform, and
hydrochlorofluorocarbons (HCFCs). These gases—
emitted anywhere around the globe—may eventually circulate from the troposphere to the stratosphere.

Unlike chlorine from natural sources, such as
volcanoes and ocean spray, which dissolves in rain
and returns to the surface, CFCs are not water
soluble and do not "wash out" of the troposphere.
Because they are chemically stable, they do not
break down in the lower atmosphere, and may have
a lifetime in the troposphere of over 100 years.
They inevitably reach the stratosphere through atmospheric circulation.

When CFCs reach the stratosphere, the chlorine
is released and destroys ozone by pulling an oxygen
atom from the ozone molecule. The two most important ozone-depleting chlorinated substances are

CFC–11 and CFC–12. More recently, scientists developed HCFCs as a less destructive substitute for CFCs.

Halons, another type of ozone-depleting substance, contain bromine which attacks the ozone molecules in a similar fashion to chlorine. Halons, however, destroy four to sixteen times more ozone than CFC–11 during their atmospheric life. Methyl bromide, unlike other controlled ozone-depleting chemicals, has both natural and human-made sources—including emissions from biomass burning and soil fumigation. A final culprit, carbon tetrachloride is a non-chlorinated ozone-destroying compound whose ozone depleting potential is approximately equal to that of CFC–11. Once employed in dry cleaning, its application in industrialized countries is now restricted because of its toxicity, but it still finds common use in other countries [*Ozone-friendly?*, Discover, Feb.1995, at 20].

D. ENVIRONMENTAL IMPACTS

A decrease in the ozone layer means an increase in the amount of harmful ultraviolet radiation that reaches humans, animals and plants on the earth's surface and an increase in its attendant damage. Ultraviolet radiation causes cell damage in humans and animals, resulting most notably in skin cancer, cataracts and depressed immune systems. It also has been linked to crop damage, phytoplankton destruction with repercussions up the food chain, increased ground-level ozone pollution, and increased damage to photo-reactive materials like plastics.

The EPA has calculated that for every 1 percent decrease in stratospheric ozone, there would be a 5 percent increase in non-malignant skin cancer—an increase of 10,000 to 20,000 additional cases each year. Malignant melanoma skin cancer has not been directly linked to ultraviolet radiation, but research indicates that it, too, would increase. One study found that a 1 percent decrease in stratospheric ozone would cause an additional 25,000 cases of potentially blinding cataract disease each year.

E. REMEDIAL OBJECTIVES

In order to restore the ozone shield and prevent the further enlarging of the ozone hole, it is necessary to prohibit the use of damaging chemicals [*supra* § II.B.]. Beginning with the Vienna Convention for the Protection of the Ozone Layer (Vienna Ozone Convention), Mar. 22, 1985, 26 I.L.M. 1529 (entered into force Sept. 12, 1988) the international community has instituted such controls, and we have seen the development of a comprehensive scheme for phasing out CFC's by the year 2010 and restoring the ozone-shield. The legal response to the problem of ozone depletion remains one of the most striking achievements of international environmental law. A number of factors have contributed to this success, including (1) a growing scientific consensus as to the threat posed to the ozone layer by the release of human-made chemicals into the atmosphere; (2) the existence of a relatively small number of producing nations whose industry, after limited objections, eventually backed international controls; (3) the role played by "hegemon" or "leader" states like the United States, which had begun controlling CFC's before negotiations for both the Vienna Ozone Convention and the Montreal Protocol on Substances That Deplete the Ozone Layer (Montreal Protocol), Sept. 16, 1987, 26 I.L.M. 1550 (Entered into force Jan. 1, 1989); and (4) the development of innovative institutional mechanisms that have attracted reluctant parties and have allowed for more flexible decision-making. [*see generally, Chronology of International Cooperation to Protect the Ozone Layer*, Env't, Mar. 1995 v.37 n.2, at 20].

F. LEGAL RESPONSE

1. THE OZONE CONVENTION

Following the recent trend, the ozone regime reflects the framework approach to international law-making (*see* Chapter 6, Climate Change). Also known as the convention-protocol approach, this method proceeds from a treaty of generalities, signed by a range of parties, who then create a protocol (or protocols) of more specific and stringent application. In this case, the Vienna Ozone Convention attracted over 25 signatories in the first two years, including all the major producers of ozone-depleting chemicals except Japan. With the science still uncertain in 1985, the parties negotiated a

treaty without specific controls that instead
stressed cooperation and research [*see* arts. 2–4]. Of
greatest significance, the treaty empowered its Conference of the Parties (COP) to adopt future protocols dealing with such controls [art. 6(4)(h); art.
2(2)(c)]. This was achieved in 1987 with the Montreal Protocol.

2. MONTREAL PROTOCOL

A milestone in the field of international law, the
Montreal Protocol creates institutional mechanisms
and incentives now included in virtually every environmental convention. It should also be seen as a
prime example of the precautionary approach; even
though scientists had linked CFC's and halons to
potential global ozone depletion and had identified
the Antarctic ozone hole, the atmospheric models
remained inconclusive with no direct evidence of
physical harm to humans or the environment. Still,
in 1987 the parties adopted a protocol with firm
national commitments regarding the reduction of
CFCs and halons. Over the years the parties have
strengthened these commitments and added others,
most particularly the Montreal Protocol Parties:
Adjustments and Amendments to the Montreal Protocol on Substances that Deplete the Ozone Layer
(London Amendments), June 29, 1990, 30 I.L.M.
537 (1991), and the United Nations: Montreal Protocol on Substances that Deplete the Ozone Layer—
Adjustments and Amendments (Copenhagen
Amendments), November 23–25, 1992, 32 I.L.M.

874 (1993). A look at the difference between Adjustments and Amendments provides a window into the dynamic institutional machinery of the regime.

3. ADJUSTMENTS AND AMENDMENTS

The Montreal Protocol, as updated through the Seventh Meeting of the COP (12/95) sets specific consumption and production controls for seven types of chemicals: CFCs [art. 2A, 2C], halons [art. 2B], carbon tetrachloride [art. 2D], methyl chloroform [art. 2E], hydrochlorofluorocarbons (HCFCs) [art. 2F], hydrobromofluorocarbons (HBFCs) [art. 2G], and methyl bromide [art. 2H]. Originally, the protocol dealt only with halons and certain CFCs, and added articles 2C–2E in 1990, and articles 2F–2H in 1992 by amendment. Other amendments have included the listing of new Annexes, and changes involving trade restrictions and transfer of production allowances. Though the COP may pass amendments by a two-thirds majority, these may not bind a party against its will [Vienna Ozone Convention arts. 9(3), 9(4)]. Instead, following the traditional rule of consent in international law, each party must sign on to and ratify each amendment before becoming obligated [art.9(5)].

Once an amendment is adopted under the Montreal Protocol, however, each party relinquishes its ability to avoid "adjustments." Adjustments include changes in the reduction and/or phase-out schedules of all controlled chemicals, described in articles 2A–2H and listed in Annexes A to C & E, as well as changes in the ozone-depleting potentials of particular chemicals [art. 2(9)(a)]. Significantly, the COP passes adjustments by a two-thirds majority vote, representing separate majorities of developed and developing countries, and the adjustments remain binding on all the parties [art. 2(9)(c)]. In this way, the Montreal Protocol commits parties to specific numerical controls, regardless of whether they have voted for/or against a successful adjustment. Some scholars have perceived such informal decision-making as an end-run around the formal doctrine of consent in international law. Others have argued that the parties have simply consented in the protocol to be bound against their consent to adjustments. Regardless, the COP has made many such adjustments over the years, and Table 1 reflects the current requirements for all parties who have adopted both the London and Copenhagen Amendments. Obviously, except for these adjustments, the Montreal Protocol would remain a much slower and more inflexible mechanism for dealing with the ozone depletion problem.

In the following Table 1, one notices that the Montreal Protocol offers special arrangements for developing countries. These nations generally have less stringent requirements under the Protocol, including later base level dates and longer phase-out periods. The Montreal Protocol also provides developing country parties with security that phase-outs will not leave them lacking necessary chemicals, as both developed and developing countries in most cases may continue production beyond a chemical's reduction date so as to meet the "basic domestic needs" of developing countries (*see* Table 1). These "basic domestic needs" provisions have helped to allay third-world fears of being left without proper substitutes under the Montreal Protocol.

Additionally, all parties, not just developing nations, are allowed "essential use" exemptions after the 100 percent reduction phase-out date for most chemicals. These exemptions are granted by the parties under Annex VI and cannot be taken unilaterally. For the year 1997, for example, the Technology and Economic Assessment Panel has authorized 2,606 tons of CFC–11 "essential use" exemptions to developed countries, including 331 tons to the US and 1,991 tons to the EU, respectively. As the parties as a whole approve such exemptions, the prospect of abuse or the development of significant loopholes is forestalled.

TABLE 1

TIMETABLE OF ADJUSTMENTS TO THE
MONTREAL PROTOCOL

(FOR PARTIES ADOPTING BOTH THE LONDON
AND COPENHAGEN AMENDMENTS)

(AS OF 1/96)

	DEVELOPED COUNTRIES	DEVELOPING COUNTRIES
CFCS Article 2A (Annex A, Group I) Applicable to Production and Consumption	Base Level: 1986 100% reduction: 1/1996 + 15% (of base level allowed to be produced to meet "basic domestic needs" of developing countries)	Base Level: Average of 1995–1997 Freeze: 7/1999 + 10% (of base level allowed to be produced to meet "basic domestic needs" of developing countries) 50% Reduction: 1/2005 + 10%

	DEVELOPED COUNTRIES	DEVELOPING COUNTRIES
		85% Reduction: 1/2007 + 10% 100% Reduction: 1/2010 + 15%
Halons Article 2B (Annex A, Group II) Applicable to Production and Consumption	Base Level: 1986 100% Reduction: 1/1994 + 15%	Base Level: Average of 1995–1997 Freeze: 1/2002 + 10% 50% Reduction: 1/2005 + 10% 100% Reduction: 1/2010 + 15%
Other Fully Halogenated CFCs Article 2C (Annex B, Group I) Applicable to Production and Consumption	Base Level: 1989 100% Reduction: 1/96 + 15%	Base Level: 1998–2000 20% Reduction: 1/2003 + 10% 85% Reduction: 1/2007 + 10% 100% Reduction: 1/2010 + 15%
Carbon Tetrachloride Article 2D (Annex B, Group II) Applicable to Production and Consumption	Base Level: 1989 100% Reduction: 1/1996 + 15%	Base Level: Average of 1998–2000 85% Reduction: 1/2005 + 10% 100% Reduction: 1/2010 + 15%
Methyl Chloroform Article 2E (Annex B, Group III) Applicable to Production and Consumption	Base Level: 1989 100% Reduction: 1/1996 + 15%	Base Level: Average of 1998–2000 Freeze: 1/2003 + 10% 30% Reduction: 1/2005 + 10% 70% Reduction: 1/2010 + 10% 100% Reduction: 1/2015 + 15%
HCFCs Article 2F (Annex C, Group I) Applicable Only to Consumption	Base Level: 1989 HCFC Consumption + 2.8% of 1989 CFC Consumption Freeze: 1996 35% Reduction: 1/2004 65% Reduction: 1/2010 90% Reduction: 1/2015 99.5% Reduction: 1/2020 + "Service Tail" Allowing Servicing of Existing Refrigeration and Air-conditioning equipment 100% Reduction: 1/2030	Base Level: 2015 Freeze: 1/2016 100% Reduction: 1/2040
Hydrobromoflourocarbons (HBFCs) Article 2G (Annex C, Group II) Applicable to Production and Consumption	100% Reduction: 1/1996	100% Reduction: 1/1996

	DEVELOPED COUNTRIES	DEVELOPING COUNTRIES
Methyl Bromide Article 2H (Annex E) Applicable to Production and Consumption, Excluding Quarantine and Pre-shipment Applications	Base Level: 1991 Freeze: 1/1995 + 10% 25% Reduction: 1/2001 + 10% 50% Reduction: 1/2005 + 10% 100% Reduction: 1/2010 + 15%	Base Level: Average of 1995–1998 Freeze: 1/2002 + 10%

4. TRANSFERS

The Montreal Protocol originally allowed small-producing parties to transfer or receive production in excess of the prescribed limits, as long as the combined levels of the two parties engaged in the transfer did not exceed production standards. The London Amendments extend this right to all parties, not just small producers, and for all controlled substances except HBFCs [art. 2(5)]. Identified in the protocol as industrial rationalization, this mechanism attempts to enhance efficiency between producers, allowing a shift of reduction and phase-out burdens from those least capable to those in the best position to do so. For those controls already at 100 percent reduction, this has the practical effect of allowing a transfer from one producer to another of that excess deemed necessary for the basic domestic needs of developing countries. With regard to HCFCs, the Copenhagen Amendments permit developed country parties who are small consumers to transfer excess consumption to other developed country parties [art.2(5)bis.]. Again, as with all the provisions for industrial rationalization, the nations involved must notify the Secretariat of the terms and period of the transfer.

In a further nod to economic efficiency, regional organizations such as the EU may also "jointly fulfill" their consumption obligations as long as the combined levels remain within the mandated limits [art. 2(8)]. This resembles the notion of "joint implementation" developed under the Climate Change Convention (*see* Chapter 6)—by which parties may more efficiently share the burden of compliance.

5.   TRADE RESTRICTIONS

Though in possible violation of the 1994 WTO Agreement (formerly the GATT), the Montreal Protocol as augmented by the London and Copenhagen Amendments (and through the adjustments at the Seventh Meeting of the COP) bans all import of controlled substances from non-parties, except HCFCs and methyl bromide [arts. 4(1), 4(1)bis., 4(1)ter.]. In addition, the protocol now bans all export of these substances to non-parties [arts. 4(2), 4(2)bis., 4(2)ter.], and discourages the export of technology for their production or utilization [art. 4(5)]. The protocol also bans the import from non-parties of products containing the above substances—though a party who makes a timely objection to the Annex listing such products will not be bound [arts. 4(3), 4(3)bis., 4(3)ter.]. Finally, the parties through the COP must in the future consider the feasibility of so-called "process" trade restrictions, which disallow the import of products produced with, but not containing, the above controlled substances [arts. 4(4), 4(4)bis., 4(4)ter.].

6. TECHNOLOGICAL AND FINANCIAL ASSISTANCE

By way of the London Amendments, the Montreal Protocol became the first environmental treaty to link the compliance of developing countries with the provision of technological and financial assistance by developed countries. Accordingly, the protocol now operates a "financial mechanism," including a Multilateral Fund to meet all "agreed incremental costs" of compliance by developing country parties [art. 10]. Though what constitutes "incremental cost" within a particular situation remains highly debatable, the term refers to the cost of compliance which a party would not incur but for its adherence to the Montreal Protocol. In this way, developing nations need not simply rely on the protections offered by article 5, but have a new incentive both to sign on to the protocol and to meet the relevant control provisions. The Multilateral Fund remains under the ultimate control of the COP, but the World Bank, UNEP and UNDP share in its administration.

B. MULTILATERAL

CHAPTER EIGHT

ANTARCTICA

A. THE GEO–PHYSICAL CHARACTER OF ANTARCTICA

Antarctica is the earth's fifth largest continent with an approximate size of the United States and Mexico combined. The continent is the coldest, windiest, and driest in the world [FRANK G. KLOTZ, AMERICA ON THE ICE, ANTARCTIC POLICY ISSUES 85 (1990)]. Coastal temperatures average 0°C in the summer and −20°C in the winter, while interior temperatures average −20°C in the summer and −65°C in the winter [Colin Deihl, *Antarctica: An International Laboratory*, 18 ENVTL. AFFAIRS 423, 425–26 (1991)]. Winds often exceed 200 km/hr. An ice sheet covers 98% of the land mass, extending over 14 million square kilometers and plunging to a depth of over two kilometers [Jacques–Yves Cousteau & Bertrand Charrier, *Introduction: The Antarctic, A Challenge to Global Environment Policy, in* THE ANTARCTIC ENVIRONMENT AND INTERNATIONAL LAW 5 (Joe Verhoeven, et al. eds., 1992)]. Though the ice sheet contains 70% of the world's fresh water, the continent has a desert climate because of its low annual precipitation, averaging only five to six

167

inches of water in the form of snow. Antarctica has no indigenous human population, and no nation has a recognized claim of sovereignty over it.

B. SCIENTIFIC AND ARCHEOLOGICAL IMPORTANCE

Antarctica is important as a location for conducting scientific research of global significance that benefits virtually all scientific disciplines. Because it has been less affected by human activity than any other continent, its near-pristine environment provides a baseline for measuring pollution in populated areas of the world [James N. Barnes, *Protection of the Environment in Antarctica: Are Present Regimes Enough?*, *in* THE ANTARCTIC TREATY SYSTEM IN WORLD POLITICS 212 (Arnfinn Jorgensen–Dahl & Willy Ostreng eds., 1991)]. Antarctic ice sheets hold valuable records of past global climates and help us to understand the effects of human activities on the global environment. Core samples, in which each year is represented by a thin layer of ice that once was snow, show evidence of industrial pollution and radioactive fallout, as well as volcanic eruptions from around the world. Meteorites, valuable for their planetary information, are easier to find in Antarctica because they accumulate and are more noticeable on the ice sheets. The continent has terrestrial and freshwater ecosystems, unique in their simplicity, which provide valuable models for studying biological processes. Many important global environmental problems, such as stratospheric ozone depletion and global warming, can be better studied in polar regions.

C. ECONOMIC IMPORTANCE

Some scientists theorize that Antarctica may contain rich oil and mineral resources similar to those found in Australia and South Africa. These speculations are based, primarily, on the similarity of geologic formations and the continental drift theory. Actual scientific data also suggests the presence of oil and gas beneath Antarctica's continental shelf. Additionally, geologists have discovered deposits of iron, copper, nickel, chromium, uranium, coal, and other minerals in rock outcroppings.

The current international legal effort to prohibit oil and mineral exploration commenced some 50 years ago. It sprang from the recognition that most drilling would occur on the continental shelf, in the very heart of Antarctica's biological productivity and that an accident—made more likely by Antarctica's harsh climate—would have a disastrous effect on most Antarctic ecosystems [FRANK G. KLOTZ, AMERICA ON THE ICE, ANTARCTIC POLICY ISSUES 87 (1990)]. The principle of non-degradation of the Antarctic environment was implied in the Antarctic Treaty in 1959, which dedicated Antarctica to scientific research and peaceful purposes; the principle has been re-expressed in subsequent agreements. The Antarctic Environmental Protocol and various earlier conventions have committed the parties to a more comprehensive protection of the entire Antarctic environment [Protocol on Environmental Protection to the Antarctic Treaty (1991 Antarctic Environment Protocol), Oct. 4, 1991, art. 2, 30 I.L.M. 1461].

Still, Antarctica remains economically attractive, but dangerous. Drilling rigs and well heads would have to withstand the most severe icebergs, high winds, and violent wave conditions in the world, making the prospect of oil or mineral development on Antarctica remote. Moreover, a lack of data, high financial costs and technical obstacles introduced by increased conservation efforts stymie mineral development. On the other hand, the ice sheet covering Antarctica contains 90% of the world's glacial ice, representing 70% of the world's fresh water, and may be a potential supply of fresh water if and when technology makes this economically feasible. Furthermore, Antarctica's growing tourist industry, which attracts thousands of tourists each year, could be economically significant, but poses its own environmental difficulties.

D. ENVIRONMENTAL IMPORTANCE

Antarctica is a microcosm of global environmental problems. For instance, Antarctica's coastal areas, where land is exposed, provide critical habitat and breeding grounds for seabirds and mammals. Human activities in the form of scientific bases and support facilities have contaminated the environment and disturbed seabirds and mammals, causing them to desert their nests or breeding grounds and alter breeding cycles for the year. Humans have also introduced foreign plant and animal species that disrupt Antarctica's ecological balance by competing with and sometimes destroying native species. Additionally, the Antarctic ecosystem remains especially fragile in that just one species, the shrimp-like krill, exists as the major food source of all higher species (whales, seals, fish, squid, penguins, birds). The krill in turn feed almost exclusively on zooplankton—creating an ecosystem extremely vulnerable to pollution, or the exploitation of krill beyond a sustainable level as a food source for humans [G. Hempel, *Antarctic Marine Food Webs, in* ANTARCTIC NUTRIENT CYCLES AND FOOD WEBS 269 (W.R. Siegfried, P.R. Condy & R.M. Laws eds., 1983)].

Of further significance, the Antarctic continent exerts a fundamental influence on the world's climate by regulating the average temperature of the earth [HENRY PHILLPOT, *Climate, in* ANTARCTICA 33, 36 (W.N. Bonner & D.W.H. Walton eds., 1985)]. It is the principal "heat sink" of the global climate system, causing warmer air and ocean waters near the equator to move toward the colder air and waters at the pole, creating atmospheric and marine circulation patterns in the Southern Hemisphere (in conjunction with the rotation of the earth). Any major change in the reflective properties of the continent (its "albedo") or the volume of the Antarctic ice sheet could have dramatic effects on the rest of the world, including climate change and a rise in sea level.

E. GEO–POLITICAL IMPORTANCE

Protecting the Antarctic environment was made more difficult by the lack of recognized sovereignty over the entire continent. The primary international control strategies to protect Antarctica are collectively called the Antarctic Treaty System, initially developed by twelve countries who held conflicting views over the sovereignty of Antarctica. The Treaty System provides for cooperative international scientific projects, in which nations exchange information, facilities, and personnel. The Treaty System is a remarkable accomplishment in international cooperation. It suspends conflicting territorial claims, prohibits military uses, and preserves the continent for scientific research.

F. LEGAL RESPONSE

1. OVERVIEW

As the forbidding continent of Antarctica gradually proved more accessible during the first half of this century, questions arose as to its legal status. Given the potentially vast awards in the form of mineral and living resources, seven countries made various and conflicting claims of sovereignty. The "claimant states," as these seven have become known, were the United Kingdom (1908), New Zealand (1923), Australia (1933), France (1938), Norway (1939), Chile (1940) and Argentina (1942). These countries based their claims on a diverse assortment of theories, including the well-worn doctrine of "discovery" or "exploration," as well as "contiguity" or proximity to the Antarctic land mass. After World War II another group of five countries—all with extensive contacts to the continent—asserted that they would neither maintain nor acknowledge any territorial claims to Antarctica. Thus Belgium, Japan, South Africa, the U.S.S.R. and the United States became known as the "nonclaimant states."

Throughout the 1950's the dispute continued over who would control Antarctica. Finally, in 1959 the twelve "claimant" and "nonclaimant states" met to resolve their differences, eventually signing a compromise treaty. The result of these efforts, the Antarctic Treaty (1959 Antarctic Treaty), Dec. 1, 1959, 402 U.N.T.S. 71, 12 U.S.T. 794, T.I.A.S. No. 4780, 19 I.L.M. 860 (entered into force June 23, 1961), has since given birth to a broader international regime for the continent, which now includes the Convention on the Conservation of Antarctic Seals (1972 Seals Convention), Feb. 11, 1972, 11 I.L.M. 251 (entered into force Mar. 11, 1978); the Convention on the Conservation of Antarctic Marine Living Resources (CCAMLR), May 20, 1980, 19 I.L.M. 841 (entered into force Apr. 7, 1982); the Convention on the Regulation of Antarctic Mineral Resource Activities (CRAMRA), June 2, 1988, 27 I.L.M. 859; and the 1991 Protocol on Environmental Protection to the Antarctic Treaty (1991 Antarctic Environment Protocol).

It should be noted, however, that from the outset excluded nations have questioned the legal basis of the original parties to contract on behalf of the world community. To these nations, Antarctica exists as part of the "global commons," and though the treaty parties may bind themselves, they may not bind others by their private agreement. Though the number of parties to the 1959 treaty has grown from the original 12 to 42, it still remains unrepresentative of the entire international community as only nations who "conduct substantial scientific research" in the region achieve full voting status. Because of this exclusivity, some third world nations have suggested that the treaty system operates more as a "club" than an internationally sanctioned authority. Still, as the United Nations has not acted to co-opt or replace the present treaty system, it remains the sole governing regime for Antarctica.

2. THE 1959 ANTARCTIC TREATY

The 1959 convention only incidentally considers several environmental matters. More significantly, the treaty places in abeyance the territorial claims of all contracting parties—neither negating nor sustaining the former claims while at the same time providing that "[n]o new claim, or enlargement of an existing claim, ... be asserted while the present Treaty is in force" [art. IV]. In addition to the original "claimant" and "nonclaimant" states, the convention allows accession by any country, but again only those who conduct "substantial scientific research activity" in Antarctica may achieve full voting status [art. IX(2)]. In effect, this system has created two classes of participants to date, 26 Consultative Parties (voting) and 16 Non-consultative Parties (non-voting).

Concerning the environment, the treaty does prohibit nuclear explosions on the continent, as well as the disposal there of radioactive wastes [art. IV]. The treaty also names the "preservation and conservation of living resources" as a possible topic of further measures by the parties [art. IX(1)(f)]. The latter in fact has led to the Certain Recommendations of Third Antarctic Treaty Consultative Meeting, Annex: Agreed Measures for the Conservation of Antarctic Fauna and Flora (1964 Agreed Measures), June 13, 1964, 17 U.S.T. 992. These measures designate the continent a "Special Conservation Area," and provide safeguards for both "specially protected species" and "specially protected areas." (As presented below, the 1991 Antarctic Environment Protocol alters and improves on these designations.)

For species, the 1964 Agreed Measures limit the taking of all animals, except with a permit, and disallow the issuing of a permit for "specially protected species" (listed in Annex A) except for a "compelling scientific purpose" that neither threatens the ecosystem nor the survivability of that species [art. VI]. The 1964 Agreed Measures also severely limit the bringing into Antarctica of any non-indigenous plant or animal species [art. IX], and require that at all times parties take precautions not to disturb or disrupt the animals living there [art. VII].

Within "specially protected areas," listed in Annex B, parties have more stringent requirements. In these areas access is restricted, as parties must not allow their nationals to collect plants or drive vehicles except with a permit [art. VIII]. More recently, in 1989 the consultative parties added multiple-use planning areas (MPAs) to the protections offered under the 1959 Antarctic Treaty—establishing a larger zone for which parties must develop a management plan. In this way, and as altered and improved upon by the 1991 Antarctic Environment Protocol, the treaty now requires the parties to work more closely together in the coordination of all activities within a given locale.

3. 1972 CONVENTION FOR THE CONSERVATION OF ANTARCTIC SEALS (1972 SEALS CONVENTION)

Within the 1959 Antarctic Treaty area, the 1972 Seals Convention limits harvesting of three species of seals (Crabeater, Leopard, Wedell), and prohibits harvesting of three others (Ross, Southern Elephant, *Artocephalus* Fur seals). In point of fact, since the inception of the convention no commercial sealing has taken place—whether driven by the convention itself, politics or economics. As a result, the convention remains something of a "sleeping treaty"—but not one with the negative connotation that term generally implies.

In addition to the harvesting measures, the convention creates both a season, sealing zones (which allow limited taking) and sealing reserves (which do not) for the harvestable species. A loophole, however, exists with regard to all seal species, for which a party may issue a special permit that allows taking for reasons of scientific research or to provide specimens for museums, educational or cultural institutions [art. 4]. If a party issues a permit under article 4, it must then report the number of seals killed or captured under these permits to the Scientific Committee on Antarctic Research (SCAR). SCAR also remains in charge of assessing the annual reports of the parties, as well as suggesting amendments to its technical provisions.

Should nations decide to resume commercial sealing in Antarctica, the parties would have to reconcile the provisions of the 1972 Seals Convention with those of the 1991 Antarctic Environment Protocol (see below).

4. 1980 CONVENTION ON THE CONSERVATION OF ANTARCTIC MARINE LIVING RESOURCES (1980 CCAMLR)

The objective of the 1980 CCAMLR is the conservation of all living resources found south of the Antarctic Convergence, encompassing "fin fish, molluscs, crustaceans and all other species of living organisms, including birds" [art. I(2)]. In effect, the CCAMLR provides an early, rather rudimentary example of the ecosystem approach to conservation—an approach that aspires to protect ecosystems as a whole rather than focusing on individual species. The treaty, though not defining conservation, explains that the term "includes rational use" and lists "the following principles of conservation:

(a) prevention of decrease in the size of any harvested population to levels below those which ensure its stable recruitment. For this purpose its size should not be allowed to fall below a level close to that which ensures the greatest net annual increment;

(b) maintenance of the ecological relationships between harvested, dependent and related populations of Antarctic marine living resources and the restoration of depleted populations to the levels defined in subparagraph (a) above;

and

(c) prevention of changes or minimization of the risk of changes in the marine ecosystem which are not potentially reversible over two or three decades, taking into account the state of available knowledge of the direct and indirect impact of harvesting, the effect of the introduction of alien species, the effects of associated activities on the marine ecosystem and of the effects of environmental changes, with the aim of making possible the sustained conservation of Antarctic marine living resources."

CCAMLR art. II.(3).

The treaty thus mandates a method of conservation that focuses on the specific species, the interrelation between species, and the entire marine ecosystem. In addition, the mention of "sustained conservation" suggests an early move toward the concept of "sustainable development" in international law.

In order to implement these principles, the treaty creates two significant institutions—the Commission and the Scientific Committee. The Scientific Committee acts as the consultative body to the Commission, making recommendations concerning conservation matters [art. XV]. Here the CCAMLR makes an early gesture toward environmental impact assessment, requiring that among its duties the Scientific Committee gauge the "effects of proposed changes in the methods or levels of harvesting and proposed conservation measures" [art. XV(2)(d)]. The Commission then acts on the Scientific Committee's recommendations at its annual meeting, including the formulation of specific measures on the quantity of harvesting, method of harvesting, and the designation of protected species [art. IX].

Interestingly, the CCAMLR binds its contracting parties to the important provisions of the 1959 Antarctic Treaty—whether or not they are parties to that treaty [art. III, IV]. The CCAMLR also requires its parties to adhere, "when appropriate," to the 1964 Agreed Measures [art. V(2)]. The convention, however, makes clear that it does not derogate from the rights and obligations under either

the International Convention for the Regulation of
Whaling (ICRW), Dec. 2, 1946, 161 U.N.T.S. 366
(entered into force Nov. 10, 1948) or the Convention for the Conservation of Antarctic Seals (1972
Antarctic Seals Convention), Feb. 11, 1972, art. VI,
11 I.L.M. 251 (entered into force Mar. 11, 1978).
And, as we shall see, the CCAMLR remains intact
after the 1991 Antarctic Environment Protocol,
though parties to both must cooperatively reconcile
the differences between the two instruments.

5.   1988 ANTARCTIC MINERAL RESOURCES CONVENTION (CRAMRA)

In contrast to the CCAMLR, CRAMRA never
received the full support of its own signing parties,
as both France and Australia refused to ratify the
instrument because it appeared too weak in terms
of its protection. Originally intended to establish a
framework for ascertaining whether the wise utilization of Antarctic lands included the prospecting,
exploration and development of minerals resources,
CRAMRA in its final form set forth an extensive
range of measures aimed at protecting the environment. In fact, the CRAMRA's provisions concerning
liability for environmental damage, environmental
impact assessment, and dispute resolution will continue to serve as models for future international
environmental law treaties. In the end, however,
the convention never came into force and so remains a dead letter, presumably supplanted forever
by the 1991 Antarctic Environmental Protocol.

6.   1991 ANTARCTIC ENVIRONMENT PROTOCOL

As CRAMRA's prospects faded, and amid growing fears that the continent faced imminent environmental degradation, the Antarctic Treaty Consultative Parties chose to create an environmental protocol to the 1959 treaty. The 1991 Protocol, broad and ambitious in scope, incorporates a number of progressive environmental ideals and principles. Most significantly, the protocol establishes Antarctica as a "natural reserve, devoted to peace and science" and commits the parties "to the comprehensive protection of the Antarctic environment and dependent and associated ecosystems" [art. 2]. Though some nations lobbied for the designation of the continent as a "World Park"—a designation which presumably would offer greater protection—the classification of Antarctica as a natural reserve marks a first for any substantial area within the global commons. Among other principles the protocol places a premium on the planning and conducting of activities so as not to cause significant harm—an objective mandating prior assessment, effective monitoring and cooperation among the parties. Furthermore, the protocol acknowledges the intrinsic value of the continent, including its wilderness, aesthetic and scientific values [art. 3(1)]. In fact, some critics see an over-emphasis on scientific value, worrying that the "priority" given to scientific research in articles 3(1) & 3(3) could outweigh the prohibition against causing significant harm.

As for substantive requirements, the protocol adopts a 50 year moratorium on "any activity relating to mineral resources, other than scientific research" [art. 7]. Thus the protocol forbids all mineral exploration except that done for scientific purposes. While some parties sought a permanent ban on such activities, others, notably the United States, preferred some flexibility to pursue mineral resources in the future. As a result, after 50 years any Consultative Party may call a Review Conference to amend art. 7 (or any other provision), at which the parties may adopt any such amendment by a weighted majority [art. 25]. Otherwise, to change the moratorium before the expiration of the 50 year period, only the unanimous consent of the Consultative Parties will suffice [arts. 25(1); 12(1)(a) & (b)].

Other substantive provisions include the establishing of contingency plans in response to environmental emergencies [art. 15] and the filing of annual reports by each party outlining the measures it has taken to comply with the protocol's various requirements [art. 17]. In this regard, the protocol creates no international authority to verify and enforce compliance, instead relying on the adoption of national measures by the individual parties. The protocol, however, does create a Committee for Environmental Protection (the Committee)[art. 11]— the primary function of which is "to provide advice and formulate recommendations" to the Antarctic Treaty Consultative Meetings on the specific operations of the protocol [art. 12]. In general, the Committee must oversee, though not verify or enforce, the more detailed substantive requirements found in the protocol's annexes. To date, annexes have been adopted on Environmental Impact Assessment [Annex I], Conservation of Antarctic Fauna and Flora [Annex II], Waste Disposal and Waste Management [Annex III], Prevention of Marine Pollution [Annex VI] and Area Protection and Management [Annex V].

(a) Environmental Impact Assessment (EIA)

The protocol makes EIA an integral part of each party's obligation to protect the ecosystem, subjecting all relevant activities to the assessment procedures set out in Annex I [art. 8]. Though the procedures themselves are fairly detailed, the parties conduct the evaluations without international oversight. First, if an activity is determined to have "less than a minor or transitory impact," then no further assessment need take place and the activity may proceed [Annex I, art. 1(2)]. If, however, the party cannot make such a determination, then it must prepare an Initial Environmental Evaluation (IEE). Again, the purpose of the IEE—which includes a consideration of alternatives and impacts— is to assess whether the activity will have "less than a minor or transitory impact" [Annex I, art. 2]. If the IEE suggests the activity may have more than minor repercussions, then the party must prepare a much more extensive draft Comprehensive Environmental Evaluation (CEE). The draft CEE must contain very thorough investigations and conclusions about the possible impacts through the entire duration of the activity and beyond [Annex I, art. 3].

The party then must allow public comment for a period of 90 days while simultaneously forwarding the draft CEE to the Committee for consideration [Annex I, art. 3]. If the Committee chooses, it may then pass the document on to the Antarctic Treaty Consultative Meeting for further consideration [Annex I, art. 3]. In effect the party always retains the right to go forward with its proposed activity, but only after intense public scrutiny at various levels. Finally, if the party does go forward after preparation of a final CEE, it must continue to monitor the activity, assessing and verifying the project's consequences [Annex I, art. 5].

(b) Conservation of Antarctic Fauna and Flora

The protocol also includes an Annex on the conservation of plants and animals, which revises the relevant provisions of the 1964 Agreed Measures. In keeping with the protocol's focus on national control, each party oversees its own endeavors and issues its own permits through an appropriate authority. Annex II prohibits the taking or harmful interference of both fauna and flora except with a permit (the 1964 Agreed Measures had concentrated on fauna)[Annex II, art. 3]. The Annex additionally contains an Appendix A which lists "Specially Protected Species" which cannot be taken without a permit, and then only for a "compelling scientific purpose" that neither jeopardizes the species nor uses lethal force [Annex II, art. 3(5)]. Further, the

Annex precludes the introduction of exogenous plants and animals except with a permit and for all species but those listed in an Appendix B [Annex II, art. 4]. In actuality Appendix B names very broad categories—"domestic plants" and "laboratory animals and plants including viruses, bacteria, yeast and fungi"—thus the requirement remains primarily one of applying for a permit. And lastly, in a devastating blow to polar companionship, the Annex outlaws dogs from the continent, banning all canines from the Antarctic Treaty Area as of 1994 [Annex II, art.4(2)].

(c) Waste Disposal and Waste Management.

In Annex III the parties have attempted to deal with the difficult problem of waste from human activities in Antarctica. As general obligations each party must strive to reduce the amount of wastes, to remove wastes, and to clean up past and present disposal and work sites [Annex III, art. I]. More specifically, the annex creates three categories of wastes requiring different disposal methods. First, the most hazardous wastes—such as radioactive materials, fuel, and acutely toxic wastes—must be removed by the generating party [Annex III, art. 2(1)]. Second, for less hazardous liquid wastes and sewage and domestic liquid wastes, the generating party must work to remove these from the continent "to the maximum extent practicable" [Annex III, art. 2(2)]. Third, for other plant and animal residue, the generator must either remove or incinerate, autoclave or sterilize such products [Annex III, art. 3(2)].

Thus the annex leaves some room for disposal of non-Article 2(1) wastes by incineration, on land and in the sea. The parties must phase-out incineration by the 1998/1999 season, and until then shall "to the maximum extent practical reduce harmful emissions" [Annex III, art. 3]. Concerning other waste disposal on land, the annex allows no disposal onto ice-free areas or into fresh water systems [Annex III, art. 4(1)], and "to the maximum extent practicable" no disposal of article 2(2) wastes onto ice-covered areas except by stations into deep-ice pits [Annex III, art. 4(2)]. On the other hand, a party may still discharge sewage and domestic liquid wastes directly into the sea in most circumstances [Annex III, art. 5].

To keep track of these requirements, the annex compels each party to prepare a waste management plan that catalogues the procedures for waste reduction, storage and disposal at each site [Annex III, art. 8(2)]. In addition, each party must annually review and update its plan, which it then submits for non-binding review to the Committee [Annex III, art. 9].

(d) Prevention of Marine Pollution

Annex IV of the protocol creates rules for the prevention of pollution from ships in the Antarctic Treaty area. The annex applies to all ships flying a party's flag and to any other ship engaged in Antarctic operations [Annex IV, art. 2], but not to warships or other ships owned or operated by a state-party and used for government service [Annex

IV, art. 11]. The annex envisions four specific types of discharges, that of oil, noxious liquid substances, garbage and sewage. For oil, the annex prohibits the release of oil or oily mixture from a ship, except in cases permitted under Annex I of MARPOL 73/78 [Annex IV, art. 3; *see* Chapter Eleven, Vessel–Based Pollution]. The prohibition does not apply to discharge due to damage to a ship or its equipment. For noxious liquid substances—a category of more hazardous substances—the annex disallows discharge in any amount causing harm to the marine environment [Annex IV, art. 4]. Similarly all garbage release remains prohibited except for food wastes, which each ship must discharge at least 12 nautical miles from land or the nearest ice shelf [Annex IV, art. 5]. As for sewage, a ship may not dispose of any untreated wastes at sea within 12 nautical miles of land or ice-shelves, except where such a prohibition would "unduly impair" Antarctic operations [Annex IV, art. 6]. The qualifier, "unduly impair," obviously allows flexibility on the part of each party's implementation of article 6.

The annex further states that it does not derogate from any specific rights and obligations under MARPOL 73/78 [Annex IV, art. 14], and requires the parties to develop contingency plans for combating marine pollution, including oil spills from ships [Annex IV, art. 12].

(e) Area Protection and Management

In Annex V the protocol clarifies and updates the 1964 Agreed Measures, as well as later adoptions of the consultative parties, concerning area protection and management. The annex offers two types of designations—Antarctic Specially Protected Areas (ASPAs) and Antarctic Specially Managed Areas (ASMAs). An area may be approved as an ASPA so as "to protect outstanding environmental values, scientific, historic, aesthetic or wilderness values, any combination of those values, or ongoing or planned scientific research" [Annex V, art. 3]. The primary protection afforded by an ASPA designation, which includes areas formerly designated Specially Protected Areas and Sites of Special Scientific Interest, is to prohibit all access except by a permit [Annex V, art. 3]. On the other hand an ASMA, which may include one or more ASPAs, does not require a permit for entry but instead seeks to coordinate activities and improve cooperation among the parties [Annex V, art. 4]. A third designation, which is not an area designation as such, allows a party to propose a site or monument of recognized historic value as a Historic Site or Monument [Annex V, art. 8]. The value of such a listing protects these locations from damage, removal or destruction [Annex V, art. 8(4)].

To propose an area designation, any party (or certain institutions within the treaty system) must submit a detailed Management Plan to the Antarctic Treaty Consultative Meeting [Annex V, art. 5]. The Management Plan should contain the necessary measures to protect each area as appropriate, and the annex provides extensive guidelines in this regard. Thus the annex contains considerable potential protections, but again potential pitfalls remain. Perhaps the most significant drawback—a further example of the emphasis on national enforcement throughout the protocol—exists in the reliance on each party's appointment of "an appropriate authority" to issue permits for access to the critical ASPAs [Annex V, art. 7]. This of course leaves a great deal of discretion to the individual interpreter concerning what activities do and do not take place within the most fragile areas of the continent.

The United States recently ratified the 1991 Antarctic Environment Protocol, passing implementing legislation in September 1996. The bill, The Antarctic Science, Tourism, and Conservation Act of 1996, 16 U.S.C.A. §§ 2403a, 2413 (West 1997) [H.R.3060], mandates the application of National Environmental Policy Act (NEPA), 16 U.S.C.A. §§ 2401, et seq. (West 1997) procedures for all governmental and non-governmental activities on the continent. As of this writing, only three consultative parties had failed to ratify the Protocol—which is expected to enter into force sometime in 1997.

CHAPTER NINE

TOXIC AND HAZARDOUS SUBSTANCES

A. NATURE OF THE PROBLEM

Large quantities of almost any chemical substance can harm humans, living organisms, and the environment. Toxic and hazardous substances, on the other hand, can cause significant damage in small, even minuscule, amounts. There is no universally adopted or accepted definition of a hazardous or toxic substance, despite the fact that they are among the pollutants responsible for transboundary air and water pollution, as well as land-based pollution and dumping. Overlapping definitions and meanings attached to them have resulted in the terms toxic and hazardous being used interchangeably, conjunctively, and even disjunctively.

In general, the toxicity of a substance is identified by a number of factors including the length of time it will persist in the environment, how it tends to bioaccumulate or build up in the tissues of lower species, the extent to which it reacts with other substances to form a more harmful contaminant, and whether it produces a carcinogenic (cancer-causing), mutagenic (gene-altering), or teratogenic (birth defect-causing) effect in humans [FAO International Code of Conduct on the Distribution and Use of Pesticides, 23 FAO Conf. Res. 10/85]. Similarly, a chemical substance is considered hazardous where it exhibits certain characteristics that can cause injury, disease, economic loss, or environmental damage.[G. TYLER MILLER, LIVING IN THE ENVIRONMENT A46–A53 (6th ed.1989)].

The two terms have been variably defined even within national legal systems. For example, in the United States the term "hazardous" is defined differently for each class of pollutant and for differing regulatory schemes within a plethora of controlling statutes that include: the Occupational Safety and Health Act, 29 U.S.C.A. §§ 651–678 (West 1985); Clean Air Act, 42 U.S.C.A. §§ 7401–7671 (West 1995); Clean Water Act, 33 U.S.C.A. §§ 1251–1376 (West 1986); Federal Insecticide, Fungicide, and Rodenticide Act, 7 U.S.C.A. §§ 136.–136y (West 1980); Toxic Substances Control Act, 15 U.S.C.A. §§ 2601–2629 (West 1982 & Supp. 1996); Hazardous Materials Transportation Act, 49 U.S.C.A. §§ 5101–5127 (West 1997); Federal Hazardous Substance Act, 15 U.S.C.A. §§ 1261–1276 (West 1982 & Supp. 1996); Resource Conservation and Recovery Act of 1976 (RCRA), 42 U.S.C.A. §§ 6901–6991k (West 1995); and the Comprehensive Environmental Response, Compensation and Liability Act (CERCLA or Superfund), 42 U.S.C.A. §§ 9601–9675 (West 1995).

Specifically, hazardous waste is defined by RCRA as any solid waste which because of its concentration, quantity, or physical, chemical, or infectious characteristics may cause or significantly contribute to an increase in mortality or contribute to irreversible or incapacitating illness [RCRA, 42 U.S.C.A. § 6903]. Hazardous air pollutants are defined by the Clean Air Act as air pollutants which may present a threat of adverse health effects, including those substances which may be carcinogenic, mutagenic, teratogenic, neurotoxic, or those that cause adverse environmental effects through bioaccumulation or deposition [42 U.S.C.A. § 4712 (b)(2)(B)].

A few salient developments surrounding hazardous and toxic substances shed light on their meaning. First, if a material is regulated domestically, it will also be treated as hazardous under the Basel Convention on the Control of Transboundary Movements of Hazardous Wastes and their Disposal (Basel Convention), Mar. 22, 1989, 28 I.L.M. 657 (entered into force May 5,1992) and the Bamako Convention on the Ban of Import into Africa and the Control of Trans-boundary Movement and Management of Hazardous Wastes Within Africa (BamakoConvention), Jan. 29, 1991, 30 I.L.M. 775 (not in force). Second, the Basel Convention defines hazardous waste to include substances which are explosive, flammable, oxidizing, poisonous, infectious, corrosive, toxic, ecotoxic, or any substance capable of forming another material which possesses any of the previous characteristics after disposal. Third, in addition to contaminants that possess these characteristics, a number of treaties such as the Basel Convention, [art. 1 & Annex I] and the Bamako Convention [art. 2 & Annex I] contain a list of wastes that have previously been identified as hazardous, including medical waste, organic chemicals or hydrocarbons, radioactive wastes, and materials that contain traces of heavy metals.

B. SOURCES

About 95 percent of all hazardous pollutants are created by industries that generate four primary groups of toxic and hazardous chemicals. They are: toxic metals, petrochemicals, pesticides and radioactive materials (a discussion of radiation is excluded from this chapter because it is dealt with in Chapter Seventeen).

Toxic metals include heavy metals and trace metals. Heavy metals are those metals such as mercury, cadmium and lead whose densities are at least five times greater than water. Trace metals are those metals present in the environment or the human body in very low concentrations such as zinc, copper and iron [JOHN HARTE, ET AL., TOXICS A TO Z 103 (1991)]. Metals are present in nearly all rock types, are concentrated in ores, and enter the environment naturally through erosion and volcanic activity. Human activities have altered the natural cycle of metals and in many instances contributions from humans surpass those from natural sources. Metals, for example, are natural contaminants of coal and oil and when burned these fuels release vast quantities into the air. Ore refining, trash burning and cement production also result in airborne metals. Additionally, discarded materials in dumps can leak metals into underground aquifers and groundwater, while arsenic and cadmium, found in pesticides and fertilizers, can enter our waters through run-off.

We use and find petrochemicals in goods as varied as food, medicine, cosmetics, lumber, household appliances, fuels, plastics, papers and innumerable other manufactured products. Chemical compounds are divided into two groups: organic and inorganic. Organic compounds are based on carbon atoms usually in combination with hydrogen, and the better known include ethylene, methylene chloride, formaldehyde, benzene, DDT, and polychlorinated biphenyls (PCB's). Inorganic compounds are not based on carbon, and examples of such substances include sulfuric acid, aluminum, and chromium. Chemical products enter the environment in a number of ways. The principal among these are intentional use as in the case of pesticides, incidental and operational releases of liquid discharges and gaseous emissions during the manufacturing process, accidental spills, and waste disposal.

Most pesticides are produced by the petrochemical industry, but their importance as a source of pollution arising from individual and agricultural use, calls for separate treatment. Approximately 2.3 million metric tons per year of these pesticides are used worldwide to kill, repel, or control undesirable living organisms [G. TYLER MILLER, LIVING IN THE ENVIRONMENT 550 (6th ed. 1989)].

Humans use pesticides as pest killers, and to date over 50,000 pesticide products exist. They include:

insecticides (insects), herbicides (plants), fungicides (molds and mildew), rodenticides (rats and mice), acaricides (mites and ticks), bactericides (bacteria), avicides (birds), and nematicides (roundworms).

The most widely used insecticides fall into one of four chemical groups: organochlorines, organosphosphates, carbamates and botanicals. The most dangerous of these are organochlorines (chlorinated hydrocarbons) which contain chlorine, carbon, and hydrogen. Examples of organochlorines include insecticides such as DDT, chlordane, lindane, aldrin/dieldrin, and heptachlor. These compounds are considered persistent because they do not readily break down in the environment. They also tend to bioaccumulate in plant and animal tissues [JOHN HARTE, ET AL., TOXICS A TO Z 112–140 (1991)].

Pesticides contain both inert and active ingredients. The active ingredient is the portion of the chemical that actually kills or controls the target organism [TRAVIS WAGNER, IN OUR BACKYARD 239–49 (1994)]. Presently, 700 active ingredients function within the 50,000 different types of pesticides on the market. Because pesticides are designed to kill a broad spectrum of organisms, they present a threat not only to the target organism but also to other animals, including humans [WORLD RESOURCE INSTITUTE, WORLD RESOURCES 1994–95 113 (1994)]. Unfortunately, less than 0.1 percent of insecticides and 5 percent of herbicides applied to crops by spraying actually reach the target organism. The remaining chemicals become toxic contaminants as they vaporize into air, run off into water, or leach into soil and groundwater [G. Tyler Miller, Living in the Environment 553 (6th ed. 1989)].

C. ENVIRONMENTAL IMPACTS & PATHWAYS

1. IMPACTS

Toxics often impact ecological food chains by bio-accummulating in the tissues of aquatic organisms. The process of bioaccumulation begins when a toxic contaminant present in the soil or water is absorbed by plants that are later ingested by a lower animal. If not readily excreted by it, the contaminant will gradually increase in that animal beyond the level of the surrounding environment. This process of growing accumulation continues up the food chain. Generally, the higher the concentration of a toxic substance in the environment, the more it will be taken up by plants and passed from plants to plant-eating animals, culminating in very high concentrations in predatory animals [John Harte, et al., Toxics A to Z 86–90 (1991)].

In the 1960's, for example, in the United States bald eagles, peregrine falcons, and other predatory animals died as a result of reproductive failure caused by excess DDT in their tissues. These birds did not feed on the farmlands where farmers had originally used DDT, but on fish that were at the end of a long food chain in which DDT had bioaccu-mulated. Rain run-off had carried the DDT into lakes and ponds where the pesticide passed from algae to plankton, eventually aggregating in fish which retained rather than excreted the poison. Finally the birds that fed on these fish developed even higher concentrations of the deadly chemical.

High concentrations of toxic metals in the environment also present a danger to human health. Metals exist as a unique contaminant because they are elemental compounds which never decompose. Therefore, they remain a threat that can resurface at any time. Human activities that move these elements into the air, water, and soil may do so at concentrations toxic to humans.

The tragedy that took place in Minamata, Japan, in the 1950's offers a painful example. Japanese villagers in the fishing village of Minamata were poisoned by mercury (a heavy metal) that had been discharged into the water by a nearby chemical company, and had bioaccumulated in fish eaten by the villagers. This resulted in approximately fifty deaths and several thousand cases of permanent nervous disorders.

Toxic metals like mercury, cadmium, lead, and arsenic find their way into the air through the burning of coal and oil for energy, ore refining, trash burning, cement production, and the use of automobiles [JOHN HARTE, ET AL., TOXICS A TO Z 116–118 (1991)]. These elements can also leach into the soil and water when metal-containing products are buried in landfills. Fertilizers and pesticides often contain arsenic and cadmium which can run off into surface waters and may eventually end up in groundwater. The specific health effects of high metal levels in humans depend on both the type of metal and the organ involved. Lead poisoning can cause convulsions, brain damage or degeneration, and death. Arsenic, beryllium, cadmium, and chromium causes lung cancer. Long term exposure to metal dust may result in the formation of scar tissue in the lungs or cystic fibrosis [G. TYLER MILLER, LIVING IN THE ENVIRONMENT 472 (6th ed. 1989); JOHN HARTE, ET AL., TOXICS A TO Z 104 (1991)].

Toxic chemicals are believed to cause long term health effects in humans, like cancer and cirrhosis of the liver, at low dosages over a long period of time. DDT and other organochlorine insecticides pose the greatest threat to human health because they persist in the environment from 2–15 years and tend to bioaccumulate in food chains [WORLD RESOURCE INSTITUTE, WORLD RESOURCES 1994–95 114 (1994)]. Rarely used in the United States now, these chemicals still remain in extensive use in lesser developed countries that export a large amount of agricultural products. One notorious type of organochlorine herbicide, 2,4,5–T or Agent Orange, contains dioxin, one of the most toxic chemicals ever made by humans. Studies indicate that dioxin can cause soft-tissue sarcoma, Hodgkin's disease, fetal death, and birth defects [JOHN HARTE, ET AL., TOXICS A TO Z 116–18 (1991); G. TYLER MILLER, LIVING IN THE ENVIRONMENT 554–55 (6th ed. 1989)]. Organophosphate and carbamate insecticides find more frequent use in the United States. These types do not bioaccumulate and tend to break down more quickly, though often they remain more acutely toxic to vertebrate animals.

Toxic and hazardous wastes take many forms: liquid, solid, semi-solid (sludge), and containerized gas. They are neutralized or sequestered through various physical, chemical, and biological processes of treatment and disposal. Some physical waste treatment or remediation technologies change the form of the waste and reduce its volume and weight. Biological and chemical facilities use living organisms (microorganisms) to stabilize waste materials employing aerobic (oxygen-using) and anaerobic (non-oxygen-using) methods [ENCYCLOPEDIA OF THE ENVIRONMENT 314–315, 795–803 (Ruth Eblan & William Eblan eds., 1994)]. During remediation, the treatment process itself can constitute a source of pollution by creating gaseous and solid residues that need to be discharged into landfills, underground injection wells, or the oceans.

A typical example of treatment is to place the waste in large surface impoundments such as pits, ponds, or lagoons where it is filtered, solidified, degraded, or neutralized. If not properly lined, however, the surface impoundment or landfill may leach or migrate into the groundwater. Also, the waste may simply run off into surface waters if the cap on the structure breaks down. With regard to household waste and small scale industrial waste, because the generator's quantities remain small these wastes are not typically treated as hazardous waste, and therefore these often end up in landfills not designed to prevent migration into surface or groundwaters [TRAVIS WAGNER, IN OUR BACKYARD 135–36 (1991)].

Incineration is a more expensive method of treatment and disposal, in which wastes are burned at high temperatures. Depending upon the waste involved, incineration may offer a relatively safe disposal method, though the ash generated can contain toxic materials that require disposal. Furthermore, in some circumstances toxic gaseous and particulate materials may escape at harmful levels. [E. WILLARD MILLER, ENVIRONMENTAL HAZARDS: TOXIC WASTE AND HAZARDOUS MATERIAL 38 (1991)].

Wastes are also discharged into water bodies, such as rivers, lakes and estuaries. Where hazardous and toxic chemicals are so disposed we have seen how they can bioaccumulate in the tissues of aquatic organisms. When humans consume animals with elevated concentrations of contaminants in their tissues the result may be serious health effects or even death [G. TYLER MILLER, LIVING IN THE ENVIRONMENT 325 (6th ed. 1989)].

Wastes not successfully dealt with by any other means may be stored in waste piles or tanks and then disposed of in landfills, in surface impoundments, or in deep wells. Deep-well injection involves the pumping of liquid waste into a well or a geologic formation located below underground sources of drinking water. Unfortunately, injected hazardous wastes may eventually migrate into the groundwater through cracks or fissures [JOHN HARTE, ET AL., TOXICS A TO Z 161 (1991)].

2. PATHWAYS

We have dealt with the environmental movements, or the routes or journeys traveled by chemicals through air, water or land, and their advance through food chains. By pathways we now consider their points of entry into, and passage through human bodies toward target organs, giving rise to disease and harm to human health. When discharged into the environment, pollutants affect humans through three routes. A person may inhale a substance, ingest it through water or food, or absorb it through the skin.

Once it enters the bloodstream, the contaminant circulates to all of the organs in the body. However, the extent of harm depends on the concentration and type of contaminant present. Some contaminants are easily metabolized by the body and become detoxified. Other contaminants, typically cancer-causing substances, become more toxic after metabolization. This is called bio-activation. The body may also reduce the toxic effect of a substance by storing it in fat tissue, but adverse effects may still occur if the body utilizes a large amount of fat for energy at one time. The acute effects of a contaminant may disappear because a number of chemicals will naturally bind with proteins in the bloodstream, thereby reducing the amount free to attack a certain organ. Nonetheless, this process may result in a chronic effect because the chemical may stay in the body longer, becoming unbound and harmful at a later date.

All substances can become toxic if they impact humans in sufficient concentrations, and scientists engaged in ascertaining the risk posed by a chemical try to measure the linkage between exposure to a chemical and disease by employing both epidemiological and toxicological data. Epidemiology involves the study of human populations to discover the relationship between various risk factors and the occurrence of disease in that population. Toxicology uses data collected from laboratory experiments on animals, bacteria, and cell or tissue cultures to identify the mechanism of disease and the way that the contaminant causes harm.

Establishing linkages is particularly difficult for a number of reasons. The potency of a substance, the degree of exposure, and the fact that certain groups of people are more sensitive to particular toxic substances complicates such assessments. A fourth difficulty exists for toxicological data derived from high dosages administered to test animals. A researcher must extrapolate such high dosages onto a fact situation involving humans, who possess different metabolisms than animals, and whose contact occurs at a lower level of the suspect substance [JOHN HARTE, ET AL., TOXICS A TO Z 27–32 (1991)].

Real-life exposure to toxic and hazardous contaminants can result in both chronic and acute health effects in humans. Acute effects, such as skin burns, rashes, and kidney damage, appear shortly after introduction to a large dose or concentration of a contaminant. Chronic effects are those which do not appear initially, but tend to last for many years after long-term exposure to low concentration levels or short-term exposure to extremely high concentrations [G. TYLER MILLER, LIVING IN THE ENVIRONMENT 450 (6th ed. 1991)]. Contact with certain types of toxic or hazardous contaminants can result in chronic health effects such as cancer, inheritable diseases, birth defects, heart and lung disease, and nerve or behavioral disorders. Carcinogens remain extremely difficult to identify because of the complex nature of cancer as a disease and the broad range of chemicals and environmental factors encountered by humans. To date, common examples of these substances include asbestos, carbon tetrachloride, arsenic, and benzene. Mutagens, such as benzo-pyrene and ozone, can alter an organism's genetic code resulting in cancers or inheritable diseases like cystic fibrosis. Other chemicals and certain metals, including lead, cadmium, arsenic and mercury are classified as teratogens. [JOHN HARTE, ET AL., TOXICS A TO Z 30–33 (1991)].

D. REMEDIAL OBJECTIVES

Hazardous chemicals and wastes are the inevitable consequence of modern living. The life style enjoyed in developed countries depends to a significant degree on the use of chemicals for a variety of purposes. So many of the goods taken for granted— ranging from simple articles like knives, forks, and instant food, to more complex machines such as motor cars or computers—involve the use of chemicals. Chemicals are used in the extraction and refining of raw materials needed for these products as well as in the manufacturing and packaging process. They also find their way into the environment when these products are discarded or dumped.

The dangers associated with the use of hazardous or toxic chemicals and the generation of waste can be controlled by a number of strategies. A primary goal should be to reduce demand for products that entail the use of such substances. Demand management exists as a painful but necessary step in any concerted attempt to find solutions. Second, it is necessary to adopt a comprehensive view of the problem by regulating and managing local, regional and global material and energy flows in products, processes and industrial sectors. Third, and this may be the more practicable of the objectives, integrated as distinct from fragmented pollution controls should be adopted.

Many international conventions have attempted to control pollution within the environmental media (air, land or water) in which it is found. Such a fragmented approach fails for a number of reasons. It concentrates on moving the pollution generated by polluting activities from one place to another. Unfortunately, such pollution transfers ignore the basic law of physics that matter is indestructible. The initial destination of pollutants may be altered, but ultimately they re-enter the flow of material within the environment.

Limitations on discharges in one medium, such as air, while correcting the immediate pollution problem within that medium, often do little more than shift the pollution from air to land without recognizing the adverse impact of transferred pollution. Such transfers can create even greater problems in the medium to which they are moved. Thus, control technologies aimed at achieving specific limits to pollution generate new streams of residuals which have adverse effects on other media. This is evidenced by the massive quantities of sludge created by existing pollution controls in the United States. For example, the provisions of the United States Clean Air Act directed at reducing sulphur dioxide require the use of 'scrubbers' in smoke stacks. Huge quantities of lime, limestone solution, and water are sprayed on exhaust gases as they flow up power plant smokestacks. Sulphur dioxide in the gas then reacts with the spray and forms a solution from which the sulphur dioxide is later removed, strained, and disposed of in the form of sludge. The Environmental Protection Agency (EPA) has estimated that three to six tons of scrubber sludge may be produced for each ton of sulphur dioxide removed from the flue gas. Consequently, the problem of sulphur dioxide in the air has been replaced by the problem of sludge disposal. Municipal wastewater treatment and sewage treatment plants also produce large quantities of sludge. Some of this sludge contains toxic substances which are nondegradable and bioaccumulable.

Direct transfers are compounded by indirect transfers resulting from physical, chemical, and biological forces. Usually, fragmented controls assess the risk of a pollutant on the basis of a single chemical causing exposure in a single medium, but they do not consider the risk to people multiply exposed in different mediums. Most international treaties ignore the multi-media risk posed by even a single substance. The bewildering and aggravated risk presented by the synergistic effects of thousands of substances circulating in the environment simply falls outside the pale of reckoning.

The present fragmented approach also lacks economic efficiency. Pollution controls already in place ensure that wastes cannot be discharged according to the best environmental option. This may led to inefficient use of the assimilative capacity of the environment. In the example previously considered we observed how the implementation of the Clean Air Act might lead to the creation of large quantities of sludge. Sludge can be disposed of in a number of ways. It can be discharged into a river or directly into the sea, or piped into a lagoon to settle and dry out as solid waste. What is germane is the possibility that current air pollution requirements might lead to water discharges, or solid waste disposal problems that cause greater overall damage to the environment than might be the case if the air pollution standards had been cognizant of cross-media impacts. In addition, water pollution and land waste disposal laws also could prevent the discharges into water or disposal as solid waste without further treatment. Setting independent standards for each medium that ignore the assimilative capacity of the environment imposes unnecessary and unjustified costs on the manufacturing process.

A more efficient and cost effective method of pollution control would be to distribute the wastes between the three media of water, air, and land in a manner that makes optimum use of the environment, and of any special or particular assimilative capacity it might possess. This policy would lead to a balanced approach to pollution control which would avoid the problems of standards that are overly stringent in some areas and unduly lax in others.

An increasingly urgent need for safe and cost efficient methods of disposal has arisen as industrialized countries continue to strengthen regulations on the disposal of hazardous waste. In the past, industrialized countries have either dumped this waste directly into the ocean or buried it upon the land, but increased awareness of the dangers associated with these methods led to strict regulation, forcing industries to look to lesser developed countries for a solution.

Industry has targeted countries located primarily in Africa, Latin America, and the Caribbean because these countries normally have less stringent pollution control regulations and are usually more willing to accept these wastes as a method to raise revenues. The cost of disposing of wastes in these countries is usually significantly lower than either instituting waste minimization techniques at the source or utilizing an approved disposal facility located in the generating country.

Obviously, however, this practice is not a solution to the waste problem because it merely transfers the environmental cost from industry to a group of people less qualified to bear it. Most countries that import hazardous wastes lack information as to the risks these wastes pose to human health and the environment, and also lack the knowledge or administrative capacity to manage them properly. In fact, in the past many countries have accepted hazardous chemicals for use and disposal without knowing that the chemicals have been banned in the generating country. Because of this overall lack of knowledge, developing countries may utilize disposal techniques that are not adequate to control the risks that these wastes present to their citizens and their environment. In addition to the dangers posed by improper disposal techniques, the long distance transportation of hazardous wastes across land and water presents an increased risk of harm to transit states and the marine environment from accidental spillage.

Waste trade with developing countries continues to decline as industrialized countries have developed and utilized waste minimization techniques. Further, nations have enacted a number of treaties and regional agreements in order to deal with the problems associated with the trade of hazardous waste. As we shall see, treaties such as the Basel Convention indicate that these countries increasingly agree to dispose of hazardous wastes at the source as long as the disposal can take place in an environmentally sound manner [arts. 4(2) (c), (d), (e),(g), 7, 8].

Therefore, both the Basel and Bamako Conventions allow for trade between similarly situated party states, but only if the exporting state lacks the capacity to dispose of the waste in an environmentally sound manner and the importing state gives its Prior Informed Consent (PIC) (see below). The importing state must also possess the ability to dispose of the waste in an environmentally sound manner and if an illegal trade occurs, the exporting state must accept the waste for re-import [Basel, arts. 6, 9; Bamako, arts. 4, 6, 7, 9].

These conventions correctly seized the basic concepts underlying an integrated approach when they called upon all parties to reduce the generation of hazardous and toxic wastes to a minimum. This can only be done by reducing the source of such wastes and "sources" embrace demand for a product. They also call for "environmentally sound management" which opens the door to integrated pollution control. Unfortunately, as detailed below, these requirements are left in the soft limbo of aspiration rather than of hard legal duty.

The Bamako Convention calls for a prohibition on the importation of hazardous waste into their regions from non-parties and attempts to regulate trade between parties to the convention. The right of states to ban imports is supported by other agreements such as the African, Caribbean and

Pacific States — European Economic Community: Fourth Lome Convention (Lome Convention), Dec. 15, 1989, 29 I.L.M. 783 (entered into force Sept. 1, 1991), which prohibits exports of hazardous waste to African, Caribbean, and Pacific state parties from the European Union. While the prohibitions on exports or imports of wastes express valuable if controversial aspects of IEL, it is well-settled that the requirement of Prior Informed Consent codifies existing customary law (see below).

A number of organizations—including the International Labour Organization (ILO), the Organization for Economic Cooperation and Development (OECD) and the European Union have participated in the international effort to control the harmful effects of pesticides and other toxic chemicals. In addition, the World Health Organization (WHO) has developed important guidelines for classification, and WHO works with both UNEP and the ILO in promoting the International Programme in Chemical Safety.

Another significant contribution is presently being made by the Codex Alimentarius Commission, which has developed regional and international standards regarding chemical residues in foods. The Codex Alimentarius standards, it should be noted, generally remain substantially less restrictive than those of developed states and are relied upon by developing countries when alleging the formers' protectionist restrictions of trade disguised as health and safety concerns. On the other hand, some domestic environmental organizations of developed countries have used the Codex standards as a rallying point against free trade agreements such as NAFTA and GATT/WTO. The work of the Food and Agricultural Organization (FAO) and UNEP, however, has had the greatest impact on the behavior of nations.

E. LEGAL RESPONSE

1. TOXIC AND HAZARDOUS SUBSTANCES IN GENERAL

At present, no international treaty exists regarding the distribution and use of hazardous substances across all media. In the absence of such a treaty, the FAO and UNEP have striven to fill this gap through two sets of voluntary guidelines. These influential regulations—prime examples of "soft law"—predominantly focus on the relative obligations of developed and developing nations regarding trade. Both sets of rules adopt a regulated trade approach to the interaction between exporter and importer, allowing transfers of substances banned in another country under the principle of Prior Informed Consent.

This approach contrasts with that taken by the 1991 Bamako Convention negotiated by the Organisation of African States. The Bamako Convention, discussed in detail in the section on hazardous wastes, prohibits African countries from importing *all* banned or restricted pesticides and chemicals from outside the continent.

2. PESTICIDES

(a) 1985 FAO International Code of Conduct on the Distribution and Use of Pesticides (Amended in 1989)(1985 FAO Code of Conduct)

As pesticide exports continued to accelerate during the 1980s, the United Nations FAO sought to limit the harmful effects of improper use in developing countries. The 1985 FAO Code of Conduct, amended in 1989, forges a compromise between exporting and importing nations. As the Code identifies in article 1(1.1), it seeks to "set forth responsibilities and establish voluntary standards of conduct for all public and private entities ... particularly where there is no or an inadequate national law to regulate pesticides." The Code— which deals only with pesticides and not other hazardous substances—embraces the "necessary and acceptable use" of these chemicals, while striving to prevent "significant adverse effects on people or the environment" [art. 1(1.2)]. Non-binding in nature, the Code consequently employs hortatory and sometimes vague aspirational language.

Under the Code, governments retain ultimate responsibility for the distribution and use of pesticides in their countries, but also the pesticide industry—including manufacturers, marketers and traders—plays a significant role. Regarding testing, for example, manufacturers should follow well-recognized procedures in assessing the risk of their products and should evaluate the applicability of their products in anticipated regions of use [art. 4]. Manufacturers should then make available all such information to the proper government authorities in the countries in which their products are offered for sale [art. 4]. In order to receive and evaluate these reports, governments of importing countries should possess or have access to effective analytical facilities [art. 4]. Governments of exporting nations, as well as international organizations, should strive to assist developing countries in establishing facilities capable of undertaking product and residue analysis [art. 4].

The Code also states that governments of importing countries should develop necessary regulatory legislation for the control of pesticides, including registration [art. 6] and rules on availability and safe use [art. 7]. For its part industry should make sure that the exported product remains subject to the same quality standards of comparable domestic products, and should ensure that their products are traded by and purchased from reputable traders [art. 8]. The FAO Code of Conduct additionally requires that all pesticide containers be clearly labeled according to international guidelines (e.g. the FAO Guidelines on Good Labeling Practice, 1985) [art. 10]. In this regard industry should use labels that include appropriate symbols and pictograms whenever possible, in addition to written instructions, warnings and precautions [art. 10]. Likewise, the packaging, storage and disposal of pesticides should conform in principle to the applicable guidelines formulated by FAO and WHO, respectively.

Undergirding the provisions of the Code of Conduct is the principle of Prior Informed Consent (PIC). This principle requires that no pesticide banned or severely restricted by any government in order to protect human health or the environment be imported without the knowledgeable acquiescence of the importing country. FAO has in fact developed Guidelines on the Operation of Prior Informed Consent (1990), and the importing country's decision should be made in accordance with these [art. 9]. To implement the PIC procedure, exporting countries that ban or severely restrict the use or handling of a pesticide should notify the FAO, which then relays this information to other participating governments [art. 9]. The Code of Conduct also requires FAO to maintain a database with UNEP regarding control actions and decisions [art. 9].

In making PIC decisions the governments of importing countries must ensure that any decision does not run afoul of WTO (formerly GATT) in creating an unfair trade barrier masked as an environmental or health concern [art. 9]. Governments of exporting countries, on the other hand, must take appropriate measures as allowed under domestic law to ensure that exports do not occur contrary to the decision of the importing country [art. 9].

As a soft law instrument that only provides voluntary standards of behavior, the FAO Code of Conduct must rely on persuasion rather than the threat of legal consequences. The FAO has steadily provided sound advice concerning the management of pesticides, and the institution has developed a considerable and well-respected expertise in the area. Though the Code, as such, has achieved broad political acceptance, NGOs have in fact documented routine violations of its provisions in developing countries.

3.   OTHER TOXIC CHEMICALS

(a) 1987 UNEP London Guidelines for the Exchange of Information on Chemicals in International Trade (1987 UNEP London Guidelines)

In substance the 1987 UNEP London Guidelines, UNEP/PIC/WG.2/2 at 9, UNEP ELPG No. 10, UNEP/GC/DEC/15/30 (1987) closely resemble the voluntary standards of the FAO Code of Conduct. Providing a broad definition of the term, the Guidelines state that " 'chemical' means a chemical substance whether by itself or in a mixture or preparation, whether manufactured or obtained from nature and includes such substances used as industrial chemicals and pesticides" [art. 1(a)]. Concerning pesticides, however, the Guidelines in fact defer to the FAO which it acknowledges as the primary source of guidance for the management of pesticides internationally [Intro 7]. Thus the Guidelines seek in non-duplicative fashion to supplement and cooperate with the FAO regarding pesticides, while establishing the primary system of voluntary controls for other hazardous chemicals.

As an overriding principle, the London Guidelines state that both importing and exporting countries should protect human health and the environment against potential harm by exchanging information on chemicals [2.(a)]. To this end the Guidelines also promote the principle of Prior Informed Consent (PIC) and establish formal PIC Procedures. On the other hand, the Guidelines make clear that nations may participate in the information exchange procedures without participating in the more formal PIC Procedures [7.1(a)].

The Guidelines establish the International Register of Potentially Toxic Chemicals (IRPTC) as the general information clearinghouse and require all states, having taken action to ban or severely to restrict a chemical, to notify the IRPTC with information surrounding that action [6]. Particularly an exporting state having taken any action should provide the Designated National Authority of the importing state with the relevant information through the IRPTC [8]. Additionally an importing state participating in the PIC Procedures, when responding using the official PIC forms, "will have the opportunity to record their decisions regarding future imports of banned or severely restricted imports in a formal way" [7.1]. For its part the IRPTC relays the decision to the exporting country, maintains a database of all important information, and provides such information for inclusion in the regular updates of the UN Consolidated List of Products whose Consumption and/or Sale have been Banned, Withdrawn or Severely Restricted by Governments [7.4].

Beyond the use of the clearinghouse, states of export should directly provide information, advice and assistance to importing states regarding the sound management of hazardous chemicals [13.(b)]. States of export should, for example, as far as practicable supply precautionary information in the principle language(s) of the importing state, accompanied by suitable pictorial aids and labels [13.(d)]. The Guidelines recognize the desirability of exporting states using no less stringent requirements of classification, packaging and labeling than in their own countries—and in the absence of standards in the importing state, that the exporter employ classification, packaging and labeling standards in conformity with internationally harmonized procedures [14]. Importing states, on the other hand, have responsibilities with regard to their own citizens, and should take measures to ensure that users at all levels are given the necessary information, advice and assistance to manage these chemicals safely [13.(c)].

The London Guidelines therefore closely follow the substantive standards offered by the FAO Code of Conduct, with FAO and UNEP working jointly to implement the PIC procedure. In fact, negotiations are presently underway to create a PIC Convention and in 1995 the Inter-Organization Programme for Sound Management of Chemicals (IOMC) was established to coordinate the efforts of all international and intergovernmental organizations involved in chemical safety. Even with such improvements, the distribution and use of hazardous substances remains one of the most under-regulated areas of international environmental law. As we shall see below, the world community has so far placed more energy and attention on the transboundary movement and trade in hazardous wastes.

(b) Hazardous Wastes

i. Overview

To date, international attention has focused primarily on the transboundary movement and trade in hazardous wastes. In 1987 UNEP adopted the Governing Council Decision on Cairo Guidelines and Principles for the Environmentally Sound Management of Hazardous Wastes (Cairo Guidelines), UNEP/GC/DEC/14/30, UNEP ELPG no. 8 (1987), which function as "soft law" standards similar to the 1987 London Guidelines, discussed above. The same UNEP working group then developed the text of the 1989 Basel Convention on the Control of Transboundary Movements of Hazardous Wastes and Their Disposal (1989 Basel Convention), which came into force in 1992. Like the Cairo Guidelines, the Basel Convention originally adopted a broad managed-trade approach to hazardous wastes—allowing all transboundary transfers based on the principle of Prior Informed Consent. Opponents complained that the Basel Convention did little to restrict trade, and instead functioned more as a tracking system for continued transfers to developing countries, in effect licensing the dumping of hazardous wastes in the third world. Particularly African countries were most vocal against the managed-trade approach of the Basel Convention and collectively in 1991 adopted the Bamako Treaty—which strictly bans the import of hazardous wastes from outside the continent (see below). Since its inception, however, the Basel Convention has been amended (in 1995) to prohibit trade in hazardous wastes between OECD and EU states on the one hand, and all non-OECD and non-EU states on the other [art. 4A]. This provision, as well as other enhancements discussed below, has gradually gained third world support for the convention—which now has over 100 parties including a handful of African nations.

ii.   *The Basel Convention on the Control of Transboundary Movements of Hazardous Wastes and Their Disposal (Basel Convention)*

Environmentally Sound Management

The Basel Convention, though primarily dealing with the transboundary movement and trade in hazardous wastes, also contains general provisions regarding the environmentally sound management of such wastes. Under the convention "hazardous waste" means those substances or objects included in the categories set out by Annexes I and III, as well as those defined or considered as hazardous wastes by the domestic legislation of the party of export, import or transit [art. 1(1)]. Other substances or objects included in the categories of Annex II, such as those collected from households, are known as "other wastes" [art. 1(2)]. Under the treaty "environmentally sound management" is de-

not constituting an environmentally sound management of hazardous wastes ..." [pmbl. 7 bis]. Parties additionally must not allow export to parties which have prohibited all imports, or which cannot manage the particular wastes in question in an environmentally sound manner [art. 4(2)(e)]. Likewise, importing parties must prevent import if the wastes cannot be managed in proper fashion [art. 4(2)(g)]. The convention also prohibits any transfers between parties and non-parties [art. 4(5)], except transfers that do not derogate from environmentally sound management as provided by the convention and are communicated to the Secretariat [art. 11]. (This latter provision is the loophole by which the United States, a signatory that has not ratified the convention because it has not passed appropriate implementing legislation, continues to export hazardous wastes to parties). In fact, the convention only allows transfers between parties in the following circumstances:(a) the state of export cannot dispose of the wastes adequately; (b) the wastes in question are required as raw material for recycling or recovery industries; or (c) the transfer is in accordance with other criteria to be decided by the Parties [art. 4(9)]. Finally, as remarked above the amended convention prohibits all transboundary movements of hazardous wastes not designated for recycling from all OECD and EU states to all non-OECD and non-EU states [art. 4A(1)]. Hazardous wastes designated for recycling must likewise be phased out between the same states by the end of 1997 [art. 4A(2)].

When transboundary movement does take place, the parties must conduct such transfers in a manner protecting human health and the environment [art. 4(2)(d)]. In this regard parties must ensure that packaging, labeling and transport conform with generally accepted international rules and standards [art. 4(7)(b)]. More broadly, in no way may generating states transfer the duty to manage wastes in an environmentally sound manner to states of import or transit [art. 4(10)].

In addition to these general obligations, the Basel Convention establishes a global paper trail for any transboundary movement of hazardous or other wastes. The state of export must notify (or require the generator or exporter to notify) any state of transit or import concerning the details of the transaction [art. 6(1)]. This is done by way of written instrument through each state's designated "competent authority" [art. 6(1)]. The written notification must contain all the declarations and information specified in Annex V A [art. 6(1)]. Upon receipt the state of import must respond to the notifier in writing—consenting to the movement with or without conditions, denying the movement, or requesting additional information [art. 6(2)]. Until the notifier has received written permission as well as confirmation of an environmentally sound contract from the importing state, the exporting state may not allow shipment [art. 6(3)]. The state of export must also receive written consent from the state of transit, though provisions are made for a state of transit which is also a party to opt out of this requirement [art. 6(4)]. With written consent of the states concerned, the state of export may use a less detailed general notification for regular shipments over a twelve month period [arts. 6(6)–6(8)]. Finally, if informed by the importing state that the contract cannot be completed as drawn, the state of export must receive the shipment back unless other arrangements can be made, and neither the state of export nor any party of transit may hinder that return [art. 8].

As a framework treaty, the Basel Convention has benefitted from the cooperative impetus and flexible decision-making power built into the framework approach. Informal decisions of the Conference of the Parties, meaning those that do not call for ratification or other formal approval by each state, have led to a number of innovative mechanisms. Such innovations include "Model National Legislation" for the transboundary movement and management of hazardous wastes, a "Manual for the Implementation of the Basel Convention," and "Draft Forms" for the identification and tracking of illegal trade. In addition, the COP has swiftly moved to implement specific provisions of the convention, including the development of a Draft Protocol on Liability and Compensation, and the establishment of regional and sub-regional centers for training and technology transfer regarding both the management of wastes and the minimization of generation. In short, under UNEP guidance the Basel Convention has quickly evolved from a poorly ratified treaty into a relatively effective, if under-funded, hazardous waste regime.

iii. *The Convention on the Ban of Imports Into Africa and the Control of Transboundary Movement and Management of Hazardous Wastes Within Africa (Bamako Convention)*

Though born out of disapproval with the Basel Convention's managed-trade approach, the Bamako Treaty in fact closely follows its predecessor in most respects. It does however create more stringent rules for its African parties in several ways. The most significant difference from the original Basel Convention lies in the Bamako Convention's banning of all hazardous wastes into Africa from non-parties [art. 4(1)]. Of course this difference has narrowed considerably given the recent amendment to the Basel Convention involving OECD and EU nations. Additionally, "hazardous wastes" is defined more broadly and even includes banned or strictly regulated hazardous substances [art. 2(1)]. The convention also provides for unlimited liability as well as joint and several liability on hazardous waste generators [art. 4(3)(b)]. Other differences include a stronger commitment to the Precautionary Approach that emphasizes clean production methods rather than permissible emissions [art. 4(3)(f) & (g)], and the disallowal of general notification procedures for regular shipments of the same wastes [art. 6(6)]. Though the Bamako Convention creates more stringent conditions than the Basel Convention, an African nation may nonetheless become party to both. The Basel Convention clearly allows a party to impose "additional requirements ... in order to better protect human health and the environment" [art. 4(11)], and the Bamako Convention permits a party to enter into other agreements as long as these do not "derogate from the environmentally sound management of hazardous wastes" as required by the convention [art. 11(1)]. Therefore, as long as an African party follows the strict procedures of the Bamako Convention, it may also benefit from the transfer of resources through the Basel Convention. Indeed a handful of African nations have ratified both treaties as of this writing.

iv. *Other Regional Agreements*

In North America, the United States has signed two pre-NAFTA agreements with its hemispheric trading partners. The Canada—United States Agreement Concerning the Trans-boundary Movement of Hazardous Waste, Oct. 28, 1986, 11099 T.I.A.S. 496 (amended in 1992) allows the "export, import, and transit of hazardous waste" across the border [art. 2], and requires notification of the importing country for any planned transfers [art. 3]. In a twist on the principle of Prior Informed Consent, however, silence is deemed consent and the exporter may proceed with the shipment if the importing country does not respond to the notification within thirty days [art. 3].

In a more traditional version of Prior Informed Consent, and one more in adherence with the relative positions of developed and developing countries, the Mexico—United States Agreement for Co-operation on Environmental Programmes and Trans–Boundary Problems, Nov. 12, 1986, 26 I.L.M. 25 (entered into force Jan. 29, 1987) (Annex III to the 1983 US–Mexico Agreement on Cooperation for the Protection and Improvement of the Environment in the Border Area) (Mexico–U.S. Hazardous Waste Agreement) prohibits transfer of hazardous waste without approval by the importing country [art. III]. For its part, the importing party must respond within forty-five days and may choose to accept, accept with conditions, or reject the planned shipment [art. III].

Another significant regional instrument, the 1989 Lome IV Convention, prohibits all exports of hazardous wastes from EU states to African—Caribbean—Pacific (ACP) states [art. 39(1)]. In fact the treaty, which defines hazardous wastes according to Basel Convention standards [art. 39(3)], mandates that ACP states prohibit the import of hazardous wastes from all countries [art. 39(1)]. The obligations of art. 39(1), however, are without prejudice to other international obligations.

CHAPTER TEN

LAND–BASED POLLUTION

A. NATURE OF THE PROBLEM

At least 80 percent of all marine pollution comes from sources that are located on land [*Agenda 21*, June 13, 1992, U.N. Doc. A/CONF. 151/26, ch. 17]. Pollutants generated on land travel through numerous environmental pathways such as the atmosphere, rivers, canals, underground watercourses, and outfalls before eventually finding their way to the ocean. Urban expansion into coastal areas has exacerbated the problem of land-based marine pollution. Twenty two of the world's 35 largest cities are on the coast of an ocean or sea. Of these, seventeen are in developing countries. Sixty five percent of the cities with populations over two and one half million are situated on a coast. These urban centers and their supporting agriculture and development create various forms of pollutants that end up in the marine environment [Pilomene Verlan, *The Role of Public Health in Coastal Zone Management, in* Oceans Yearbook 287 (1994)]. Land-based pollution has loomed more problematic to the extent that urban growth has departed from principles of sustainable development, and environmental protection has been ignored or minimized by economic growth.

B. SOURCES AND ENVIRONMENTAL IMPACTS

In general, there are eight groups of pollutants that are deposited into the ocean from land-based sources: 1) chemical nutrients; 2) sewage and bacterial agents; 3) oil; 4) organic chemicals; 5) metals; 6) sediments and litter; 7) radioactive substances; and 8) heat. Nutrients, such as phosphorus and nitrogen compounds, are introduced into the marine environment by runoff from fertilized agricultural lands, discharges of domestic sewage, industrial effluents, and atmospheric emissions. Excessive nutrient concentrations can accelerate the naturally occurring process of eutrophication by which waters are enriched by nutrients. The introduction of excessive nutrients into the ocean, however, can unnaturally increase the productivity of the waters and lead to uncontrolled phytoplankton growth [ANDREW GOUDE, THE HUMAN IMPACT ON THE NATURAL ENVIRONMENT 212 (1994)].

Uncontrolled growth of these species is popularly known as a red tide. This process will eventually cause the decomposition of organic materials which will in turn result in a serious depletion of the oxygen content of the waters and possibly the death of fish and many important species of marine life. Large fish kills create an even greater demand for oxygen as the fish decompose. Additionally, some species of phytoplankton emit toxins which, if present in high concentrations, will contaminate shellfish and damage certain types of fish. In the ocean, increased algal growth and a lack of dissolved oxygen may have a detrimental effect on coral reefs, which function as important repositories of biological diversity (See chapter five).

Sewage and bacterial agents account for a significantly large portion of all marine pollution [Philomene Verlaan, *The Role of Public Health in Coastal Zone Management, in* OCEAN YEARBOOK 290 (Mann Borgese, Norton Ginsburg & Joseph Morgan eds. 1994)]. The principal pollutants contained in sewage include organic materials, nutrients, pathogens and trace metals. In developed countries, sewage is usually treated to remove solids and is sometimes chemically or biologically treated to produce a less harmful effluent. However, in lesser developed countries raw sewage is often discharged directly into watercourses. The pathogens present in sewage contaminate shellfish and may lead to serious gastrointestinal disorders. Recreational activities may also be affected in areas in which sewage discharge has led to high pathogen concentrations. Finally, the organic materials and nutrients in sewage lead to accelerated eutrophication.

Oil tanker spills are a highly publicized source of marine pollution, but the bulk of organic chemicals enter the marine environment from less publicized land-based sources such as industrial discharges, sewage disposal, river runoff, and atmospheric fallout from fossil fuel combustion. Natural seepages also have a significant impact [ANDREW GOUDIE, THE HUMAN IMPACT ON THE NATURAL ENVIRONMENT 214 (1994)]. For a more complete discussion of the aquatic effects of oil pollution, see Chapter Eleven, Vessel–Based Pollution.

Organic chemicals, such as DDT and PCBs, are introduced into the marine environment through rivers, pesticide runoff from agricultural land, atmospheric deposition, and municipal and industrial discharges. High concentrations of metals in the marine environment can be toxic to marine life and present dangers to human health. The principal sources of metals in the ocean are industrial and municipal discharges into rivers, coastal discharges, and atmospheric emissions. Concentration levels of these metals tend to be greatest in industrial areas and estuaries. The characteristics and impacts of these toxic metals, and how they advance up the food chain are also discussed in Chapter Nine, Toxic and Hazardous Substances.

Metals are a particularly vexing pollutant because they are elements which do not degrade. Even when they are diluted, they can be bioaccumulated to toxic concentrations. For a fuller discussion, see Chapter Nine, Toxic and Hazardous Substances at pages 197–8.

Litter and debris from human activities enter the ocean through rivers, municipal drainage systems, and coastal recreational areas. Plastics are the major type of litter present in the marine environment. Marine fish and mammals are injured or killed by plastics when they ingest or become entangled in the debris. In addition, the debris often ends up on coastal areas where it mars the beauty of the natural environment [DANIEL G. MAROWSKI, ENVIRONMENTAL VIEWPOINTS 233–34 (1992)]. Soil sediments from agriculture can cover and destroy the bottoms of rivers, estuaries, bays and even entire sections of ocean gulfs. An example of this phenomena is found in the Chesapeake Bay in the United States. Agricultural sediments have damaged the Chesapeake marshes, fisheries and bottom ecologies [CHARLES GOLDMAN & ALEXANDER HORNE, LIMNOLOGY 327 (1983)].

Land-based radioactive waste is often dumped into the oceans from ships. Russian nuclear wastes have been dumped into the oceans, and this dumping blurs the distinction between land-based pollution and dumping [LAKSHMAN GURUSWAMY, GEOFFREY PALMER & BURNS WESTON, INTERNATIONAL ENVIRONMENTAL LAW AND WORLD ORDER 576 (1994); *see also* Chapter Twelve, Dumping].

Some percentage of the radioactive material in each nuclear power plant escapes to the environment during normal operation, and finds its way into the oceans. The marine impact of radioactive wastes disposal is illustrated by the case of the Savannah River in the United States which divides South Carolina from Georgia. Radioactive waste dumps and military nuclear processing facilities along the Savannah River have introduced so much fissionable material to the river that it has been measured in the flesh of fish [William Booth, *Ecosystem Paradoxically Glows at Former Atomic Bomb Factory Site*, Washington Post, May 26, 1996, at A3]. These radioactive materials are carried in water, sediments and biota of the Savannah River into the Atlantic Ocean. Moreover, nuclear bomb testing—particularly atmospheric testing—has introduced enormous quantities of radioactive material into the marine environment.

Electric power generation creates large quantities of excess heat. As a result, most power plants are located on or near large sources of water. The marine ecology surrounding the power plant is severely impacted. Still, the dangers of heat discharge remain relatively unexplored and undiscussed. The concept of heat pollution thus illustrates the need for a flexible, working definition of pollution [CHARLES GOLDMAN & ALEXANDER HORNE, LIMNOLOGY 55 (1983)].

With any polluting substance, the impact on the marine environment primarily depends on whether the pollutants are present on the open seas or in a semi-enclosed or coastal area. Pollutants in the open seas tend to have a less detrimental effect than pollutants in coastal areas because of the open sea's natural capacity to assimilate and dilute large amounts of pollution [ANDREW GOUDIE, THE HUMAN IMPACT ON THE NATURAL ENVIRONMENT 232 (1994)]. However, the ocean's assimilative capacity is not infinite because time must pass before the pollutant can be dispersed, diluted, or sedimented. In addition, some pollutants are impossible to transform into less harmful substances and others may tend to bioaccumulate in marine animals. Coastal areas are usually more sensitive to pollution because they receive higher levels of pollutants from more concentrated sources and tend to be more biologically productive [id.].

C. REMEDIAL OBJECTIVES

The control of land-based pollution is the most daunting task facing the international community for a number of reasons. First, it is the result of domestic pollution in all it aspects, embracing the three media of air, land, and water. Controlling land-based pollution thus exists as a proxy for controlling the sovereign rights of states to pollute their own territory—a restraint that states rarely accept. The problem stems from the extreme reluctance of states to surrender even a modicum of sovereignty with respect to actions within domestic boundaries, strongly preferring to retain control at the national level.

Second, the scientific difficulties of demonstrating pathways and sources are immense except in cases of single source direct outfalls and pathways. In situations with more than one set of contributors, apportioning responsibility to individual polluters is fraught with uncertainty. As an additional complication, chemicals released into air or water interact with each other and give rise to synergistic reactions and effects. The impact of such synergistic effects is greater than the sum of their individual effects, making it very difficult to establish cause and effect relationships. DDT, for example, is extremely soluble in oil but not in water, greatly multiplying the exposure for marine organisms in oil-polluted waters [THE ENCYCLOPEDIA OF THE ENVIRONMENT, 686 (RUTH A. EBLAN & WILLIAM R. EBLAN eds., 1994)]. Thus, where different nations are responsible for land-based discharges of DDT and oil, respectively, they often resist control measures by arguing that another state is the more culpable agent. Nations thus find it easier to resist controls arguing that the actions required to arrest land-based pollution often involve surmise and guess-work .

Third, environmental controls on the sources of land-based pollution—run-off from rivers, estuaries, and pipelines—generally require extremely expensive measures entailing significant economic sacrifice. Nations invariably balk at accepting such self-imposed controls. In light of these difficulties, states have focused less on the remedial objective of solving land-based pollution, and more on maintaining the widest possible flexibility to adopt measures as they see fit.

D. LEGAL RESPONSE

Though land-based sources contribute the highest percentage of marine pollution, for the above reasons the international commitment to controlling these wastes remains low. As it stands at the international level, there exists little more than a framework for future regulation of land-based marine pollution, with occasional calls for a legally binding instrument on the subject. The most effective agreements remain regional ones, and these do not comply with the rigorous standards imposed both internationally and regionally with regard, for example, to dumping and vessel-based pollution.

1. THE UNITED NATIONS CONVENTION ON THE LAW OF THE SEA (UNCLOS)

UNCLOS, defines pollution as:

the introduction by man, directly or indirectly, of substances or energy into the marine environment, including estuaries, which results or is likely to result in such deleterious effects as harm to living resources and marine life, hazards to human health, hindrance to marine activities, including fishing and other legitimate uses of the sea, impairment of quality for use of sea water and reduction of amenities....

Dec. 10, 1982, art. 1(4), 21 I.L.M. 1261 (entered into force Nov. 16, 1994).

Despite this broad definition, UNCLOS provides only a general scheme for states to follow in attempting to reduce land-based marine pollution. The convention requires states to adopt measures "to prevent, reduce and control" such pollution, "taking into account internationally agreed rules, standards and recommended practices and procedures" [art. 207(1)]. The mandate that states "take into account" international constraints of course has little normative value, as states need only consider and not follow such rules. Regardless, no formal standards even exist at the global level for land-based pollution, and states have only simple recommendations to look to under the Montreal Guidelines for the Protection of the Marine Environment Against Pollution from Land–Based Sources (Montreal Guidelines) [UNEP/GC.13/9/ Add.3, UNEP/GC/DEC/13/1811, UNEP ELPG No. 7 (1985)]. UNCLOS also provides that states "[s]hall endeavor to harmonize their policies ... at the appropriate regional level" [art. 207(3)], and "shall endeavor to establish global and regional rules, standards and recommended standards and procedures" [art. 207(4)]. Again, however, that states "shall endeavor" does not mean that states "must" act to facilitate these ends. Moreover, the rules for enclosed or semi-enclosed seas [arts. 122–123]— areas which tend to be the most susceptible to Land–Based marine pollution—only offer the slightly more forceful requirement that states "should cooperate" in coordinating protective action.

2. MONTREAL GUIDELINES FOR THE PROTECTION OF THE MARINE ENVIRONMENT AGAINST POLLUTION FROM LAND–BASED SOURCES

The Montreal Guidelines are a set of recommendations compiled by a Working Group of Experts under UNEP auspices. Adopted as a UNEP Governing Council Decision in 1985, they present a broad range of specific suggestions which states may adapt to national legislation, regional agreements or any future global agreement on land-based pollution. As such, the Montreal Guidelines elaborate on the generalities of UNCLOS article 207—providing for the basic obligations to protect the marine environment, to adopt control measures, to cooperate with other states, and to not cause transboundary harm. The Montreal Guidelines also state the need to establish "specially protected areas" and to assist developing countries in their efforts to combat pollution. Interestingly, in an early recognition of integrated pollution control, the Montreal Guidelines warn against simply preventing one type of pollution (i.e. land-based marine pollution) by creating another (e.g. hazardous waste landfills). Additionally, the Montreal Guidelines echo UNCLOS' expansive definition of marine pollution referred to above [Montreal Guidelines § 1(a); *see also*, UNCLOS, art. 1(4)].

To give more specific advice to governments, the Montreal Guidelines provide fairly detailed information in the three Annexes attached to the document. Annex I, "Strategies for Protecting, Preserving and Enhancing the Quality of the Marine Environment," gives a substantial account of the three control strategies of environmental quality standards, emission standards and environmental planning. In developing a program to combat marine pollution, the annex suggests that governments individually tailor an approach combining all three strategies. Annex II, "Classification of Substances," provides an overview of the typical method of rating harmful substances, advising the creation of a "black list" for dangerous substances, and a "grey list" for less dangerous substances. Annex III, "Monitoring and Data Management," presents valuable recommendations toward the creation of effective technical programs, gleaned from the experiences of the better regulated states.

3. REGIONAL TREATIES

A number of regional treaties have addressed the problem of land-based pollution, including those for the Baltic Sea, the North–East Atlantic Ocean, and the North Sea. As a general rule, states have had a difficult time in developing regional standards, and even when developed the standards do not bind objecting parties. Furthermore, even when parties agree to regional standards no higher authority exists to compel action, as all enforcement power remains in the hands of the national governments.

To date, the Convention for the Prevention of Marine Pollution from Land–Based Sources (1974 Paris Convention), June 4, 1974, 13 I.L.M. 352 (entered into force May 6, 1978) is perhaps the most developed and comprehensive example of regional cooperation on the subject.

Covering the area of the North–East Atlantic and the North Sea, the 1974 Paris Convention calls for the elimination of pollution from a "black list" of dangerous substances, and the strict limitation of pollution from a "grey" list of less harmful substances [art. 4]. A supervisory body known as the Paris Commission (PARCOM) amends the contents of both lists binding parties who vote for its decisions, but not reluctant parties [art. 18]. Over the years PARCOM has adopted a considerable number of broadly accepted measures, including a phased-out reduction of PCBs and a strong endorsement of the precautionary principle as applied to integrated ecosystem protection [PHILIPPE SANDS, PRINCIPLES OF INTERNATIONAL ENVIRONMENTAL LAW 21 (1995)].

The 1974 Paris Convention will be replaced, along with the Convention for the Prevention of Marine

Pollution by Dumping from Ships and Aircraft (1972 Oslo Convention), Feb. 15, 1972 932 U.N.T.S. 3 (entered into force Apr. 7, 1974), by the Convention for the Protection of the Marine Environment of the North East Atlantic (OSPAR Convention), Sept. 22, 1992, 32 I.L.M. 1069 upon the ratification of all members of the prior two treaties (*see* Chapter Twelve, Dumping). Upon its entry into force, the OSPAR Convention will consolidate efforts to combat land-based pollution with those to control dumping—creating a single commission to oversee both activities. The 1992 OSPAR Convention should do more to control land-based pollution, where appropriate requiring "best available techniques" (BAT) and "best environmental practice" (BEP) for point sources [Annex I, art. 1(1)].

In determining what constitutes BAT and BEP in a specific circumstance, the Commission first looks to the guidelines provided in Appendix I, with BAT as state of the art technology and BET as the most appropriate mix of measures and strategies taking environmental, social and economic factors into account. Next, in the setting of specific programs and time scales for the control of a specific substance, the Commission considers a series of criteria listed in Appendix 2, including persistency, toxicity and tendency to bioaccumulate. In this way, the Convention dispenses with the "black list—grey list" method, providing only a single, non-exhaustive list of substances to be regulated. This approach appears to offer more flexibility in controlling any particular substance and consequently may lead to greater acceptance of the Commission's arrived at standards. Even so, objecting parties still are not bound by the Commission's official decisions with regard to the annexes and appendices [art. 13], nor its amendments to the annexes [art. 17] or appendices [art. 19]. Without a doubt, however, the OSPAR convention does present a better chance for more effective control than the 1974 Paris Convention, though the latter remains the governing document at the current time.

A small group of the UNEP Regional Seas Conventions have spawned specific protocols dealing with land-based pollution, including the Protocol for the Protection of the Mediterranean Sea Against Pollution from Land Based Sources, May 17, 1980 (entered into force June 17, 1983), and the Protocol for the Protection of the South–East Pacific Against Pollution from Land–Based Sources, July 23, 1983 (entered into force Sept. 23, 1986). In general, these protocols have followed the format of the 1974 Paris Convention—employing both "black" and "grey" lists for specific controls. For "black" list substances, the Parties must undertake to eliminate such discharges while requiring national authorization for any limited release of "grey" list substances. In not setting specific obligatory standards for reluctant parties, these protocols function more as a forum for future cooperation than an effective mandate for immediate control.

CHAPTER ELEVEN

VESSEL–BASED POLLUTION

A. NATURE OF THE PROBLEM

Thousands of miles separate the bulk of the world's oil resources from their markets, and giant oil tankers crisscross the oceans of the world carrying massive quantities of oil to distant destinations. The deliberate release of oil by such tankers in the course of routine shipping operations, and oil spills caused by tanker accidents, threaten marine living resources and ecosystems [see ROBERT CLARK, MARINE POLLUTION (3d ed. 1992)]. Vessels also pollute the oceans with intentionally discharged garbage, of which plastic debris presents the most serious threat to marine life.

The gross volume of oil that is spilled into the sea is declining. In 1971, 6.3 million metric tons of oil were lost to the sea. In 1980, the figure was 3.2 million tons, and in 1989, the figure dropped further to 560,000 million tons [RONALD MITCHELL, INTENTIONAL OIL POLLUTION AT SEA 70 (1994)]. Shipping operations and accidents are responsible for approximately 35 percent of the oil pollution in the marine environment. Of this 35 percent, tanker accidents account for only 5 percent of total marine oil pollution, but the harm caused by these accidents is dramatic because of the large volume of oil released in a small area. In comparison, land-based sources, including dumping and atmospheric fall-out, contribute approximately 45 percent of all oil pollution (these sources are discussed in Chapter Ten). Natural sources (such as seepage) account for about 10 percent and coastal refineries and offshore oil production account for approximately 1–5 percent of all oil pollution. In any event, less than 1/100 of 1 percent of all of the oil that is traded is lost at sea [*id.*].

Thus vessel-based pollution is not the most dangerous form of marine pollution and often does not present as large a risk to human health compared to pollutants released by land-based activities or dumping. It is being treated as a separate subject in this book primarily to reflect the international attention given to it. A number of reasons account for the international response to vessel-based pollution. Oil spills create dramatic and frightening visual effects and lend themselves to graphic photographs and media attention. Such publicity is heightened by the harm suffered by sea birds and other marine creatures. The wide publicity given to killed and maimed birds provokes public indignation and tarnishes the image of the oil industry. Such an impression is worsened by the fact that oil slicks washed ashore effectively prevent the use of beaches and prohibits sea bathing. In response, ship owners, operators of oil tankers and oil companies— who do not cherish their tarnished environmental image—have been willing to take steps to control vessel pollution and to set up their own compensation schemes.

B. ENVIRONMENTAL IMPACTS

1. HARM CAUSED BY THE PHYSICAL PROPERTIES OF OIL

The physical properties of oil make it harmful to marine life. Oil spilled or discharged at sea changes its composition as it spreads over the surface of the water in a thin layer called an *oil slick*. Some components evaporate or dissolve, while others break down and disperse as small droplets. Under some water conditions a thick, sticky mass may form on the surface of the water. The heavy residues of oil from the discharge of oily bilge and ballast water may form tar balls.

Oil that becomes stranded near shore smothers small marine animals and destroys plant life. Heavier oils and mousse-like emulsions clog the bodies of small marine animals, interfering with respiration, feeding and movement. Seabirds, sea otters, and other small marine animals that spend much of their time on the surface of the water, and rely on the insulating properties of feathers or fur to survive, are particularly vulnerable [*see* DWIGHT HOLING, COASTAL ALERT, ECOSYSTEMS, ENERGY, AND OFFSHORE OIL DRILLING 28 (1990)]. Oil destroys the water repellence of a sea bird's plumage, causing it to become waterlogged and drown, or freeze to death from the loss of thermal insulation. Over 30,000 seabirds died as a result of the 1989 *Exxon Valdez* oil tanker accident in Alaska, but many more seabirds die each year from non-accidental releases of oil in the Northeast Atlantic. Sea otters, which rely on the trapped air in their dense fur for survival in the cold, are likewise vulnerable to floating oil. A sea otter will die of hypothermia if 20–30 percent of its body is covered with oil. The *Exxon Valdez* oil spill caused the deaths of over 1,000 sea otters.

2. HARM CAUSED BY THE TOXIC PROPERTIES OF OIL

Crude oils as well as refined petroleum products contain toxic substances detrimental to the health of sea birds, animals, and fish [*see* A. NELSON-SMITH, OIL POLLUTION AND MARINE ECOLOGY 100–102 (1973)]. Oil-coated seabirds and otters swallow oil when attempting to remove it from their feathers or coats, and this can have detrimental effects in the form of poisoning, decreased reproduction, or genetic mutations. Oil can also kill filter-feeding marine animals that ingest it when filtering water to gain nutrients.

Oils that are dissolved or dispersed in the water can easily penetrate the delicate skin of fish gills, while its aromatic components can irritate and clog the respiratory systems of fish. Adult fish may be able to avoid areas of floating oil, but fish eggs and immature fish that inhabit surface waters cannot do so, and absorb hydrocarbons that cause reduced hatching and early death. Oil that reaches the sediments on the bottom of the ocean impacts the very base of the marine food chain by reducing the production of aerobic bacteria, on which the benthic (bottom-dwelling) organisms depend for their diet.

C. CAUSES OF VESSEL–BASED OIL POLLUTION

It is estimated that intentionally discharged tanker oil accounts for up to one third of all ship-generated pollution [RONALD MITCHELL, INTENTIONAL OIL POLLUTION AT SEA 70 (1994)]. Tanker accidents and discharges from non-tankers account for the remaining pollution. Other than land-based sources, tanker de-ballasting and cleaning constitute the major source of oil pollution. When a tanker delivers its cargo, a thin layer of oil remains in the tanks as "clingage." On the return voyage, tankers fill empty cargo tanks with sea water as ballast to stabilize them. They also use sea water in high pressure cleaning procedures to wash down the tanks before receiving a new consignment of oil. Additionally, oil and lubricants from the ship's engines leak into the bilges (bottoms) of tankers and become mixed with sea water. Prior to their arrival at port, captains traditionally discharged the resulting oil/water solutions (or "slops") at sea.

As part of routine operations, ships discharge garbage in addition to oil-contaminated bilge and ballast water. [ROBERT CLARK, MARINE POLLUTION 4 (3d ed. 1992)]. Non-biodegradable plastic debris is an especially serious problem because it may remain in the ocean for 100 years [*see* TONY HARE, POLLUTING

THE SEA 14 (1991)]. An estimated 6.5 million tons of plastic per year were discarded by ships in the early 1990's. Seabirds, fish, and mammals die from drowning or injury by getting tangled in plastic packaging, such as six-pack rings and sheeting, or by swallowing plastic objects.

D. REMEDIAL OBJECTIVES

Remedial objectives for routine operational discharges should include ship design changes, as well as port facilities for receiving "slops." Most tanker accidents occur in high risk areas near shore and close to port entrances where the high volume of shipping traffic multiplies the risk of a collision, and natural hazards such as reefs and rocks increase the risk of ships going aground. Accident prevention should concentrate on construction standards, such as double-hulled oil tankers, and safety standards that ensure seaworthiness and prevent navigational errors that might result in a collision or grounding [BIRNIE & BOYLE at 263–273]. Ships should be prepared for emergencies and provisions need to be made for intervention in case of an accident. As we shall see, there has been a positive legal response to these issues.

Efforts should also be made to control and contain spilled oil and prevent its reaching land. Floating booms (similar to short curtains) may be used in an attempt to deflect and contain the spilled oil until it can be pumped off the surface, but are most useful in protecting small areas. Devices for mopping up oil slicks, called "slick-lickers," can handle small spills but are not effective on the open sea.

Dispersal techniques need to be improved. All of the components of crude oil are degradable by bacteria but at vastly different rates depending on the state of the oil. The breakdown of oil into droplets that will more easily biodegrade can be accelerated by spraying dispersants on oil slicks. The dispersants are less toxic than in the 1970's, when the surfactants used in the dispersants caused erosion of fish gills and organs. To further accelerate nature's own cleanup mechanism, a new technique, *bioremediation*, stimulates the growth of the naturally occurring oil-eating bacteria.

More progress needs to be made in shore cleaning techniques which have sometimes proven more damaging to the flora and fauna than the oil itself [ROBERT CLARK, MARINE POLLUTION 1 (3d ed. 1992)]. Beach cleaning techniques include high-pressure water, steam, and dispersants. Physical forces, heat, and cleaning-chemical toxicity may kill most naturally occurring organisms on the beach that have not already been killed by the effects of the oil. Physically mopping up the oil on the beach is only partially effective because most of the oil spilled eludes recovery or clean up. Moreover, clean ups are often more apparent than real because the oil is not removed, but drained away or forced to a few inches below the surface. Here, without oxygen to degrade the oil, it may remain for over a year.

"Ex ante" regulations based upon new technology need to be implemented by a liability regime that enables injured parties to seek relief against polluters. As we discuss below, the international response to vessel pollution has been more satisfactory than in many other areas.

E. LEGAL RESPONSE

The law has responded to the two different manifestations of vessel pollution: (1) in the general operation of commercial shipping; and (2) in the occasional accident occurring at sea (*see* Chapter Ten, Land–Based Pollution).

1. OPERATIONAL POLLUTION

As we have noted, most vessel pollution of the marine environment arises from the daily operation of ships, not from the highly publicized, but infrequent, catastrophe. To address this type of pollution, the international community has developed two fundamental and related schemes of governance. The first is the International Convention for the Prevention of Pollution from Ships (MARPOL), Nov. 2, 1973, 12 I.L.M. 1319 signed in 1973 and amended by Protocol of 1978 Relating to the International Convention for the Prevention of Pollution from Ships, [Feb. 17, 1978, 17 I.L.M. 546 (entered into force Oct. 2, 1983)]. These documents set out specific regulations for, among other things, the permissibility of pollution discharge as well as construction requirements for ships. The second important legal regime is the United Nations Convention on the Law of the Sea (UNCLOS), Dec. 10, 1982, 21 I.L.M. 1261 (entered into force Nov. 16, 1994) which potentially alters the jurisdictional structure of MARPOL while generally deferring to its other provisions .

(a) The 1973/1978 International Convention For the Prevention of Pollution From Ships (MARPOL)

Created under the auspices of the International Maritime Organization (IMO)—formerly the Inter-Governmental Maritime Consultative Organization—MARPOL provides an innovative framework for the prevention of marine pollution. It covers all commercial ships, excluding only government and military vessels, and the parties to the convention account for nearly all of the world's merchant fleet. In this sense MARPOL does not suffer from the lack of international participation which so often plagues environmental treaties.

The MARPOL treaty and its protocols (most significantly the 1978 Protocol Relating to the International Convention for the Prevention of Pollution from Ships) supply general duties for parties, which it supplements with five more detailed Annexes that are themselves supplemented by Appendices to Annexes. In this way, MARPOL creatively deals with the problem of balancing general duties with specific obligations. The regime also provides a flexible approach to law-making, as various combinations of a two-thirds majority in either the IMO or a convened Conference of the Parties can effectively amend the Treaty, Protocols, Annexes or Appendices [see art. 16(f)(I-v)].

Annex I covers the regulation of oil discharge from ships, mandating both construction requirements and release allowances. The technical requirements of construction and readiness are fairly intricate, and attempt to provide minimum safety standards with respect to tankers. Significantly, recent regulations 13[f] and 13[g] call for "double-hulls" on all new oil tankers—a feature long sought by environmentalists to prevent spillage in case of rupture. As for release allowances, Annex I quantitatively limits discharge from all ships, and essentially prohibits discharge in most circumstances near the coastline [Reg. 9]. The Annex also severely limits the release of oil in special environmentally sensitive areas, including the Baltic, Mediterranean, Black and Red Seas [Reg. 10].

In allocating responsibility for the monitoring of its regulations, MARPOL creates a role both for the flag state and the port state. To fulfill its obligations, the flag state must certify each ship's compliance with MARPOL's construction and readiness guidelines by issuing an International Oil Pollution Prevention Certificate for each vessel [Reg. 5(2)]. In addition, the flag state must update the certificate, conducting periodic surveys of each ship to ensure continued observance of the regulations [Reg. 4]. The port state, for its part, may inspect any ship within its ports or off-shore terminals in order to verify "that there is on board a valid certificate" [art. 5]. If "clear grounds" exist for believing that the condition of the ship does not correspond to the certificate, the port state may then conduct a full inspection of the vessel [art. 5(2)]. If it finds a violation, the port state must prevent the ship from setting sail until the vessel "can proceed to sea without presenting an unreasonable threat of harm to the marine environment" [art. 5(2)].

Concerning the investigation of discharge violations, the port state has even more latitude than in construction and readiness inspections. In this case, the port state does not need "clear grounds" upon which to proceed with an inspection, but in fact may examine any and all ships within its jurisdiction. When coupled with some reliable evidence, the port state may also investigate any violation alleged by another party to the convention, regardless where the claimed illegal discharge has occurred [art. 6(5)]. If an inspection indicates a violation of MARPOL discharge rules, the port state immediately submits a full report to the flag state [art. 6(4)]. The flag state must then institute appropriate actions against the violating ship, and must notify both the port state and the IMO of the disciplinary steps taken [art. 6]. In applying its own law, the flag state must not allow more lenient treatment of its flag ships, but must impose penalties "adequate in severity to discourage violations" of the MARPOL regime [art. 4(4)].

(b) The United Nations Convention on the Law of the Sea (UNCLOS)

As previously discussed, UNCLOS of 1982 significantly alters the jurisdictional scheme of the world's oceans. Concluded after MARPOL, UNCLOS makes potentially broad changes in the application of the former, especially in regard to coastal state power under the expanded Exclusive Economic Zone (EEZ). MARPOL does not compel extension of coastal state jurisdiction beyond the territorial sea, but neither does it forbid such an extension. Instead, MARPOL simply gives deference to future application of UNCLOS to its own provisions, stating that "the term 'jurisdiction' ... shall be construed in the light of international law in force at the time of application or interpretation of the present Convention" [MARPOL 9(3); BIRNIE & BOYLE, at 273].

As a jurisdictional matter, the question arises as to when a coastal state may adopt stricter pollution provisions than those provided in MARPOL. Based on traditional notions of sovereignty, UNCLOS codifies a long-held customary rule that a coastal state may adopt more stringent discharge rules in both its internal waters and territorial sea [art.211(3), 211(4)]. The rigor of these laws, however, must not interfere with a foreign vessel's right of innocent passage [art. 24]. Innocent passage remains a time-honored right, and UNCLOS defines the term as movement which is "not prejudicial to the peace, good order or security of the coastal state" [art. 19(1)]. On the other hand, a coastal state may not adopt stricter construction or readiness requirements for foreign vessels traveling in its internal waters or territorial sea, as clearly this would dramatically hinder the right of innocent passage by limiting access to only certain types of vessels [art. 21(2)].

In the EEZ, in contrast, a coastal state may not adopt more exacting discharge rules than those already in place under MARPOL [art. 211(5)]. In this way, UNCLOS limits the sovereignty of a coastal state within its own jurisdiction. Even for environmentally sensitive areas, a coastal state must first seek approval of the IMO to adopt special pollution discharge rules and, if approved, the adopted rules must follow IMO recommendations [art. 211(6)(a)].

Concerning enforcement of discharge violations, UNCLOS offers several variations from the more limited MARPOL regulations, though nations have yet to put these expanded powers into practice. Under UNCLOS, coastal states have a type of graduated authority in dealing with pollution violations. For example, if "clear grounds" exist for believing a vessel has committed a state or MARPOL violation in the territorial sea, then the coastal state may undertake physical inspection of the ship, detain the vessel, and institute proceedings against it [art. 220(2)]. For minor violations in the EEZ, a coastal state may only require the ship to provide information concerning its identity as well as its last and next ports of call [art. 220(3)]. However, when "clear grounds" exist for believing a ship has committed "a substantial discharge causing or threatening significant pollution of the marine environment" in the EEZ, then the coastal state may commence an inspection if the vessel fails to provide satisfactory information about the incident [art. 220(5)]. Finally, in the most egregious circumstances, if "clear objective evidence" exists that a vessel has committed a violation causing "major damage or threat of major damage to the coastline," the coastal state may then undertake a broader physical inspection of the ship, detain the vessel, and institute proceedings against it [art. 220(6)].

UNCLOS also gives expanded enforcement jurisdiction to the port state, but again in practice states have yet to employ these powers. Understandably, a port state may institute proceedings against any vessel voluntarily in port that has committed a violation within that state's territorial sea or EEZ [art. 220(1)]. Additionally, however, UNCLOS conveys a qualified universal jurisdiction on the port state, which may institute proceedings against any ship that has committed a MARPOL discharge violation on the high seas or within the jurisdiction of another state, if the latter so requests [art. 218]. The result is an expanded role for the port state, much beyond that bestowed by MARPOL. The universal jurisdiction remains limited only by that of the flag state, which always retains a right of preemption under Article 228, except in cases of "major damage" to coastal states. Whether the international community actually adopts the expanded jurisdictional powers of the port and coastal states remains to be seen, though states now possess the legal wherewithal to do so under UNCLOS. In the meantime, the legal regimes of MARPOL and UNCLOS must take significant credit for the fact that routine shipping operations, once responsible for releasing an estimated 3—6 million metric tons of crude oil each year in the 1970's, have declined recently to only 10 to 20 percent of that level [RONALD MITCHELL, INTENTIONAL OIL POLLUTION AT SEA 70 (1994)].

2. ACCIDENTAL POLLUTION

Over the years, accidental pollution of the marine environment—especially in the form of oil spills— has given rise to an extensive system of international agreements for the prevention and containment of such disasters. At the most general level, UNCLOS provides a requirement that states notify other affected states in the case of imminent danger or damage to the marine environment [art. 198], as well as mandating that states cooperate in the development of contingency plans to respond to these emergencies [art. 199]. To this end, states have added a number of safety protocols to the UNEP Regional Seas Conventions—providing a framework for collaboration and the creation of specific response plans. In addition to these protocols, an international treaty has recently come into force, the International Convention on Oil Pollution Preparedness, Response and Co-operation (OPRC), which establishes a broader role for the IMO in coordinating action among parties [Nov. 30, 1990, 30 I.L.M. 773 (entered into force May 13, 1995)].

(a) International Convention on Oil Pollution Preparedness, Response and Co-operation (OPRC)

Heavily backed by the United States following the *Exxon Valdez* oil spill, OPRC creates a certification program that ties into the 1973/1978 MARPOL provisions. Under the treaty each party must require its flag ships to carry on board "an oil pollution emergency plan" that adheres to the criteria put forth in MARPOL Annex I, Regulation 26 [*see* art.3(1)(a)]. These ships then remain subject to inspection by the port state in accordance with MARPOL art. 5 & 6 [*see* art. 3(1)(b)]. Moreover, operators of offshore units—such as drilling rigs—must now have oil pollution emergency plans [art. 3(2)]. At the state level, each party must develop a "national contingency plan for preparedness and response" as part of a national and regional system designed to deal with major oil spills [art. 6]. Parties also have quite specific procedures for reporting oil pollution incidents [art. 4] and for acting on such reports [art. 5]. Buttressing each of these obligations, the OPRC provides a strong oversight role for the IMO—a function designed to foster efficient use of the organization's expertise, and to effect fairness and universal compliance with its provisions.

(b) International Convention Relating To Intervention on the High Seas In Cases of Oil Pollution Casualties (1969 Intervention Convention and 1973 Protocol)

To clarify extra-jurisdictional powers of states, the international community created one of the earliest environmental pollution treaties with the 1969 Intervention Convention, Nov. 29, 1969, 26 U.S.T. 765 (in force May 6, 1975). Developed in response to another major oil spill, the *Torrey Canyon* disaster, in which a tanker mishap caused massive damage to the coastlines of Britain and France, the 1969 Intervention Convention lays down the requirements for a coastal state's intervention during a high seas accident. Under the treaty parties may take measures on the high seas as necessary "to prevent, mitigate, or eliminate grave and imminent danger to their coastline" [art. I(1)]. The treaty also provides mandatory notification and consultation procedures, except in cases of extreme urgency, with regard to flag states and other interested parties [art. III]. All actions taken by an intervening coastal state must be proportionate to the actual or threatened damage, or the state may be liable to those unreasonably harmed [art. V, VI].

In the 1973 Protocol Relating to the Intervention on the High Seas of Pollution by Substances Other Than Oil (1973 Intervention Protocol), Nov. 2, 1973, 34 U.S.T. 3407 (in force Mar. 30, 1983), the parties extended the rules of the original convention to other hazardous substances. The protocol creates a list of such substances, but also allows action to control any accident involving "those other substances which are liable to create hazards to human health, to harm living resources and marine life, to damage amenities, or to interfere with other legitimate uses of the sea" [art. I(2)]. Concerning the latter group of unlisted substances, the burden of proof shifts to the intervening coastal state to prove a "grave and imminent danger" analogous to that of a listed substance [art. I(3)].

The 1982 UNCLOS drops the requirement of "grave and imminent danger" and allows a coastal state the right to take any measures proportionate to the actual or threatened damage [art. 221]. Note that no reference is made here to the coastal state's EEZ. Therefore, UNCLOS appears to apply the same standard of proportionality to actions taken in the EEZ, as to those taken on the high seas under the 1969 Intervention Convention and 1973 Intervention Protocol. The only significant difference exists in UNCLOS discarding the "grave and imminent danger" threshold for both the EEZ and high seas.

3.   LIABILITY

(a) State Responsibility

The responsibility of states for actions with respect to the marine environment remains a well-settled rule of international law. UNCLOS codifies the principle in article 235(1), asserting that "states are responsible for the fulfillment of their international obligations concerning the protection and preservation of the marine environment." Therefore, both flag and coastal states may find themselves liable for actions taken or not taken in accordance with international law. As to the specific liability imposed, most commentators consider the standard one of "due diligence" rather than "strict liability" [BIRNIE & BOYLE, at 291 (1992)]. In fact, although several instances exist in which flag states have paid compensation for oil tanker accidents, injured parties have not targeted states concerning marine pollution. Instead, given the elaborate compensation scheme outlined below, nearly all claimants for oil pollution accidents have looked to private entities to make them whole.

(b) Civil Liability

i. *1969 International Convention on Civil Liability for Oil Pollution Damage (1969 CLC)*

The 1969 CLC, Nov. 29, 1969 973 U.N.T.S. 3 (entered into force June 19, 1975) creates a system for awarding compensation as well as limiting the liability incurred by the owner of a ship involved in an oil pollution accident. Upon the coming into force of the 1992 Protocol to the 1969 CLC, the treaty will become the 1992 International Convention on Civil Liability for Oil Pollution Damage, 1992 WL 602598, (1992 Liability Convention). Unlike the 1969 CLC, the 1992 Liability Convention clarifies that "pollution damage" includes damage to the marine environment, though "compensation for impairment of the environment other than loss of profit from such impairment shall be limited to costs of reasonable measures of reinstatement actually undertaken or to be undertaken" [art. I(6)(a)]. In other words, claimants will not receive speculative awards for environmental damage, but will only obtain compensation for actual restoration of the marine ecosystem.

According to an allocation procedure based on gross tonnage, the total compensation of a ship owner remains limited for any particular accident. In arriving at the right total some calculation is involved. For example, each "unit of tonnage"— computed in accordance with measurement regulations—corresponds to a certain number of "units of account." Under the 1992 Liability Convention, this translates into three million units of account for the first 5,000 units of tonnage, and 420 units of account for each unit of tonnage thereafter [art. V(1)]. A ceiling of 59.7 million units of account exists for any specific accident. To qualify for the ceiling, the owner must deposit a fund with the appropriate court constituting the total amount of its liability— converting the specified units of account (or "Special Drawing Rights" (SDR) as defined by the International Monetary Fund (IMF)) into national currency according to IMF procedures. Claimants then receive compensation from the fund "in proportion to the amounts of their established claims" [art. V(4)].

Under the 1969 CLC, the owner cannot take advantage of the limit on liability if the owner's "actual fault or privity" caused the accident [art.

V(2)]. The 1992 Convention would change this provision, only disallowing the limit on liability when the owner's actions or omissions intentionally or recklessly caused the pollution damage. Under both conventions, the owner of a tanker must hold insurance in the amount of its potential fund contribution, and the ship must carry a certificate attesting to that fact on board at all times [art. VII]. Significantly, during the transitional phase when the 1969 CLC still remains in force, the 1992 Liability Convention would mandate the satisfaction of claims first from the 1969 CLC and then the 1971 Fund Convention (mentioned below) before allowing claims under its own provisions [art. XII *bis*].

ii. *International Convention on the Establishment of an International Fund for Compensation for Oil Pollution Damage (1971 Fund Convention)*

The 1971 Fund Convention, Dec. 18, 1971, 1971 U.N. Jur. Y.B. 103 (entered into force Oct. 16, 1978) creates a burden sharing system in which the owners of oil cargo, such as oil companies, contribute to the overall cost of a tanker accident. In this way ship owners do not shoulder the entire cost of such a catastrophe. The convention adopts most of the definitions of the 1969 CLC, and by protocol in 1992 incorporates the definitions of the 1992 Liability Convention. Upon the entry into force of the 1992 protocol, the convention will be known as the 1992 International Convention on the Establishment of an International Fund for Oil Pollution Damage (the 1992 Fund Convention). To date, under the

1971 Fund Convention much confusion has occurred concerning the application of the term "pollution damage" to environmental harm; however, in adopting the definition of the 1992 Liability Convention as discussed in the preceding section, the 1992 Fund Convention will now allow compensation for "reasonable measures of reinstatement actually undertaken or to be undertaken" [art. I(2)].

One should remember that the 1971 Fund Convention and its 1992 counterpart exist solely as additional sources of restitution for injured "persons"—whether individuals, corporations or states. To this end, such persons have access to the 1992 Fund Convention only if "unable to obtain full and adequate compensation" under the 1992 Liability Convention for the following reasons: (a) the 1992 Liability Convention is inapplicable; (b) the owner or its insurance company cannot pay; or (c) the damage exceeds that allowed under the 1992 Liability Convention [art. 4(1)]. As in the 1992 Liability Convention, the 1992 Fund Convention itself establishes a limit on the total contribution the Fund might make to a particular accident, in most cases in the amount of 135 million "units of account" (or "SDRs") as converted into national currency by the International Monetary Fund [art. 4]. An insurance mechanism that attempts to spread the cost of a single accident among all oil cargo owners, the Fund obtains its own contributions from these entities through the contracting parties, basing each assessment on the number of tons of oil cargo received during the preceding year.

CHAPTER TWELVE

DUMPING

A. NATURE OF THE PROBLEM

The wastes generated in today's world need to be neutralized or disposed of in some fashion. We have noted that such disposal, or neutralizing of wastes through conversion systems, utilizes the absorptive capacity of the environment and includes the emission of gases and particles into the atmosphere, discharges of sludge and liquid effluent into the aquatic environment, and burial on land (*see* Chapter Nine, Toxic and Hazardous Substances). To this list must now be added the "dumping" of wastes into the sea. Approximately 10 percent of the pollutants and toxic materials that enter the ocean do so in this way [INTERNATIONAL MARITIME ORGANIZATION, THE LONDON DUMPING CONVENTION: THE FIRST DECADE AND BEYOND 44 (1991)].

"Dumping" is term of art referring to a particular form of marine pollution that is not included in land-based (*see* Chapter Ten), or vessel-based pollution (*see* Chapter Eleven; *see* § D 2, *infra* for a legal definition). Specifically, it has been confined to a form of marine pollution in which wastes, often containing toxic materials, are taken by ship and dumped, or incinerated, in the high seas. "Dumping" has not, therefore, typically referred to land-based pollution through discharges of wastes into the sea, estuaries or rivers from direct outfalls, or vessel-based pollution caused by accidental or deliberate discharges by oil tankers or other ships. However, since what is dumped is generated on land, it is difficult to refute the rationale of the Convention for the Protection of the Marine Environment of the North East Atlantic (OSPAR Convention), Sept. 22, 1992, 32 I.L.M. 1069 that treats dumping as a species of land-based pollution.

In the past, dumping hazardous waste into the ocean was seen as an acceptable method of disposal because of the relatively low economic costs and the perception that oceans could readily assimilate unlimited quantities of waste. Ocean dumping became less favored as its effects on marine ecology became apparent. Questions have also arisen concerning the reasonableness of allowing industrialized countries to utilize a shared resource (the oceans) without regard to the risks and costs imposed on future generations [PATRICIA BIRNIE & ALAN BOYLE, INTERNATIONAL LAW AND THE ENVIRONMENT 320 (1992)].

B. SOURCES AND ENVIRONMENTAL IMPACTS

Hazardous wastes—such as industrial sewage, effluents, sludges, radioactive wastes and dredged spoils—are being dumped or discharged directly into the oceans and rivers [MICHAEL R. GREENBERG, A PRIMER ON INDUSTRIAL ENVIRONMENTAL IMPACT 256

(1979)]. A more detailed review of the characteristics of these materials is provided in Chapters Nine (Toxic and Hazardous Substances) & Ten (Land–Based Pollution).

C. REMEDIAL OBJECTIVES

As we have noted in Chapter Nine, dumping is a symptom of the malaise of ever-spiraling wastes. Remedial objectives should focus on ways of dealing with its root cause: demand for products which can only be met by generating toxic and hazardous wastes. We have also noted the need for an integrated approach to waste disposal and pollution control.

We shall see that the United Nations Convention on the Law of the Sea (UNCLOS), Dec. 10, 1982, 21 I.L.M. 1261 (entered into force Nov. 16, 1994), and the Convention on the Prevention of Marine Pollution by Dumping of Wastes and Other Matter (1972 London Convention), Dec. 29, 1972, art. 3(1), 1046 U.N.T.S. 120 (entered into force Aug. 30, 1975) do not prohibit all ocean dumping. Instead, they attempt to control it by prohibiting the disposal of particular wastes based on their toxicity, persistence, bioaccumulation, and likelihood of widespread environmental exposure. By far the most encouraging of the regional conventions is the 1992 OSPAR Convention, which takes an integrated approach and deals with land-based pollution and dumping in one treaty. This treaty points the way to the future and could serve as a pilot project for more ambitious undertakings.

D. LEGAL RESPONSE

The international attitude toward ocean dumping has moved from an initial stage of acceptance, through strict regulation, to the present general trend prohibiting the dumping of particular kinds of wastes. Especially in recent years, as in the banning of all radioactive dumping at sea, the international community has tightened the rules relating to dumping. As for the legal regime, UNCLOS sets forth a framework of rules for states to follow. The 1972 London Convention, a global treaty, more specifically governs actions, and a system of regional agreements facilitates compliance.

1. UNITED NATIONS CONVENTION ON THE LAW OF THE SEA

UNCLOS mandates that all states adopt measures "to prevent, reduce and control pollution of the marine environment by dumping" [art. 210(1)]. However, in creating such measures, states may not establish standards that are "less effective" than global rules and standards [art. 210(6)]. In this way, UNCLOS establishes a "floor" of minimum protection that all states must follow, and that floor exists as the 1972 London Convention. Yet within its own territorial sea, Exclusive Economic Zone (EEZ) or continental shelf, a state has the right to institute more stringent requirements than those of the London Convention [art. 210(5)]. Furthermore, in codifying customary international law, UNCLOS provides the coastal state with the right of prior approval to any dumping within its sovereign waters, which of course now includes both the EEZ and the continental shelf [art. 210(5); PATRICIA W. BIRNIE & ALAN E. BOYLE, INTERNATIONAL LAW AND THE ENVIRONMENT 326 (1992)].

2. CONVENTION ON THE PREVENTION OF MARINE POLLUTION BY DUMPING OF WASTES AND OTHER MATTER (1972 LONDON CONVENTION)

The 1972 London Convention exists as the primary vehicle for the international regulation of dumping. As defined by the convention, dumping includes the "disposal of wastes or other matter from vessels, aircraft, [and] platforms" as well as the deliberate sinking of those structures themselves as a method of disposal [art. III(1)]. "Dumping," however, does not include the discharge of oil and other harmful substances in the normal operation of those structures, which in general is covered by the International Convention for the Prevention of Pollution from Ships (1973/1978 MARPOL Convention), Nov. 2, 1973, 12 I.L.M. 1319 (entered into force July 1, 1992).

In governing the disposal of wastes, the 1972 London Convention employs a listing and permit system which intends to cover the entire spectrum of dumping at sea. For substances listed in Annex I, or the "black list," dumping is prohibited except in emergency situations [art. IV(1)(a), V(2)]. In addition to dangerous substances such as mercury, cadmium and crude oil, this list includes "netting and ropes" which may "interfere materially with fishing, navigation or other legitimate uses of the sea" [Annex I(4)]. In contrast, the convention allows the dumping of substances on Annex II, or the "grey list," but requires a prior "special permit" to do so. Materials on this list include trace amounts of the toxic substances listed in Annex I, as well as less hazardous wastes such as chromium and nickel [art. IV(1)(b)]. The convention allows the dumping of all other wastes at sea, simply requiring that the vessel obtain a "general permit" [art. IV(1)(c)]. In considering whether to grant either type of permit, the designated authorities must look to the broad dictates of Annex III, which mandates that they take into account both the characteristics of the material dumped and the dump site. The responsibility for issuing these permits, and thereafter reporting the information to the IMO, falls upon the appropriate authorities of a party for all wastes loaded in its territory [art. VI(2)]. On the other hand, when a flag ship loads wastes in the territory of a state not party to the convention, then the responsibility for permitting and reporting remains with the flag state [art. VI(2)].

Especially for an older treaty, the 1972 London Convention creates an innovative and flexible rule-making system. Consultative Meetings of the Parties may adopt an amendment to the treaty by a two-thirds majority of those present, but such a change only comes into force for those parties who accept it [art. XV(1)(a)]. For an amendment to any

Annex—which must be based on scientific or technical considerations—again a two-thirds majority at the Consultative Meeting passes the change, but the burden shifts as only parties who denounce the amendment within a certain time frame remain unbound [art. XV(2)]. Finally, a Consultative Party may adopt non-binding resolutions as it sees fit [*see* art. XIV(b)-(f)].

In considering the special example of radioactive waste dumping, we can see the flexibility of the above system at work. For instance, the convention originally placed high-level radioactive wastes on Annex I, and low-level radioactive wastes on Annex II. In 1983, however, and then again in 1985, the Consultative Meeting passed a non-binding resolution that installed a moratorium on the dumping of all radioactive wastes, including low-level wastes. From this point on the political and scientific debate intensified concerning the potential harm of radioactive dumping, culminating with the Russian admission that the former Soviet Union had repeatedly dumped both high-and low-level wastes for decades. As a final measure, in 1993 the Consultative Committee amended Annex I to include all "radioactive wastes or other radioactive matter" [Annex I(6)]. In response only Russia officially filed a declaration of non-acceptance with the IMO, in effect allowing it legally to continue the disposal of low-level radioactive wastes at sea. For all other parties, the dumping of radioactive material of any type remains illegal.

The case of radioactive dumping therefore, while reflecting the flexibility of the 1972 London Convention system, also reveals its limitations in controlling all dumping of an environmentally damaging nature. Furthermore, though in theory the permit and reporting system covers the entire spectrum of dumping at sea, nations have had a difficult time in controlling illegal dumping by their own nationals [PHILIPPE SANDS, PRINCIPLES OF INTERNATIONAL ENVIRONMENTAL LAW 310 (1995)]. Nonetheless, as a general rule commentators point to the convention as one of the most successful environmental treaties to date—having played a significant role in reducing quantitatively the worldwide disposal of wastes at sea [PATRICIA BIRNIE & ALAN BOYLE, INTERNATIONAL LAW AND THE ENVIRONMENT 330 (1992)].

3. REGIONAL TREATIES

A number of regional treaties have dealt with the question of dumping, and in some cases these agreements have led to a tightening of standards beyond those of the 1972 London Convention. These regional treaties include the Convention on the Protection of the Marine Environment of the Baltic Sea Area, Apr. 9, 1992,1992 WL 675165; the Convention on the Protection of the Black Sea Against Pollution, Apr. 21, 1992, 32 I.L.M. 1101, and accompanying Protocol on the Protection of the Black Sea Marine Environment Against Pollution by Dumping, Apr. 21, 1992, 1992 WL 602572; and the Convention for the Protection of the Natural Resources and Environment of the South Pacific Region, Nov. 24, 1986, 26 I.L.M. 38 (entered into force Aug. 22, 1990), and the accompanying Protocol for the Prevention of Pollution of the South Pacific by Dumping, Nov. 24, 1986, 26 I.L.M. 38 (entered into force Aug. 22, 1990).

The most developed of the regional treaties, however, remains the Convention for the Prevention of Marine Pollution by Dumping from Ships and Aircraft (1972 Oslo Convention), Feb. 15, 1972, 932 U.N.T.S. 3 (entered into force Apr. 7, 1974). This treaty covers the area of the North–East Atlantic and the North Sea. The 1972 Oslo Convention, moving beyond the minimum standards of the London Convention, in 1989 took the lead in prohibiting the disposal of industrial wastes in the North Sea by 1990, and in the North–East Atlantic by 1996. By contrast the 1972 London Convention only added the full panoply of industrial wastes to Annex I beginning in 1996. Upon its entry into force, the 1992 OSPAR Convention will supersede the 1972 OSLO Convention, folding both dumping and land-based pollution protection into a single document. The 1992 OSPAR Convention takes a more comprehensive ecosystem approach to protection, and more clearly defines the strong presumption against dumping by disallowing the practice entirely—*except* for a small number of listed substances [OSPAR Annex II, Art. III].

CHAPTER THIRTEEN

CONSERVATION OF MARINE LIVING RESOURCES

A. NATURE OF THE PROBLEM

Ninety percent of marine life exists within ecosystems located in shallow waters above the continental shelves. While the oceans cover 70 percent of the earth's surface, the continental shelves are submerged extensions of the coastline at the edge of the continents, forming only a small fragment of the oceans. The proximity of these shallow waters to land exposes marine resources and ecosystems to increasing environmental impacts from human activities (*see* Chapter Four, Population Growth; and Chapter Ten, Land–Based Pollution). Burgeoning population and economic growth gives rise to oceanic over-exploitation, pollution, and habitat destruction that threatens the health and bounty of the environment. Protecting marine living resources and ecosystems from these forces is important not only for maintaining the world's ecological balance, but also for meeting the food needs of an increasing world population [TONY HARE, POLLUTING THE SEA 5 (1991); D. Alastair Bigham, *Pollution from Land–Based Sources, in* THE IMPACT OF MARINE POLLUTION 203 (Douglas Cusine & John Grant eds., 1980)].

B. SOURCES AND IMPACTS

First, over-exploitation has caused a serious decline in biodiversity in the world's fishing regions. Unsustainable takings have depleted edible fish stocks, while changing the balance of the predator-prey relationship within marine ecosystems. Modern fishing technologies that yield a harvest rate exceeding the reproductive rate of fish have resulted in the depletion or full exploitation of almost every commercial species of fish. Some industrial techniques can be especially harmful. In driftnet fishing, for example, the nylon mesh nets extend for miles and indiscriminately catch all creatures too large to pass through them. The result includes the illegal catch of undersized, pre-reproductive fish of the target species, and non-target species that are then thrown back into the ocean to die. Such illegal and unwanted fish, called "by-catch," may amount to as much as 30 percent of the legal catch. In addition, thousands of marine mammals, seabirds and sea turtles are killed by drowning or injury in fishing nets each year. Dolphins are frequent victims because commercially valuable tuna swim beneath them, and the dolphins become entangled in the nets intended to catch the tuna.

Long before driftnets became a threat, whales and seals were commercially hunted to the verge of extinction, exploited for their meat, fur, oil, and ivory [SIMON LYSTER, INTERNATIONAL WILDLIFE LAW 39 (1985)]. Perhaps two million whales were killed between 1920 and 1980, when at last serious international efforts to protect whales began [J. J. McCoy, The Plight of the Whales 11 (1989)]. The killing of perhaps three or four million seals during the 19th century resulted in the serious depletion of seal populations, and led to international efforts to protect seals in the early 1900's. Today, despite international efforts, whales and thousands of seals (including baby harp seals) are still killed illegally or under the guise of legal taking for "scientific purposes."

Furthermore, human demand for fish competes with the demand on those resources by other fish, seabirds, and marine mammals. Natural fishery environments are highly diverse, and fishing one or two commercial species causes imbalances in the many ecosystems in these environs. For example, commercial over-fishing of cod and haddock at New England's Georges Bank depleted a prime feeding area for whales. Similarly, the Antarctic marine food chain has been disrupted by fishing for krill— shrimp-like crustaceans that are an important food source for whales, seals, penguins, and seabirds [Stephen Savage, Endangered Species, Dolphins and Whales 106 (1990)].

Second, pollution threatens marine living resources by destroying marine habitat and adversely affecting the health effects of species that live there. Some land-based discharges are directly toxic to marine life. The effects of these toxins is worsened by their concentration in the surface layer of the sea containing the marine phytoplankton on which the marine food chain depends. The toxic pollution of marine life has resulted in thinner egg shells of seabirds (decreasing their survival rate), impaired reproduction in some marine mammals, and physical deformities. Other pollutants, though not toxic, contribute to rampant algae growth which kills fish by clogging their gills and depleting the water of oxygen (*see* Chapter Nine, Toxic and Hazardous Substances; and Chapter Ten, Land–Based Pollution).

Pollutants are deposited in the oceans by many mechanisms including atmospheric deposition, ocean dumping and oil contamination from commercial activities. Atmospheric deposition is responsible for over 30 percent of marine pollution. Chlorinated hydrocarbons (including pesticides, such as DDT, and PCBs) are released into the atmosphere by evaporation from the earth's surface and during crop-spraying. They also are carried on wind-borne dust. These pollutants then precipitate into the marine environment as rain or fallout.

Ocean dumping constitutes ten percent of marine pollution [INTERNATIONAL MARITIME ORGANIZATION, THE LONDON DUMPING CONVENTION: THE FIRST DECADE AND BEYOND 44 (1991)]. The most significant ocean dumping involves dredged spoils, or sediments removed from shipping channels. Because shipping areas are often industrialized, dredged spoils can contain significant amounts of heavy metals, petroleum hydrocarbons, and chlorinated hydrocarbons. Other wastes dumped at sea include sewage sludges, garbage and radioactive wastes. Overall, ocean dumping adversely affects marine habitat in two ways: the solid material settles to the bottom smothering bottom-dwelling marine life, and habitat and the toxic pollutants in the dredged spoils or wastes are released into the water (*see* chapter 12, Dumping). Oil pollution from tanker operations and accidents, coastal refineries, and offshore oil production also accounts for about ten percent of all marine pollution. For a complete discussion of these activities, please *see* Chapter Eleven, Vessel–Based Pollution.

Third, estuarine and coastal habitats, such as coral reefs, mangrove forests, and coastal wetlands, are damaged not only by chemical pollution, but also by development and accompanying soil erosion. Soil sediments clog and destroy estuarine and coastal habitats. Coral reefs, central to some of the most productive and diverse ecosystems, are especially susceptible to sedimentation damage. Mangrove forests along the reef shores that provide essential feeding and breeding habitat for young fish also remain vulnerable to the deleterious impacts of sedimentation and erosion. Additionally, human activities and subsidence destroy coastal wetlands. For example, coastal development in the Mississippi Delta—predicted to continue into the next century—devastates wetlands that act as habitat of much marine biological diversity, including the feeding and breeding ground for many species of fish [WALTER REID & MARK TREXLER, DROWNING THE NATIONAL HERITAGE: CLIMATE CHANGE AND U.S. COASTAL BIODIVERSITY 8 (1991)].

C. REMEDIAL OBJECTIVES

Marine living resources are an integral part of the biodiversity of the world, and the protection of marine biodiversity has to be approached in tandem with the preservation of terrestrial biodiversity under the Convention on Biological Diversity (Biodiversity Convention), June 5, 1992, 31 I.L.M. 818 (entered into force Dec. 29, 1993) (*see* Chapter Five, Biodiversity). A twin challenge faces the protection of both marine and terrestrial living resources and ecologies: human population growth and economic development. IEL, on the whole, has attempted to deal with over-exploitation, pollution, and habitat destruction, rather than directly address the more intransigent issues of population growth and economic development that fall within the matrix of sustainable development. This pragmatic attempt to address the more immediate issues can be seen as a necessary first step toward a more complete solution because the international community may not be willing to go further at this stage. It is important, however, that any serious attempt to address marine over-exploitation should at least open the door to a more explicit and concrete recognition of the demands of sustainable development.

It is also important, both ecologically and politically, that the conservation of marine resources be located within an integrated design for the oceans, and the United Nations Convention on the Law of the Sea (UNCLOS), Dec. 10, 1982, 21 I.L.M. 1261 (entered into force Nov. 16, 1994) has responded to this challenge by establishing such a wide reaching regime. It focuses on the protection of marine living resources as an intrinsic component of the oceanic environment, and contains a number of necessary, general obligations dealing with the protection of different marine resources. UNCLOS, and the Regional Seas Conventions that seek to give substance to its general obligations, constitute a first step in the direction of a more integrated approach to biodiversity (*see* Chapter 10, Land–Based Pollution). This potential arises from the comprehensive approach of UNCLOS to the oceans, which deals *inter alia* with land-based pollution, and sets the stage for further coordination between UNCLOS and the Biodiversity Convention. Even though we have not witnessed any dramatic movements as of yet, legal potential exists for improvement in these areas.

D. LEGAL RESPONSE

1. UNITED NATIONS CONVENTION ON THE LAW OF THE SEA (UNCLOS)

(a) Overview

Developed over a period of 30 years, including fifteen years of active negotiation leading to the present convention, UNCLOS provides an example of the comprehensive rather than the framework approach to treaty-making. As an example of the comprehensive approach, UNCLOS combines a broad codification of international law and other substantive rules in a single document, instead of separating issues out by way of additional protocols to a framework convention. UNCLOS also functions as a constitution of the oceans—an umbrella convention that brings other international rules, regulations, and implementing bodies within its canopy (*see* Chapter One, Introduction § B).

(b) Jurisdiction Zones

UNCLOS resolves a centuries-long debate concerning the jurisdictional boundaries of the world's oceans. In fact its jurisdictional pronouncements have evolved from case law, particularly the ICJ's jurisdictional guidelines as set forth in the *Icelandic Fisheries Cases* (1974) [Fisheries Jurisdiction (Federal Republic of Germany v. Iceland), 1974 I.C.J. 3; Fisheries Jurisdiction (United Kingdom of Great Britain and Northern Ireland v. Ice.), 1973 I.C.J. 302]. For the purposes of marine living resources, UNCLOS delineates four major areas: the territorial sea, the exclusive economic zone, the continental shelf and the high seas.

i. Territorial Sea

In clear language UNCLOS extends the sovereignty of a coastal state to 12 nautical miles, known as the territorial sea [arts. 2 & 3]. This means that utilization of the area remains subject to the laws and regulations of the coastal state, with few intrusions by international law. The state, for example, can prohibit all fishing in this area unless otherwise provided by agreement. In effect UNCLOS only grants other states the right of innocent passage, which the coastal state may strictly control through the adoption of laws and regulations with respect to "the conservation of the living resources of the sea" [art. 21(1)(d)].

ii. Exclusive Economic Zone (EEZ)

Potentially a major breakthrough for the preservation of marine living resources, the EEZ comprises a 200 nautical mile breadth as measured from the same baselines used to measure the territorial sea [art. 57]. UNCLOS bestows sovereignty and jurisdiction over this area to the coastal state [art. 56(1)(a)], in return for which the coastal state must perform a number of obligations, including the conservation and management of living resources in the zone [art. 61(2)]. In this way UNCLOS supersedes the former doctrine of freedom of fishing, which now applies only in limited fashion on the high seas, and which has long contributed to over-exploitation of resources.

As part of its conservation and management duties, the coastal state must determine the "allowable catch of the living resources in its exclusive economic zone" [art. 61(1)] and must take measures to ensure "that the maintenance of the living resources in the exclusive economic zone is not endangered by over-exploitation" [art. 61(2)]. In doing so, the coastal state must consider the effects of exploitation on species related to the harvested species, which includes other species caught incidentally while trying to catch commercial species [art. 61(4)]. Further, the coastal state must "promote the objective of optimum utilization of living resources" [art. 62(1)], and strive "to maintain or restore populations of harvested species at levels which can produce the maximum sustainable yield" [art. 61(3)].

After setting an appropriate "allowable catch" for a commercial species, the coastal state may then take the entire catch if it desires. If, however, the coastal state cannot harvest the full allowable catch, then the coastal state may grant access to other states in order to harvest the surplus [art. 62(2)]. Contrary to the former freedom of fishing doctrine, other states may therefore only take certain designated species in the EEZ, and then only by permission of the coastal state. In considering which states to give permission to, a coastal state must first look to the needs of developing countries and landlocked states [arts. 62(2) & (3); 69 & 70].

By extending conservation and management duties to the 200 mile limit of the EEZ, UNCLOS provides a potentially effective mechanism to prevent over-exploitation of marine living resources; according to recent figures, over 90 percent of the world's fisheries resources lie within national EEZs. Nonetheless, in practice developing countries have had technical difficulty in determining the allowable catch for all commercial species in their respective EEZs, and in enforcing both their conservation laws and their exclusive rights to development. Organizations such as FAO and UNEP have tried to assist developing countries in these efforts, but funds remain scarce. Much work still exists to fulfill this promising aspect of UNCLOS.

iii.   Continental Shelf

The coastal state will in all cases have sovereignty over the natural resources of its continental shelf [art. 77(1)]. This means that the coastal state has exclusive rights to the "sedentary species" of the seabed—those "organisms which, at the harvestable stage, either are immobile on or under the seabed or are unable to move except in constant physical contact with the seabed or the subsoil" [art. 77(4)]. In most cases the continental shelf will exist within the EEZ, and so the rules pertaining to the waters above the shelf will be those of the EEZ. In the unusual case of a continental shelf extending beyond the 200–mile limit, however, a special situation arises. The waters above the seabed will remain subject to the rules of the high seas, while the natural resources of the seabed will still fall within the sovereignty of the coastal state [art. 77(1)]. Interestingly, UNCLOS includes no explicit duty to conserve the resources of the continental shelf, but most commentators agree that a duty is implied given the strong emphasis on conservation throughout the convention.

iv.   High Seas

In the area beyond the EEZ the former doctrine of freedom of fishing still obtains, though it now exists in qualified fashion. States do have the right for their nationals to engage in fishing on the high seas [art. 116], but certain duties of conservation and management also apply. For example, as necessary states must adopt measures for their respective nationals regarding the conservation of living resources on the high seas [art. 117]. In addition, states have a duty to cooperate with each other concerning the conservation and management of these resources; as appropriate this may include the creation of regional fisheries [art. 118]. Furthermore, through such cooperative arrangements states must endeavor to set "allowable catche[s]," again designed to maintain or restore harvested species at levels of maximum sustainable yield, and take any other conservation measures regarding harvested species [art. 119(1)(a)]. In doing so states must also protect incidentally captured species from becoming "seriously threatened" [art. 119(1)(b)].

The above general obligations have recently been further defined by the 1995 Agreement for the Implementation of the Provisions of UNCLOS Relating to the Conservation and Management of Straddling Fish Stocks and Highly Migratory Fish Stocks (Straddling and Highly Migratory Fish Stocks Agreement or SHMFSA), Dec. 4, 1995, A/CONF. 164/37, *available in westlaw*, 1995 WL 795745. States whose vessels work the high seas must now follow the regulations of SHMFSA, outlined directly below, concerning these designated categories of fish stocks.

(c) The Species Approach

In combination with the general obligations laid down for different jurisdictional zones, UNCLOS adopts special rules for several groups of species. This approach acknowledges the wide variety of marine living resources, as well as the commensurate difficulties in dealing with such variability. Unless otherwise noted in the treaty, the general obligations regarding the EEZ and the high seas still remain—such as setting allowable catches and adopting proper conservation and management measures. However, regarding "straddling stocks" and "highly migratory fish stocks," the recent SHMFSA provides more extensive protections.

i. Straddling Stocks

"Straddling stocks" are fish stocks located both in a coastal state's EEZ and an adjacent area of the high seas. In general UNCLOS article 63(2) mandates that the coastal state and the other states fishing the stocks on the high seas enter into agreed measures "necessary for the conservation of these stocks." In practice, however, the regional fisheries have not successfully addressed this problem, and in particular they have had no power to control the consumption of non-member distant water flagships. In the Northwest Atlantic, for example, when the member states of the Northwest Atlantic Fishing Organization (NAFO) actually reduced their total allowable catch on the high seas (excluding squid) by 8.7 percent from 1986–1992, non-member states over the same period increased their own take by 27.7 percent.

In addressing such difficulties, the 1995 SHMSFA compels greater cooperation between coastal states and distant-water flag states. Coastal States and States fishing on the high seas must "adopt measures to ensure the long-term sustainability of straddling fish stocks and highly migratory fish stocks and promote the objective of their optimum utilization" [SHMFSA art. 5(a)]. In short, this means that both coastal states and flags states must cooperate to adopt compatible "conservation and management measures" such as catch limits for certain species [SHMFSA art. 7]. In most instances this negotiation will take place through the appropriate regional or sub-regional fishery, and all flag states fishing on the high seas must either join the relevant fishery or at least agree to abide by the measures established by that organization [SHMSFA art. 8].

The new SHMFSA also provides for enforcement mechanisms on the high seas. This is a major step with regard to the management of high seas fishing. In effect, a member of a subregional or regional fishery organization may board and inspect a flag state ship on the high seas "for the purpose of ensuring compliance with conservation and management measures ... established by that organization ..." [SHMSFA art. 21(1)]. The inspecting state must notify the flag state of any alleged violation [SHMSFA art. 21(2)], such as failing to maintain accurate catch data or fishing for a prohibited stock, and the flag state must then respond within three working days [SHMSFA art. 21(6)]. In the meantime, inspectors may remain on board, and the flag state must choose either to inspect the matter itself or authorize the inspection by the inspecting state [SHMSFA art. 21(6)]. The result is a new approach to policing the high seas—one that requires all states to follow the rules adopted by regional and sub-regional fisheries organizations as these organizations attempt to protect straddling stocks and highly migratory fish stocks.

ii. Highly Migratory Species (HMS)

UNCLOS creates a special category for highly migratory species listed in Annex I of the treaty. This annex includes some mammals, but the primary focus is on non-mammals such as marlin, swordfish and tuna. Coastal and other fishing states must "co-operate" either directly or through organizations "with a view to ensuring conservation and promoting the objective of optimum utilization of such species throughout the region, both within and beyond the exclusive economic zone" [art. 64(1)]. In addition, states must work to establish appropriate cooperative organizations where none exist [art. 64(1)]. As made clear by article 65, the treaty excludes marine mammals from the article 64(1) requirement of promoting "optimum utilization" of such species if states, collectively or individually, opt for more stringent protection. Again, for non-mammals the 1995 SHMFSA creates further duties of cooperation between distant-water flag states and coastal states, with the focus of such cooperation taking place through relevant regional and subregional fisheries organizations.

iii. Marine Mammals

In singling out marine mammals, UNCLOS recognizes their especially fragile circumstances. Through loss of habitat, over-exploitation and incidental taking, the mammals of the oceans have proved particularly vulnerable, and as a rule their populations do not recover as quickly as fish. UNCLOS article 65 allows coastal states or any appropriate international organization "to prohibit, limit or regulate the exploitation of marine mammals more strictly than provided for" in the general articles dealing with the EEZ. UNCLOS article 120 broadens the protections offered by article 65 to include the high seas. Furthermore, states must "co-operate with a view to the conservation of marine mammals," and in the case of cetaceans (whales and porpoises) must "work through the appropriate international organizations for their conservation, management and study" [art. 65]. This latter provision has led to some confusion, both as to the identity of the "appropriate international organizations" and as to the breadth of the phrase "work through." Canada, for example, has taken the stand that it should manage the small cetaceans found in its own EEZ, and that NAFO should play a limited consultative role. Others have argued that the IWC exists as the proper institution for all cetaceans, and that its role should be determinative rather than consultative. As it turns out, a number of countries have instituted outright bans on the taking of many marine mammals, but small cetaceans especially remain at risk of continued depletion without a coherent framework of protection. (For more on the role of IWC, *see* § 3 below).

The Special Case of Seals.

The extension of national jurisdiction under UNCLOS has largely supplanted international efforts to protect seals, as nearly all seals live within the 200–mile limit of the EEZ. Formerly, however, the conservation of seals for later exploitation purposes very much occupied the minds of fur industry nations. As early as 1911, Japan, the United States, Russia and Canada signed a treaty to share in the taking of certain Pacific Ocean species [Convention between the United States of America, the United Kingdom of Great Britain and Northern Ireland and Russia, for the Preservation and Protection of Fur Seals]. July 7, 1911, VIII I.E.P. 3682:29 (entered into force Dec. 15, 1911). With the expiration of this convention in 1941, the same parties (Russia replaced by the Soviet Union) concluded the Interim Convention on Conservation of North Pacific Fur Seals, Feb. 9, 1957, 314 U.N.T.S. 105 (entered into force Oct. 14, 1957). The parties amended and renewed this convention a number of times, though the last agreement of 1984 has now expired. In the Atlantic, two different instruments protect seals in the northeast and northwest Atlantic, respectively, though again their importance as conservation instruments has waned. More recently, the treaty for the Conservation of Seals in the Wadden Sea entered into force in 1991 between the Netherlands, Denmark and Germany—a treaty which takes an ecosystem approach to habitat protection and pollution control, while also prohibiting the taking of seals within the region.

Therefore, though bilateral and small multilateral agreements may help in the coordination of regional protection of seals, the more wide-ranging and inclusive treaties of the past no longer possess their former appeal. In the future, more effective protection may be afforded by the listing procedures of both CITES and the Bonn Convention. Finally, for the protection of seals living outside of national jurisdiction in the Antarctic, please see the Chapter Eight, Antarctica.

iv. Anadromous Species

Anadromous species are those species, such as salmon, which spawn in freshwater rivers, migrate to the high seas, and finally return to the same freshwater rivers to reproduce. UNCLOS allocates a dual role for the state of origin, which has both a "primary interest in and [a] responsibility for such stocks" [art. 66(1)]. This means that the state of origin, after negotiations with other interested states, may set a total allowable catch for such species [art. 66(2)]. The state of origin therefore obtains the first right to exploit these species, and all taking should occur landward of the outer limits of its EEZ. However, other states that might experience economic dislocation without harvesting the species may by agreement receive special allowance to participate in the taking—either in the EEZ or on the high seas [art. 66(3)(a)]. In return for the right to utilize the species, the state of origin has the obligation to "ensure their conservation" by proper regulatory measures [art. 66(2)]. This includes the creation of conservation regulations for all takings landward of its EEZ, and the good faith attempt to establish conservatory agreements for all takings beyond that limit.

v. Catadromous Species

These are species spawned on the high seas, such as eels, who then migrate to freshwater rivers and lakes. For these species the UNCLOS gives the coastal state—"in whose waters catadromous species spend the greater part of their life cycle"—the responsibility for "management" [art. 67(1)]. Harvesting by any party is prohibited on the high seas [art. 67(2)]. In waters landward of the outer limits of the EEZ, the coastal state assumes the rights and obligations generally allocated for other types of fishing in its EEZ. This means that the coastal state sets an allowable catch and other states may only participate in the harvest by agreement [art. 67(2)].

2. UNEP REGIONAL SEAS PROGRAMME

An umbrella program of UNCLOS, the regional seas programme of the United Nations Environment Programme (UNEP) has evolved into an extremely broad system of marine protection. Covering a number of seas or coastal regions—a majority involving developing countries—the Regional Seas Programme often functions as the primary means for coordinating environmental action within the geographic area.

In implementing the programme, UNEP had made use of the convention-protocol approach to international law-making. First, UNEP develops an Action Plan for the region, which the potential parties then use to create a framework treaty. Subsequently, the parties negotiate protocols to the treaty dealing with specific areas of concern.

With regard to species conservation, though all the treaties contain general obligations to protect the marine environment, a handful have also generated protocols mandating the establishment of marine or coastal protected areas. For example, the Nairobi Protocol for the Eastern African Regional Sea Convention requires parties to cooperate in the creation of a network of protected areas with the aim of preserving both flora and fauna.

The UNEP Regional Seas Programme has proven successful in providing flexible mechanisms for the coordination of regional responses to marine problems. However, nearly all the conventions remain underfunded and the protocols continue to be unratified and/or poorly implemented. Improvement in these areas will undoubtedly lead to better protection of marine species.

3. INTERNATIONAL CONVENTION FOR THE REGULATION OF WHALING (ICRW)

Signed in 1946, the ICRW still exists as the controlling document for the regulation of whaling throughout the world [Dec. 2, 1946, 161 U.N.T.S. 72 (entered into force Nov. 10, 1948)]. Created more as an exploitation rather than conservation treaty, the ICRW has since evolved into an ideologically strict and somewhat controversial preservation regime. This shift in attitude reflects the current antiwhaling make-up of the International Whaling Commission (IWC)—the supervising body of the convention.

The ICRW creates a relatively simple institutional system. Under the treaty the IWC maintains a Schedule, which fixes "with respect to the conservation and utilization of whale resources" the following regulations [art. V(1)]:

(a) protected and unprotected species;

(b) open and closed seasons;

(c) open and closed waters, including the designation of sanctuary areas;

(d) size limits for each species;

(e) time, methods and intensity of whaling (including the maximum catch of whales to be taken in any one season);

(f) types and specifications of gear and apparatus and appliances which may be used;

(g) methods of measurement; and

(h) catch returns and statistical and biological records

The IWC may amend the Schedule at any time, but any amendments must be "necessary to carry out the objectives and purposes" of the convention [art. V(2)(a)], and must be "based on scientific findings" [art. V(2)(b)]. In addition, each party to the treaty has one vote on the IWC, and each amendment to the Schedule must carry a three-fourths majority for approval.

Originally comprised of predominantly pro-whaling states, the IWC consistently set catch limits too high, resulting in the continued depletion of commercial whale species throughout the 1970s. By 1982, however, as public outrage over whaling reached dramatic proportions, membership in the IWC came to include a majority of non-whaling states, and the commission passed a moratorium on all commercial whaling beginning three years later in 1985.

The moratorium in fact contains a double loophole. First, parties can simply object to the moratorium (or any other amendment) within a timely fashion and the moratorium will not bind them [art. V(3)]. Norway, for example, immediately did object to the 1982 action. Second, article VIII(1) of the ICRW allows continued whaling "for the purposes of scientific research"—with power to grant permits for such "scientific" action at the discretion of the flag-state. Over the years, Iceland, Japan and Norway have taken hundreds of whales under this guise, all in an attempt to keep their respective whaling industries in business pending the possible lifting of the moratorium.

Nonetheless, the moratorium has proven such a success that the IWC's own Scientific Committee recommended a partial lifting of the moratorium in 1991. The Scientific Committee proposed that up to 2,000 minke whales could be taken each year without damage to the overall viability of the species. The IWC, however, has consistently declined to heed the advice of its Scientific Committee and has refused to relax the ban. If it is assumed the Scientific Committee is correct—an assumption disputed by a number of environmental groups—this apparently flies in the face of article V(2)(b) which maintains that amendments of the Schedule "shall be based on scientific findings." As a result, Norway— which originally objected to the moratorium and so does not remain legally bound by the provision— stated that it would resume commercial whaling in 1993. Having done so, Norway has actually taken fewer minke whales than allocated to it by the Scientific Committee's Revised Management Procedure (RMP), a prospective conservation plan to be put in place upon cessation of the moratorium.

As of this writing, the IWC in 1996 again refused to lift the moratorium on commercial whaling. Iceland has dropped out of the IWC, and Japan continues to conduct its own "scientific" whaling. Japan, in fact, has taken hundreds of minke whales in the Southern Ocean Whale Sanctuary—a sanctuary specifically created in 1994 to protect whales from exploitation in Antarctica. The IWC has loudly requested that Japan stop this action.

The present impasse openly reflects the political vulnerability of some international environmental institutions. Norway, under the leadership of Prime Minister Gro Harlem Bruntland, has continued to promote high environmental standards both at home and abroad. In fact, the Bruntland report offered the original blueprint for sustainable development for the World Commission on Environment and Development in 1986. Anti-whaling states, however, who so importantly voted the moratorium into place in 1982, now find it politically impossible to reverse their position—even when confronted with strong scientific evidence. Of course these states may simply want to ban whaling altogether for a variety of valuable reasons, including moral and aesthetic ones. Nevertheless, the IWC remains committed to conservation *and utilization*, and the world remains committed to sustainable development under Agenda 21. In this case we find a high profile example of the potential conflict between preservation on the one hand, and sustainable use on the other.

4. DRIFTNET FISHING

Some recent improvement has occurred with regard to driftnet fishing—a particularly devastating method of taking in which a single boat, or several boats working together, suspend a series of nets up to 40 miles wide and 48 feet deep, catching everything (including dolphins) in their wake. The Convention for the Prohibition of Fishing with Long Driftnets in the South Pacific Nov. 23, 1989, 29 I.L.M. 1454, entered into force on May 17, 1991, entirely prohibits the fishing practice within a party's EEZ [art. 3]. In the same year, the United Nations passed a resolution calling for a moratorium on driftnet fishing on the high seas by December 31, 1992 [*UNGA Resolution on Large Scale Pelagic Driftnet Fishing and its Impact on the Marine Living Resources of the World's Oceans and Seas*, Res.46/215, reprinted in 31 I.L.M. 241 (Dec 20, 1991)]. Of course, no enforcement measure exists with the resolution, but the progressive development of soft law on the subject makes driftnet fishing on the high seas a politically unacceptable endeavor. Due to this pressure Japan and Taiwan, two of the major driftnet fishing nations, have ceased the practice altogether.

CHAPTER FOURTEEN

TRANSBOUNDARY AIR POLLUTION

A. NATURE OF THE PROBLEM

Human demands lead to a number of physical processes and activities that convert raw materials, energy, and labor into desired finished products. Diverse pollutants are introduced into the environment during various stages of these production and consumption cycles. We have noted in Chapter Nine, Toxic and Hazardous Substances that the environment is indivisible, interconnected and interdependent, and that contaminants can move within or beyond the original medium (air, water or land) into which they are introduced.

The migration of air pollutants has created major global problems such as climate change, ozone depletion, and nuclear fallout, that are dealt with elsewhere (*see* Chapters Six, Seven, and Seventeen). Pollutants transported through the air also cause problems, and in Chapter Nine, Toxic and Hazardous Substances we have discussed how pollutants cause human health and environmental problems. This chapter will focus on the residual transboundary problems caused by air pollutants not covered by regimes described elsewhere in this book. We briefly discuss problems caused by ubiquitous pollutants such as sulphur dioxide and nitrous oxides—including acid rain—and how and why they have given rise to customary and treaty regimes.

B. CAUSES AND SOURCES

Pollutants emitted into the atmosphere from industrial and commercial sources and automobile exhausts can form gases, suspensions of small liquid or solid particles, or become dissolved in cloud vapor or raindrops. Depending upon the condition of the atmosphere, these pollutants may become trapped in the air at low levels and high concentrations. Some of them react chemically to produce new or more toxic chemicals that can be transported many hundreds of miles by winds, deposited on soil or in the water (dry deposition) or returned to the earth by rainfall (wet deposition).

Once a contaminant is deposited on the soil, organisms or other chemicals present in the ground may transform it into a more toxic chemical. Whether or not this occurs, the contaminant will eventually be either absorbed by edible plants and possibly consumed by humans or other animals, carried by rainwater into a body of water, returned to the atmosphere through evaporation, or remain in the soil indefinitely.

C. ENVIRONMENTAL IMPACTS

Acid deposition, or acid rain, is a classic example of the global transportation of pollutants. In the

United States, coal and oil-fired electric plants in the midwest release gases which contain sulphur oxide dust. The dust is transported to the eastern states and Canada, where it precipitates [*see* Jurgan Schmandt, et al., *Acid Rain is Different, in* ACID RAIN AND FRIENDLY NEIGHBORS: THE POLICY DISPUTE BETWEEN CANADA AND THE UNITED STATES 31(Jurgan Schmandt, et al. eds. 1988)]. In Europe, English and French industries are a major source of sulphur, and the Scandinavian countries often receive the acid deposition [A.G. Clarke, *The Air, in* UNDERSTANDING OUR ENVIRONMENT 106 (R.E. Hester, ed. 1986)].

Acid rain is often created by the following process. Industrial plants, generally having tall stacks, distribute waste gases into the atmosphere. The gases and dusts are hot when released, so they tend to rise. Once in the atmosphere, the dusts can react with cloud water to form acids, the worst being sulphuric acid, H_2SO_4. Even if not encountering atmospheric water, the sulphur eventually falls to earth where it can react to form acids with any terrestrial water. This is called dry deposition. While the sulphur dust is high in the atmosphere the potential remains great for the acid to travel great distances and across national boundaries [*id.*].

It is important to note, however, that some acid in rain occurs naturally as part of the carbon cycle. Carbon dioxide, for example, results from respiration, fires or volcanoes. These emissions naturally react with rain water forming carbonates, making a mildly acidic solution that actually "buffers" the rain. That is, it forms a solution with the water that can absorb new sources of acidity or basicity before the pH changes. The atmospheric transport of carbon also functions as an important part of the carbon cycle, placing carbon in locations—such as rocky or nutrient poor habitats—where it might not otherwise be available [*id.* at 77].

There are scientific uncertainties associated with a discussion of acid precipitation, and recent United States government studies remain inconclusive about the seriousness of its effects [*see* Marylynn Placet, *Emissions Involved in Acidic Deposition Processes, in* ACIDIC DEPOSITION: STATE OF SCIENCE AND TECHNOLOGY; SUMMARY REPORT OF THE UNITED STATES NATIONAL ACID PRECIPITATION ASSESSMENT PROGRAM (NAPAP) 25 (1991)]. The phenomena is difficult to investigate because it traverses entire countries and even seas. However, some issues have been identified with acid deposition, and these include the acidification of nutrient poor lakes and soils, and the accelerated decay of buildings, monuments and roads. Whatever uncertainties remain, acid deposition transport clearly emphasizes that atmospheric pollution is an international issue, proving that pollutants do not respect national borders .

D. REMEDIAL OBJECTIVES

Transboundary air pollution was recognized quite early as an international pollution problem. For example, the facts of the well known *Trail Smelter Arbitration* (United States v. Canada) 3 R.I.A.A.

1938 (Mar. 11 1941) which we are about to discuss, transpired in the 1920's and 1930's. The principles derived from that case have become the bedrock of customary IEL dealing with transboundary pollution, although the arbitration itself, and the applicable law, were governed by an international agreement between Canada and the United States.

The *Trail Smelter Arbitration* presents the need for *ex ante* regulatory measures that prevent pollution, establish compliance procedures and enforcement mechanisms, as well as *ex post* grievance-remedial methods such as arbitral and judicial proceedings that are able to assign responsibility and liability for wrongful actions. As we shall see, IEL dealing with transboundary pollution is an incomplete patchwork of customary law interwoven with regional agreements of limited jurisdiction.

E. LEGAL RESPONSE

1. CUSTOM

No discussion of transboundary air pollution could begin without mention of the 1941 *Trail Smelter Arbitration* case. As suggested in Chapter Two, Sources and Forms of International Law section D, this remains one of the most significant cases in international environmental law, and the only important case dealing with air pollution. The facts actually suggest an unusual transboundary air pollution scenario, without the usual causation problems due to multiple polluters and multiple delivery streams. In this situation a single identifiable polluter—a smelter plant owned by a Canadian corporation and located in Canada—was found by an arbitral tribunal to have caused air pollution damage to a region of the State of Washington. In the next stage of the bifurcated proceedings the tribunal held Canada itself responsible for the pollution damage, providing injunctive relief and a monetary award. In doing so under the doctrine of state responsibility, the tribunal made the following summation:

> The Tribunal, therefore, finds that the above [United States domestic] decisions, taken as a whole, constitute an adequate basis for its conclusions, namely, that, under the principles of international law, as well as of the law of the United States, no state has the right to use or permit the use of its territory in such a manner as to cause injury by fumes in or to the territory of another or the properties or persons therein, when the case is of serious consequence and the injury is established by clear and convincing evidence.

Trail Smelter Arbitration (United States v. Canada) 3 R.I.A.A. 1938 ¶ 157 (Mar. 11. 1941).

This ruling has since become the basis for the general prohibition against transboundary environmental harm, most recently and definitively stated in the 1992 Rio Declaration:

> States have, in accordance with the Charter of the United Nations and the principles of international law, the sovereign right to exploit their

own resources pursuant to their own environmental and developmental policies, and the responsibility to ensure that activities within their jurisdiction or control do not cause damage to the environment of other States or of areas beyond the limits of national jurisdiction [Principle 2].

Rio Declaration on Environment and Development, Adopted by the U.N. Conference on Environment and Development, Principle 2, U.N.Doc. A/CONF. 151/26, *reprinted in* 31 I.L.M. 874 (June 13, 1992).

In this latter formulation, the parties to the Rio Declaration have discarded both the *Trail Smelter* threshold of harm ("serious consequence") and the standard of causation ("clear and convincing evidence"). The term "damage" in Principle 2, however, does suggest an actionable level of harm, and most commentators have interpreted this to mean "significant harm." As for causation much criticism has been leveled at the high degree of certainty required by *Trail Smelter*, because the "clear and convincing evidence" standard presents a potentially insurmountable obstacle for most environmental cases. Regardless, the basic premise of *Trail Smelter* has evolved into a well-settled rule of customary international law—restated in a myriad of international, regional and bilateral agreements. Taking into account the sovereign right to development, one country may not cause significant transboundary environmental harm to another.

2. CONVENTION ON LONG–RANGE TRANSBOUNDARY AIR POLLUTION (LRTAP)

(a) Overview

In the absence of a global international treaty, LRTAP—a regional treaty—emerges as the most significant legal regime in the field [Nov. 13, 1979, 18 I.L.M. 1442 (entered into force Mar. 16, 1983)]. Created under the auspices of the UN Economic Commission for Europe (ECE) in 1979, the convention counts most countries in the Northern Hemisphere as parties, including the United States, Canada and Russia. It also represents an early form of the framework convention, though its institutions lack the degree of flexibility and power inherent in more recent framework treaties. Still, LRTAP has evolved to meet the needs of its parties, adding four protocols that require specific emission limitations for sulphur dioxide (1985, 1994), nitrogen oxides (1988) and volatile organic compounds (1991). As of this writing, new protocols remain in the works for heavy metals and persistent organic pollutants, as well as an additional protocol for nitrogen oxides.

The convention, with its strong focus on combating acid rain, embraces the duty to not cause transboundary harm [LRTAP pmbl., para. 5] and mandates that the parties endeavor to limit, reduce and prevent air pollution including long-range transboundary air pollution [art. 2]. The latter phenomenon is defined as air pollution from one state "which has adverse effects in the area under the jurisdiction of another state at such a distance that it is not generally possible to distinguish the contribution of individual emission sources or groups of sources" [art. 1(b)]. As such, the Convention attempts to deal with pollution problems beyond the scope of the original *Trail Smelter* fact pattern, which identified a nearby Canadian polluter as the sole perpetrator of cross-border harm in the United States.

In addition to promoting general calls for consultations, exchange of information, and research and development on the issue, the convention endorses the existing " 'Cooperative programme for the monitoring and evaluation of the long-range transmission of air pollutants in Europe,' " known as EMEP [art. 9]. Each party is asked to join in this program of scientific monitoring and evaluation, which is overseen by a Steering Committee. The convention also establishes a Secretariat, as well as an Executive Body which resembles the Conference of the Parties of more recent framework treaties. However, unlike the newer versions of the framework approach, the Executive Body's powers remain general and unenumerated, and the convention fails to create a formal dispute resolution procedure. Still, as outlined below, the treaty has given birth to a number of substantive protocols.

(b) Sulphur Emissions

Responding to increased anxiety over the threat of acid rain, the parties have made two efforts at controlling sulphur dioxide. The Protocol to the

1979 Convention on Long–Range Transboundary Air Pollution on the Reduction of Sulphur Emissions or Their Transboundary Fluxes by at Least 30 Percent (1985 Sulphur Protocol), July 8, 1985, 27 I.L.M. 707 (entered into force Sept. 2, 1987) required parties to reduce their national annual sulphur emissions by at least 30 percent of their 1980 levels, by the year 1993. This first protocol also mandated that each party develop a national program to this end, and report its national annual sulphur emissions to the Executive Body [art. 4]. It should be noted that the parties as a group succeeded in achieving the goals of the 1985 protocol, in aggregate surpassing the 30 percent reduction called for by 1993.

The Protocol to the 1979 Convention on Long–Range Transboundary Air Pollution on Further Reduction of Sulphur Emissions and Decisions on the Structure and Function of the Implementing Committee, as well as Procedures for Review of its Compliance: United Nations; 1994 (1994 Sulphur Protocol), June 14, 1994, 33 I.L.M. 1540 as its name implies, goes beyond the measures of the 1985 protocol. To begin, parties must not exceed annual sulphur ceilings as set forth in Annex II of the protocol [art. 2(2)]. This annex also creates percentage emissions reductions, again with a base year of 1980, which each party must meet for the years 2000, 2005 and 2010. Unlike the 1985 Sulphur Protocol, however, the percentage of required reduction varies with each party—thus taking into account the different situations of individual countries. The 1994 Protocol also obligates parties to ensure, as far as possible and without excessive costs, that sulphur depositions do not exceed "critical loads"—defined as a level of "exposure to one or more pollutants below which significant harmful effects" do not occur to the environment [art. 1(8)]. In addition, the protocol sets mandatory emission limit values for new stationary combustion sources which existing sources must also strive to meet by 2004 [art. 2(5)]. Specifically, the protocol exempts Canada and the United States from the emission limit values for stationary sources, giving way to the 1991 United States—Canada Air Quality Agreement, Mar. 13, 1991, 30 I.L.M. 676 (1991) [art. 2(5)]. In any event, as of this writing the United States has yet to become a party to the protocol, remaining the only significant economic power outside of LRTAPs requirements.

(c) Nitrogen Oxides

In contrast to the relatively successful endeavor to reduce sulphur emissions, the attempt to control nitrogen oxides (NOx) has proved more difficult. The UN Protocol to the 1979 Convention on Long–Range Transboundary Air Pollution Concerning the Control of Emissions of Nitrogen Oxides or Their Transboundary Fluxes (1988 Nitrogen Oxides Protocol), Oct. 31, 1988, 28 I.L.M. 212 (entered into force Feb. 1, 1991) has only slightly reduced overall emissions, with some major industrial countries predicting emission increases up to the year 2010 (including the U.K., United States and Canada)

[*Negotiation on Pops Treaty Under Way in Geneva, to Continue in Canberra in March*, (Feb 21, 1996) 19 INT'L ENV'T REP. (BNA) 177]. For this reason, as of this writing the LRTAP parties continue negotiations on a new protocol for nitrogen oxides.

The present protocol requires all parties to control and/or reduce, using 1987 as the general baseline, their national annual emissions of NO_x by the year 1994 [art. 2(1)]. As noted above this stabilization has not occurred across the board. The protocol also mandates that the parties apply national emission standards to major new stationary sources, based on "best available technologies which are economically feasible" (BATEF)[art. 2(2)(a, b & c)]. The parties must likewise apply national emission standards to mobile sources, using the same BATEF approach [art. 2(b)]. As a guideline, the parties are encouraged to look at the Technical Annex for purposes of implementation, though the annex remains strictly recommendatory in nature [art. 10]. Perhaps most important, the protocol places a premium on research and monitoring, while also requiring strenuous reporting and review procedures—all of which may lead to a more effective protocol in the near future.

(d) Volatile Organic Compounds

An as yet unevaluated effort under the umbrella of LRTAP involves the attempt to regulate volatile organic compounds (VOXs), now embodied in the United Nations ECE Protocol to the 1979 Convention on Long Range Transboundary Air Pollution

Concerning the Control of Emissions of Volatile Organic Compounds or Their Transboundary Fluxes (the 1991 VOC Protocol), Nov. 18, 1991, 31 I.L.M. 568. This protocol provides parties with three different ways to meet the basic requirement of controlling and reducing VOX emissions, as mandated by article 2(1). First, a party may choose to reduce its national annual emissions "by at least 30 percent by the year 1999, using 1988 levels as the basis or any other annual level during the period 1984–1990" [art. 2(a)]. Second, if its damaging transboundary emissions only originate from a specified area (known as a tropospheric ozone management area or TOMA, and listed in Annex I), then it need only stabilize its total annual emissions while reducing those particularly harmful emissions using the above 30 percent formula [art. 2(b)]. Third, a small polluter may simply choose to stabilize its national annual emissions by 1999, again using 1988 as the baseline [art. 2(c)].

Concerning specific types of sources, the parties must within two years upon entry into force apply national or international standards to new stationary and mobile sources, using BATEF and taking into consideration the respective technical annexes [art. 3(a)(i) & (iii)]. Within five years of entry into force, the parties must apply BATEF to existing stationary sources located in sensitive areas [art. 3(b)(i)]. Again however, the effectiveness of these and other measures remains an open question, as the protocol has only recently arrived on the international scene.

3. UNITED STATES—CANADA

On March 13, 1991, these two countries signed the Agreement on Air Quality, Mar. 31, 1991, 31 I.L.M. 676. The end result of more than a decade of negotiations regarding transboundary air pollution, the agreement primarily attempts to engage the problem of acid rain. The treaty provides that "the parties shall establish specific objectives for emissions limitations or reductions of air pollutants and adopt the necessary programs and other measures to implement such specific objectives" [art. 3(2)(a)]. As a framework agreement, the breadth of the accord allows the United States and Canada to confront both current problems and those which may arise in the future.

Annex I establishes emissions limitations for sulphur dioxide and nitrogen oxides. As agreed, the United States must reduce by the year 2000, in accordance with Title IV of the 1990 Clean Air Act Amendments (CAAA), its annual sulphur dioxide emissions attributable to power plants by 10 million tons relative to 1980 levels [Annex I, art. 1(A)(1)]. The United States further commits to cap such emissions at 8.9 million tons per year by the year 2010 [Annex I, art. 1(A)(2)]. Similarly, Canada must limit its annual SO_2 emissions to 3.2 million metric tons annually by the year 2000 [Annex I, art. 1(B)(1)].

As for nitrogen oxides emissions, the United States must reduce by the year 2000 its total annual emissions by approximately 2 million tons, again using 1980 as the baseline [Annex I, art. 2(A)]. The United States will achieve this through the CAAA, implementing NO_x control programs for electric utility burners under Title IV, and for mobile sources under Title II. For its part, by the year 2000 Canada pledges to reduce its annual national emissions of nitrogen oxides from stationary sources by 100,000 tons below the forecast level of 970,000 tons [Annex I, art. 2(B)(1)]. Additionally, Canada must impose mobile source emissions limitations similar to those found in the CAAA [Annex I, 2(B)(2)].

Concerning institutional arrangements, the agreement establishes an Air Quality Committee to review progress in implementation [art. VIII]. The Committee compiles reports on such matters and presents these to the parties as well as the International Joint Commission (IJC)[art. IX], a body constituted under the Treaty Between Canada and the United States of America Relating to Boundary Waters and Questions Arising Along the Boundary Between the United States and Canada, Jan. 11, 1909, 36 Stat. 2496 (entered into force May 5, 1910), and intended to investigate and make recommendations regarding transboundary air pollution matters generally. The IJC invites public comment on these progress reports, and then submits a synthesis of its findings back to the parties. In this way the Agreement on Air Quality makes use of one of the oldest institutions in international law, the IJC, in an attempt to control a continuing transboundary air pollution problem.

4. UNITED STATES—MEXICO

In 1983, the United States and Mexico signed the Agreement to Cooperate in the Solution of Environmental Problems in the Border Area (La Paz Agreement), Aug. 14, 1983, 22 I.L.M. 1025. The parties agree to take measures, "to the fullest practical extent," to prevent, reduce and eliminate border pollution [art. II], and to coordinate their efforts to address the problems of air, land and water pollution in the area [art. V]. The agreement defines the border area as the region "situated 100 kilometers on either side of the inland and maritime boundaries between the Parties" [art. IV]. In effect, the La Paz Agreement functions as a framework for further action, providing for the creation of annexes to deal with specific problems.

Concerning transboundary air pollution, the La Paz Agreement now contains two separate annexes. The first, Annex IV, entered into force in 1987 and deals with air pollution from all new copper smelters located in the border region. For both parties, sulphur dioxide emissions from all new copper smelters in the area must not exceed .065 percent by volume during any six-hour period [Annex IV, art. I(1) & (3)]. To monitor compliance, smelter owners and operators must track emissions and report any violations exceeding maximum levels, while every six months an "air pollution working group" assesses the progress made in abating smelter pollution. Based on this assessment, the working group then makes specific recommendations to national coordinators in both the United States and Mexico.

Annex V to the La Paz Agreement—intended to reduce pollution caused by urban development— provides for the determination of causes of air pollution in certain United States and Mexican border cities denominated "study areas." The annex requires the United States EPA and Mexico's Social Development Secretariat (SEDESOL) to catalogue emissions from major stationary, mobile, and area sources. The two agencies must then ascertain measures necessary to bring identified pollutants within acceptable control levels (a task facilitated by ambient air quality monitoring and air modeling analysis). Such measures may include, but are not limited to, requiring a given polluter to implement pollution control technology or alter management practice in an effort to bring the polluter into compliance with emissions standards. As an ultimate goal, the parties shall "jointly explore" the harmonization of their air pollution control standards and ambient air quality standards—a process which NAFTA and its progeny may help to spur in the future [Annex V, art. V].

CHAPTER FIFTEEN

TRANSBOUNDARY WATER POLLUTION

A. NATURE OF THE PROBLEM

Waters cover the face of the earth, and the oceans occupy seventy percent of the planet's surface. In earlier chapters dealing with Toxic and Hazardous Substances (Chapter Nine), Land–Based Pollution (Chapter Ten), Vessel Pollution (Chapter Eleven), and Dumping (Chapter Twelve), we noted how wastes and pollutants created by our affluent life style are emitted into the air, discharged or dumped into rivers, streams, and the sea, or disposed of on land. While direct discharges into the aquatic environment are obvious sources of pollution, we have seen how indirect sources, such as the atmosphere, can significantly contribute to the problem. Furthermore, all the water on the earth (the hydrosphere) is continually recycled between the oceans, lakes, streams, and groundwater. This recycling process results in the movement of toxic chemicals from one water source to another [DADE MOELLER, ENVIRONMENTAL HEALTH 55 (1992)].

Pollutants can be changed for better or worse within the aquatic environment. Water is a solvent with the ability to dissolve or dilute chemicals and

314

make them harmless to human health or ecosystems. The effectiveness of the diluting process will depend on hydrologic conditions such as the type and location of a water body, the nature of the pollution load, and the concentration and characteristics of the contaminants [ENCYCLOPEDIA OF THE ENVIRONMENT 557 (Ruth Eblen & William Eblen eds., 1994); C.N. Hewitt & R.M. Harrison, *Monitoring, in* UNDERSTANDING OUR ENVIRONMENT 56 (R.E. Hester ed. 1986)]. On the other hand, water can also react with contaminants to form more hazardous or more synergistic reactions, depending on the temperature, acidity, and oxygen level of the water [H. Fish, *Water, in* UNDERSTANDING OUR ENVIRONMENT 136–7 (R.E. Hester ed. 1986)].

As we have seen, the environmental health of the oceans is critical to humanity. Rivers and streams, though they constitute less than one-half percent of the water in the hydrosphere, are essential to the proper maintenance of the global environment and human habitation [*id.* at 119]. The pollution of common pool resources such as the high seas (to which all nations have open access) can create global problems, while the use or abuse of transnational or international rivers and groundwater can cause harm to states sharing these resources. Since all the oceans and over 200 large river basins are shared by two or more countries, competition over the quality and quantity of shared waters can become very intense. In this chapter we concentrate on problems that arise when rivers, lakes, estuaries, coastlines, and groundwater are used in a manner that causes harm to other states.

B. SOURCES OF ENVIRONMENTAL HARM

Pollution introduced into rivers, watercourses, and coastal waters of one state can affect another through transport, diffusion or dispersion. As we have seen in our discussion of Hazardous and Toxic Substances (Chapter Nine), chemicals are usually discharged into waters as part of a waste stream from industrial sources such as pulp and paper mills, iron and steelworks, petroleum refineries, petrochemical industries, fertilizer factories, and other chemistry-based production installations including pharmaceutical plants [id.]. Modern agriculture relies heavily on chemical pesticides and insecticides so that significant quantities of these substances enter the aquatic environment as agricultural run-off, and irrigation waste water. Sediment, too, is swept into the aquatic environment through erosion, agricultural run-off, and irrigation overflows. [PHILLIP FRADKIN, A RIVER NO MORE: THE COLORADO RIVER AND THE WEST 64 (1984)]. In the case of transnational rivers such pollutants are carried downstream into other states or into shared coastal waters or estuaries. Apart from chemicals, organic matter such as untreated or partially treated sewage is discharged into rivers, estuaries and coastal waters [D. Alistair Bigham, *Pollution from Land–Based Sources, in* THE IMPACT OF MARINE POLLUTION 203 (Douglas Cuisine & John Grant eds. 1980)].

Indirect pollution, another major source of fresh water contamination, arises for example from the improper storage of hazardous waste resulting in the leaching of hazardous substances into underground aquifers that lie beneath common borders. Such contamination may affect an entire country's source of drinking water. Additionally, emissions of toxic metals and gases from an industrial park can be transported thousands of miles by the wind and deposited directly on a water body, or on the soil where they can then leach into the groundwater [JOHN HARTE, ET AL., TOXICS A TO Z 77 (1991)].

Both the quality and quantity of water can cause transboundary damage. Water can be extracted in such quantities as to affect its ability to sustain marine life or their supporting ecosystems. The damage caused by the reduction of water volume is not restricted to the ecological health of a river or stream. The overuse of water by an upper riparian state may deprive a lower state of essential water and lead to increased soil salinity, and may even create deserts. Extracting, impounding or diverting water into dams and reservoirs could certainly affect downstream settlements because these flow-regulating projects may restrict sources of potable or agricultural water and may affect human health [PHILLIP FRADKIN, A RIVER NO MORE: THE COLORADO RIVER AND THE WEST 64 (1984)]. In the water deprived areas of the world such as the Middle East, water conflicts may potentially bring nations to the brink of war.

C. ENVIRONMENTAL IMPACTS

The deleterious effects of water pollution vary significantly and range from chemical and biological damage, to physical damage to river beds and harbors, to pure economic loss. The chemical and biological effects of chemicals are more fully discussed under the topic of Toxic and Hazardous Substances (Chapter Nine). We take note here of the specific attributes displayed by some of these pollutants in water. For example, organo-chlorines like DDT, dieldrin, aldrin, heptachlor, and mirex are chemicals used as pesticides and insecticides that display three remarkable characteristics. First, they are toxic or poisonous in small doses; at critical concentrations they can affect the marine life in a body of water and humans who drink or are exposed to such water. Second, they are *persistent* or stable. This means that they are not readily broken down by microorganisms, enzymes, heat or ultra-violet light, and have stable and long lives in aquatic environments. Third, they *bioaccumulate*. This means that they are water insoluble, and not readily metabolized though soluble in fatty tissue, and accumulate in the fatty tissue of fish and animals upon ingestion. They then move up the food chain by aggregating in the body fat of predator fish and animals. DDT has been found, for example, to have affected condors, osprey, falcons, golden eagles, sea gulls, pelicans and even humans who have eaten such contaminated fish or mammals. A similar profile could be drawn of the impacts of industrial chemicals discharged into the aquatic environment [JOHN HARTE, ET AL., TOXICS A TO Z 86–90 (1991)].

Water polluted by sewage has substantial biological effects, including impacts on human health. Microbial agents can affect people on contact by causing skin infections and respiratory illness, while the ingestion of water or sea food contaminated by pathogens from sewage can cause severe gastrointestinal and respiratory problems. In ordinary circumstances, the microbial activity in water breaks down normal organic wastes by decomposition—a process which takes up oxygen. Large volumes of organic wastes, like sewage, introduce many nutrients to a body of water. The nutrients can spur microbial growth, resulting in an increased demand for dissolved oxygen, thus creating a Biological Oxygen Demand (BOD) that can alter the biological diversity of the body of water. This process is often called "cultural eutrophication" [CHARLES GOLDMAN & ALEXANDER HORNE, LIMNOLOGY 354 (1983)].

Rivers not only carry chemical and biological substances downstream, they also bring sediment caused by erosion, deforestation, agricultural runoff, and irrigation. Such sediment can clog up harbors and cause problems in shipping lanes. Moreover, the inflow of pollutants with attendant human health and environmental problems can adversely affect tourism, an industry upon which many developing countries are heavily dependent [D. Alistair Bigham, *Pollution from Land–Based Sources, in*

THE IMPACT OF MARINE POLLUTION 203 (Douglas Cuisine & John Grant eds. 1980)].

D. REMEDIAL MEASURES

We have observed in our discussion of Toxic and Hazardous Substances (Chapter Nine), that remedial measures should endeavor to reduce waste generation by addressing consumption demands. In order to achieve such a goal, the control of water pollution should become part of a more comprehensive attempt to integrate pollution control of atmospheric, terrestrial, and aquatic pollution. Without losing sight of this more comprehensive goal, remedial measures need also to address the more immediate problems posed by transboundary river pollution. These problems, which as we shall see have been considered by the International Law Commission (ILC), arise from the disputed rights and duties pertaining to the quality and quantity of water claimed by upper and lower riparian owners of international rivers. Furthermore, water pollution, not unlike other areas of IEL, primarily requires an *ex ante* approach supplemented by *ex post* grievance remedial mechanisms. As discussed below, various regional conventions have attempted to address this challenge.

E. LEGAL RESPONSE

1. CUSTOMARY LAW

Cooperation concerning the use of transboundary watercourses is well established. As a number of rivers and lakes demarcate international boundaries, nations have found it beneficial to arrive at cooperative relationships regarding utilization of these shared resources. As such, we can now confidently cite several broad-based rules of customary law with regard to the use of international watercourses.

The International Law Commission (ILC) has recently expounded and elaborated on these rules in the *Draft Articles on the Law of the Non-navigational Uses of International Watercourses* (ILC Draft Articles), U.N. GOAR, 46th Sess., Supp. No. 10 at 161, U.N. Doc. A/46/10, *available in Westlaw*, 1991 WL 568515 (1991). Empowered by the Charter of the United Nations, June 26, 1945, 1 U.N.T.S. xvi (entered into force Oct. 24, 1945) to "initiate studies and make recommendations for the purpose of encouraging the progressive development of international law and its codification," the ILC in its Draft Articles provides a learned roadmap both to the existing law and the law as it might be. This completed effort at codification and development is the first regarding watercourses since the Helsinki Rules on the Uses of the Waters of International Rivers (1966 Helsinki Rules), Aug. 20, 1966, 52 I.L.A. 484 (1967). In fact, in 1994 the U.N. General Assembly called for an international framework convention to be negotiated based on the Draft Articles and, after receiving comments from governments, that process will begin shortly.

For this reason we have chosen the ILC Draft Articles as our own roadmap in traversing the cus-

tomary law on the subject. Yet, in approaching the
Draft Articles one should keep in mind that the ILC
does not always distinguish between extant and
progressive development of the law, leaving room
for debate on the specifics of the present state of
affairs. In this section therefore, while entering into
the more controversial aspects of the Draft Articles,
we have also attempted to separate the general
customary law from its progressive development.
One should also take note that this writing precedes
any pronouncements the ICJ might make in the
current dispute between Hungary and Slovakia regarding the Gabcikovo–Nagymaros Project. That
matter, still pending before the court, promises
further elucidation of the customary law pertaining
to international watercourses.

(a) Communication: Notification, Consultation and Negotiation

There is no doubt that customary law, in at least
certain situations, requires communication between
and among watercourse states. In discussing these
obligations we must first outline the nature of the
terms involved. Perhaps the best approach is to
consider notification, consultation and negotiation
on a continuum of governmental interaction. Notification simply requires the providing of information
without a mutual exchange. Consultation requires a
dialogue among participants without an obligation
of reasonable compromise, or therefore of result.
Negotiation, on the other hand, requires a dialogue
with an obligation to compromise—if in good faith a
reasonable actor would so compromise—but not

necessarily an obligation of result. Of course all three terms function within a political context in which the pressures to agree (or disagree) would both inform the terms and promote an outcome.

As an overriding objective, the 1994 Draft Articles mandate communication and thus cooperation between watercourse states, requiring that they "shall, at the request of any of them, enter into consultations concerning the management of an international watercourse" [art. 24(1)]. Thus the ILC envisions the adoption of "watercourse agreements" among watercourse states, with such agreements adapted from the Draft Articles to suit the regional needs of the parties [art. 3].

Concerning the future use of a watercourse, the Draft Articles contain a high degree of specificity regarding states' obligations to communicate. The details—such as time-frames to respond—are pragmatic embellishments, but the basic obligations correspond to customary law. For example, before a watercourse state implements "planned measures" having a possibly significant adverse effect, it must provide a potentially harmed state with timely notification [art. 12]. The notifying state must allow the potentially harmed state six months in which to respond [art. 13], and may not implement the planned measures without consent during this period [art. 14]. If the notified state believes the planned measures to be unacceptable— that is inconsistent with either the rules of equitable utilization or the duty not to cause harm (discussed below)—then the parties must "enter into consultations and, if necessary, negotiations with a view to arriving at an equitable resolution of the situation" [art. 17]. Should the consultations and negotiations fail the Draft Articles offer dispute settlement provisions for impartial fact-finding (if requested by one party), and mediation or conciliation (if agreed to by both parties) [art. 33].

Given the extensive degree of cooperation found today concerning planned uses of international watercourses, the above requirements of notification, consultation and negotiation appear to follow state practice. In the Lac Lanoux Arbitration (Spain v. France), 12 R.I.A.A. 281 (Nov. 16, 1957), for instance, an arbitral tribunal stated that France could not ignore Spanish interests regarding a planned hydraulic construction project on the Carol River. The tribunal, however, did not go as far as the ILC, explaining that "if, in the course of discussions, the downstream State submits schemes to it, the upstream State must examine them, but it has the right to give preference to the solution contained in its own scheme provided that it takes into consideration in a reasonable manner the interests of the downstream State." The tribunal also disavowed as a rule of law that only a prior agreement between riparian states would allow one state to utilize the hydraulic power of a watercourse. Nonetheless, the ILC Draft Articles' mandate of consultations and negotiations (leading finally to impartial fact-finding and possibly mediation/conciliation) reflects contemporary practice in that states nearly always settle these disputes among themselves. In this regard one need only look at the proliferation of regional and bilateral watercourse agreements discussed below to appreciate how the degree of communication—and the perception of that communication as a legal requirement—has significantly increased since the 1957 *Lac Lanoux Arbitration* Case.

(b) Equitable Utilization

The concept of equitable utilization has long been a rule of law concerning international watercourses. Though speaking of a navigable river, *In re* the Territorial Jurisdiction of the International Commission of the River Oder, 1929 P.C.I.J. (Ser. A) No. 23, at 5, the Permanent Court of International Justice (PCIJ) declared that each riparian's "community of interest . . . becomes the basis a common legal right, the essential features of which are the perfect equality of all riparian States in the use of the whole course of the river and the exclusion of any preferential privilege of any one riparian State in relation to the others." In reference to non-navigational uses, the ILC Draft Articles require that "[w]atercourse States shall . . . utilize an international watercourse in an equitable and reasonable manner" [art. 5(1)]. The Draft Articles further require the resource be used "with a view to attaining optimal utilization thereof and benefits therefrom consistent with adequate protection of the watercourse" [art. 5(1)].

On its face, this universally accepted rule seems incontrovertible. Who would disagree with a requirement that one state only use a shared river or lake in an equitable and reasonable manner? Problems of interpretation arise however—as elsewhere in the law regarding standards of reasonableness—because of different operative contexts. Obviously, the very nature of a dispute means that one state does *not* consider another state's use "equitable" or "reasonable." In an effort to overcome this difficulty, the ILC Draft Articles require the "taking into account of all relevant factors and circumstances, including:

(a) geographic, hydrographic, hydrological, climatic, ecological, and other factors of a natural character;

(b) the social and economic needs of the watercourse States concerned;

(c) the population dependent on the watercourse in each watercourse State;

(d) the effects of the use or uses of the watercourse in one watercourse State on other watercourse States;

(e) existing and potential uses of the watercourse;

(f) conservation, protection, development and economy of use of the water resources of the watercourse and the costs of measures taken to that effect;

(g) the availability of alternatives, of corresponding value, to a particular planned or existing use."

[art. 6(1)].

These clearly remain helpful factors in backing up one's own position (country X's "social and economic needs"), but it is difficult to see how these do not equally aid an adversary's contrary position (country Y's social and economic needs). In other words the list simply offers a language in which to continue the consultations and negotiations mentioned above; it does, however, offer little in the way of proposing solutions. The real benefit is that it may keep the conversation ongoing so that a mutually advantageous political settlement will arise over time. Additionally, should an outside arbiter be brought into the picture, that arbiter may use the listed factors to validate its own interpretation of "reasonableness."

One might also notice the dearth of environmental factors in the list of those factors relevant to equitable and reasonable utilization. This lack is presumably balanced by the duty not to cause transboundary harm [art. 7] and the provisions against ecosystem destruction [art. 20] and pollution [art. 21]. The limited voice given to environmental factors in ascertaining equitable utilization, however, does show the continuing tension between development and environmental protection—a tension the ILC can only attempt to broker and not to resolve through the Draft Articles.

(c) Obligation Not to Cause Transboundary Harm

Like the rule of equitable utilization, the rule against causing transboundary harm has long been established for international watercourses. As early as 1937, in the case of the Diversion of Water from the River Meuse (Netherlands v. Belgium), 1937 P.C.I.J. (Ser. A/B) No. 70, at 4, the PCIJ formulated the general rule that "each of the two states is at liberty, in its own territory, to modify them [canals], to enlarge them, to transform them, to fill them in and even to increase the volume of water in them from new sources," provided that the discharge of water outside their respective territories remained at a normal level. This, of course, is an early formulation of Principle 2 of the 1992 Rio Declaration, which asserts that "States have ... the sovereign right to exploit their own resources ... and the responsibility to ensure that activities within their jurisdiction or control do not cause damage to the environment of other States."

The most recent codification in the ILC Draft Articles makes clear that the harm must be "significant" harm, and places a duty of due diligence upon watercourse states not to cause such harm. [art. 7(1)]. The difficulty—which has long plagued the ILC—is determining the proper relationship between equitable utilization [art. 5] and the no-significant-harm rule [art. 7]. What happens if the two rules come into conflict? Suppose, for example, a perceived equitable utilization in State A—such as a municipal power plant—causes significant harm to the watercourse in State B despite State A's diligent efforts to prevent that harm? The ILC offers this solution:

(d) Obligation Not to Cause Significant Harm

1. Watercourse States shall exercise due diligence to utilize an international watercourse in such a way as not to cause significant harm to other watercourse States.

2. Where, despite the exercise of due diligence, significant harm is caused to another watercourse State, the State whose use causes the harm shall, in the absence of agreement to such use, consult with the State suffering such harm over:

(a) the extent to which such use has proved equitable and reasonable taking into account the factors listed in article 6;

(b) the question of ad hoc adjustments to its utilization, designed to eliminate or mitigate any such harm caused and, where appropriate, the question of compensation.

ILC Draft Articles art. 7.

And the ILC backs this up with a further condition:

In the event of a conflict between uses of an international watercourse, it shall be resolved with reference to the principles and factors set out in articles 5 to 7, with special regard being given to the requirements of vital human needs.

ILC Draft Articles art. 10(2).

Obviously, the ILC does not convey an unequivocal priority of either rule but does soften the absolute prohibition against the causing of transboundary harm. In fact, the ILC stresses an ad hoc consultative resolution of such conflicts, which follows the trend in state practice toward negotiated settlement of such disputes. Taking the articles together, we might suggest a new formulation of the customary rule: a use is not *per se* violative of international law if it causes significant transboundary harm, as long as the use is equitable and reasonable, and the parties involved have conducted informed consultations on the matter.

Skeptics, of course, might maintain that the ILC simply offers another level of "reasonable" action in article 7—in effect a tautology which attempts to balance reasonable harm against reasonable use, all in the name of reasonableness. But to be fair the ILC has committed itself to promoting dialogue when conflicts do arise among watercourse states. It has not attempted to lay down the law rigidly with regard to specific and highly contextual problems, but instead has opted for an ongoing conversation among disputants. As long as the conversation is maintained, so the ILC seems correctly to believe, the chance for a political solution to a problem exists.

(d) Further Protections

The ILC Draft Articles provide a number of additional obligations for watercourse states which, unlike the basic rules regarding communication, equitable utilization and the duty not to cause transboundary harm, do not so clearly follow state practice. As such, these may be seen as part of the "progressive development of the law," or at least as obligations less universally recognized as examples of customary international law. These include: (1) the duty to protect and preserve ecosystems of international watercourses [art. 20]; (2) the duty to harmonize pollution prevention policies [art. 21(2)]; and (3) the duty to take all appropriate measures to prevent or mitigate conditions that may be harmful to other watercourse states, such as flood or ice conditions, water-borne diseases, siltation, erosion, salt-water intrusion, drought or desertification [art. 27]. The last duty (3), though moderated by the qualifier "as appropriate," especially expands the traditional no-significant-harm rule by holding states responsible for both natural and human causes of potential harm [art. 27].

(e) The Question of Groundwater

The ILC has long debated whether to include all types of transboundary groundwaters within the scope of the Draft Articles. As it stands, "[w]atercourse means a system of surface waters and groundwaters constituting by virtue of their physical relationship a unitary whole and normally flowing into a common terminus" [art. 2(b)]. Thus the 1994 Draft Articles exclude so-called "unrelated confined groundwaters" which by definition do not flow into a common terminus.

Though in 1994 the Special Rapporteur strongly recommended the deletion of the phrase "flowing into a common terminus" and therefore the inclusion of confined transboundary groundwaters, the Commission as a whole rejected the proposal. For his part the Special Rapporteur maintained that the

ILC should include these transboundary waters to "encourage their management in a rational manner and prevent their depletion and pollution." The Commission, on the other hand, remained reluctant to extend the scope of its work because the Draft Articles had not been formulated with confined aquifers in mind. Instead, as a compromise the ILC adopted a resolution stating its "view that the principles contained in its draft articles ... may be applied to transboundary confined groundwater." In 1986 the ILA reached a similar but more sweeping conclusion, allowing confined groundwaters within the definition of an "international drainage basin" and thus within the regulations of the 1966 Helsinki Rules. Given these two pronouncements, one may with new confidence extrapolate the rules regarding international watercourses to the special situation of confined transboundary groundwaters.

2.   REGIONAL AND BILATERAL AGREEMENTS

Though the United Nations has stated its resolve to create a global convention concerning the uses of transboundary watercourses based on the work of the ILC, as yet no such agreement has been negotiated. Over the years, however, a number of regional and bilateral arrangements have developed providing an extensive body of state practice. We have tried to highlight those most important to our prospective readers, but one should be aware that a long list of such agreements now exists. Among the agreements negotiated but not covered here include those for Lake Constance, the River Danube, the River Elbe, the Niger Basin and the Zambezi River System.

(a) 1992 ECE Convention on the Protection and Use of Transboundary Watercourses and Lakes (ECE Treaty)

The United Nations Economic Commission for Europe (ECE) recently codified basic regional rules for the protection and use of transboundary watercourses. The ECE Treaty, March 17, 1992, 31 I.L.M. 1312 (not in force) incorporates much of the customary law discussed above, while further developing the law by affirming the precautionary principle, the polluter pays principle and environmental impact assessments. Entry into force of this convention appears imminent as of this writing, and signatories include most industrialized nations of the Northern Hemisphere except the United States, Canada and Japan.

The treaty defines "transboundary waters" to mean "any surface waters or ground waters which mark, cross or are located on boundaries between two or more States" [art. 1(1)]. As such, the treaty provides broader coverage than the ILC Draft Articles, which do not officially include isolated or "unrelated" groundwaters (see above). The treaty also contains a broad definition of "transboundary impact" as meaning "any significant adverse effect on the environment" including "effects on human health and safety, flora, fauna, soil, air, water,

climate, landscape and historical monuments ...
[and] effects on the cultural heritage or socio-economic conditions" [art. 1(2)].

Part I of the convention describes the provision relating to all parties, not just riparian parties, and creates the affirmative duty to take all appropriate measures to "prevent, control and reduce any transboundary impact" [art. 2(1)]. Clearly, this would preclude an upstream state from reducing the water supply to a downstream state if such a reduction would cause significant harm. More specifically, the parties must prevent, control and reduce pollution, and ensure not only the conservation of water resources but also the conservation and restoration of ecosystems [art. 2(2)]. In guiding the obligations of the parties, the treaty also strongly affirms the concept of sustainable development.

Following customary law, the convention also imposes a duty of equitable and reasonable utilization for international watercourses. As discussed above, this principle is firmly ensconced in international law. The ECE treaty, however—as in the 1994 ILC Draft Articles—loosens the absolute prohibition against the causing of transboundary impact—in effect appearing to allow some transboundary harm perpetrated by an equitable use.

The Parties shall, in particular, take all appropriate measures:

To ensure that transboundary waters are used in a reasonable and equitable way, taking into particular account their transboundary character, in the case of activities which cause or are likely to cause transboundary impact.

ECE Treaty art. 2(2)(c).

As the ECE Treaty and the 1994 ILC Draft Articles remain the most recent and important pronouncements on the issue, we repeat again our new understanding of the customary rule: a use is not *per se* violative of international law if it causes significant transboundary harm, as long as the use is equitable and reasonable, and the parties involved have conducted informed consultations on the matter.

Balanced against the heightened profile of equitable utilization is a detailed enumeration of obligations to prevent, control and reduce transboundary impact. Among these is the requirement that each party set emission limits for discharges from point sources based on "best available technology" (BAT), and that the parties specifically tailor these limits to individual industrial sectors [art. 3(2)]. For diffuse sources, particularly from agriculture, the parties must develop and implement "best environmental practices" (BEP) to reduce the inputs of nutrients and hazardous substances [art. 3(1)(g)]. To aid in the formulation of both types of controls, the treaty defines BAT in Annex I and provides guidelines of developing BEP in Annex II. The treaty further requires parties to define water quality objectives and to adopt water-quality criteria [art. 3(3)], supplying guidelines for these actions in Annex III. As an additional general duty, parties must undertake environmental impact assessments to gauge any future level of harm [art. 3(1)(h)].

In Part II, the ECE Treaty more specifically focuses on the duties of riparian parties, especially emphasizing the need for cooperation. Riparian parties, if they have not already done so, are required to enter into bilateral or multilateral agreements in order to prevent, control and reduce transboundary impact [art. 9(1)]. These agreements must provide for the establishment of "joint bodies" to administer the agreement [art. 9(2)]. A joint body thus acts as the mechanism through which the parties can discharge numerous duties, including joint monitoring and assessment, exchange of information, and the establishment of warning and alarm procedures [art. 9(2)].

Regarding the standard customary obligations of notification and consultation, the treaty mandates that consultations be held in good faith at the request of any riparian party [art. 10], and that each country give prompt notification concerning "any critical situation that may have transboundary impact" [art. 14]. Going beyond custom, the convention also requires that riparian parties provide mutual assistance upon request should a critical situation arise [art. 15].

(b) The Rhine

The Rhine River regime offers an example of long-term regional cooperation with regard to an international watercourse. As early as 1950, the riparian European nations of the Rhine created an international commission to oversee the waterway, and in 1963 reformed that institution in the Agreement Concerning the International Commission for the Protection of the Rhine Against Pollution, (1963 Berne Convention), Apr. 23, 1963, 994 U.N.T.S. 3, (entered into force May 1, 1965). Under this agreement the primary function of the International Commission was to research the river's pollution problems and offer guidelines for improvement. Only in 1976, however, did the riparian parties more effectively attempt to arrive at solutions.

In that year the parties amended the 1963 agreement and created two more treaties—the Convention for the Protection of the Rhine against Chemical Pollution (Rhine Chemicals Convention) 1124 U.N.T.S. 375 (entered into force Feb. 1, 1979) and the Convention for the Protection of the Rhine against Pollution by Chlorides (Rhine Chlorides Convention), Dec. 3, 1976, 16 I.L.M. 265 (entered into force July 5, 1985). The Rhine Chemicals Convention is more general and mixes international and national controls.

The Rhine Chemicals Convention, for example, mandates that the parties gradually eliminate the discharge of dangerous substances listed in Annex I, and reduce the discharge of less dangerous substances listed in Annex II [art. 1]. The parties must also draw up a national list of all Annex I substances discharged into the river [art. 2], and must grant prior national approval for any such discharge [art. 3]. In granting approval the national authority must specify emission standards that do not exceed the limits proposed by the International Commission [art. 3(2)]. Any discharge of Annex II substances must also receive prior authorization, but the emission standards are to be established by the national authorities and not the International Commission [art. 6]. Finally, as is widely noted, though the convention contains a provision requiring immediate notification of the commission and affected parties in case of an accident [art. 11], the Swiss government failed to provide timely notice to either following a devastating fire at its Sandoz facility in 1986. The toxic effluent from this accident caused widespread damage to the entire ecosystem of the Rhine and led to the creation of the Rhine Action Programme in 1987 (discussed below).

The Rhine Chlorides Convention more specifically attempts to control pollution of the river by chloride ions. This convention has recently been supplemented by a 1991 protocol, which further strengthens the obligations of the parties. As it stands, each party is allocated certain discharge limits as set out in Annex IV under the protocol. The strongest measures apply to France, which must reduce its discharges where these exceed 200 milligrams per litre at the Netherlands–Germany border. The excess is to be stored on land and later discharged into the Rhine, pending favorable environmental conditions. The convention and recent protocol also provide for cost-sharing with regard to the major obligations of the parties, with percentage shares give to France, Germany, the Netherlands and the Swiss Confederation. Driving the measures of the new protocol is the 1987 Rhine Action Programme, which was adopted in the aftermath of the Sandoz incident. Though not a treaty, the Action Programme establishes as objectives: (1) the restoration of the ecosystem so as to accommodate the return of higher species; (2) the maintenance of the river as a source of drinking water supplies; and (3) the further reduction of pollution by harmful substances. The 1987 Rhine Action Programme hopes to achieve these objectives by the turn of the century.

(c) United States—Canada

A very early example of cooperation by nations with regard to shared water resources is provided by the United States and Canada. The 1909 Treaty Between the United States and Great Britain Relating to Boundary Waters, and Questions Arising between the United States and Canada (1909 Boundary Waters Treaty), Jan. 11, 1909, X I.P.E. 5158 (entered into force May 5, 1910) deals primarily with issues of navigation, the construction of dams and other diversion projects. Importantly, however, this 1909 treaty also states that the "waters flowing across the boundary shall not be polluted on either side to the injury of health or property of the other" [art. IV]. As such, the document provides one of the earliest treaty commitments to control environmental pollution in international law.

The 1909 Boundary Waters Treaty also establishes the International Joint Commission (IJC) which is composed of six commissioners—three each from the United States and Canada [art. VII]. The IJC must approve any uses, obstructions or diversions that change the level or flow of the boundary waters [art. III]. The IJC additionally acts as both an informal and formal arbiter of disputes, with the power to administer oaths and subpoena witnesses [arts. IX–XIII].

The Agreement Between the United States and Canada on the Water Quality of the Great Lakes (1978 Great Lakes Water Quality Agreement), Nov. 22, 1978, 30 U.S.T. 1383 as amended by protocol in 1987, further expands both the duties of the parties and those of the IJC. The agreement is quite detailed, with numerous annexes and appendices, and creates "General" as well as "Specific Objectives." As "General Objectives," the parties agree that the Great Lakes System should be free from substances or materials that interfere with beneficial uses and/or cause harm to human, animal or aquatic life [art. III]. So as to meet these goals, the treaty provides for "Specific Objectives" which "represent the minimum levels of water quality" for the Great Lakes System [art. IV]. These are set out in Annex 1 and mandate numerical concentration values for Persistent Toxic Substances, such as pesticides and metals, defined as any substance which has a half-life in water of greater that 8 weeks.

Augmenting the General and Specific Objectives, the 1978 Great Lakes Water Quality Agreement requires both parties to develop and implement programs and measures covering a range of problems. The requirements of these provisions are then further detailed in accompanying annexes. As such, the parties must develop programs and measures to combat pollution from municipal sources, industrial sources, non-point sources, shipping activities, dredging activities, off-shore facilities, contaminated sediments and contaminated groundwater and sub-surface waters [art. VI]. In addition, the parties must reduce and control inputs of phosphorous and other nutrients which cause eutrophication, as well as other hazardous polluting substances [art. VI]. Emphasizing the ecosystem approach to coordinated action, the treaty further requires the parties to develop and implement both Remedial Action Plans and Lakewide Management Plans [art. VI].

To administer and oversee these obligations, the 1978 Great Lakes Water Quality Agreement places more responsibilities on the IJC. Now backed up by a Water Quality Board and a Science Advisory Board, the IJC must analyze and distribute information relating to both water quality in the Great Lakes System and to pollution entering the system from outside waters [art. VII]. The IJC must also collect and analyze information concerning the General and Specific Objectives and the efficacy of adopted programs [art. VII]. To this end, the IJC is asked to provide biennial reports detailing its assessments, advice and recommendations [art. VII]. The treaty also provides the IJC with the authority to verify independently the data and other information submitted by the parties [art. VII].

To date, the parties remain far removed from achieving the ultimate goals of their General Objectives. However, the treaty regime does create a sophisticated machinery with which to engage the difficult environmental problems of this heavily industrialized region.

(d) United States—Mexico

Another longstanding relationship of cooperation regarding transboundary waters exists between the United States and Mexico. Treaties drawn in the 1880s deal with navigation, and in this century the two countries signed the 1944 Treaty between the United States and Mexico Relative to the Utilization of Waters of Colorado and Tijuana Rivers and of the Rio Grande from Fort Quitman to the Gulf of Mexico (1944 Colorado River Treaty), Feb. 3, 1944, 3 U.N.T.S. 314. This treaty considers utilization issues such as apportionment, dam construction and flood control. The treaty also establishes the International Boundary and Water Commission (IBWC) (formerly known as the International Boundary Commission by 1889 treaty), and endows this body with a number of powers and duties. These include investigating and developing plans for construction works, overseeing the respective obligations of apportionment, and resolving any disputes between the parties [art. 24]. In addition, in making specific suggestions regarding improvements to the waterways, the Commission proposes official instruments known as "Minutes" that the parties adopt through diplomatic process. In formalizing a Minute, the IBWC publicly announces a written recommendation and the governments then bind themselves to that recommendation through an exchange of diplomatic Notes. An important example of these is Minute No.242 (1973) which establishes specific responsibilities for both parties regarding the salinity of the Colorado River.

Though the 1944 Colorado River Treaty does require the IBWC "to give preferential attention to the solution of all border sanitation problems" in providing for joint use of the international waters [art. 3], this mandate by itself proved insufficient in protecting the common environment. To address this need more adequately, the parties adopted the 1983 Mexico—United States Agreement to Co-operate in the Solution of Environmental Problems in the Border Area (1983 La Paz Agreement), Aug. 14, 1983, 22 I.L.M. 1025. This agreement commits the two parties to cooperation in the field of environmental protection and conservation in the border area, obligating that they "undertake, to the fullest extent practical, to adopt the appropriate measures to prevent, reduce and eliminate sources of pollution" [art. 1]. To this end the parties conclude annexes that specify more detailed obligations, such as Annex I concerning the San Diego—Tijuana water sanitation problem. Annex I, the only addendum dealing exclusively with water pollution, requires that the parties continue appropriate consultations with regard to the construction, operation and maintenance of disposal and treatment facilities.

Recently the North American Free Trade Agreement (NAFTA) and its progeny, the North American Agreement on Environmental Cooperation between the United States, Canada and Mexico (1993 Environmental Side Agreement), Sept. 14, 1993, 32 I.L.M. 1480, have prompted more extensive cooperation regarding transboundary water resources. The latter document—in addition to restating general objectives of environmental protection—establishes a Commission for Environmental Cooperation (CEC) that oversees the environmental status of the three North American countries. The Council of the CEC considers and develops recommendations concerning pollution prevention techniques, conservation and other transboundary environmental issues [art. 10]. Building on the goals and objectives of the Environmental Side Agreement, Mexico and the United States also created the Border Environment Cooperation Commission (BECC) in 1993 [*see* Agreement Concerning the Establishment of a Border Environment Cooperation Commission and a North American Development Bank, Nov. 16, 1993, 32 I.L.M. 1545]. The BEEC works closely with the North American Development Bank and the IBWC with regard to environmental infrastructure projects, facilitating the construction and improvement of border sanitation facilities.

CHAPTER SIXTEEN

DESERTIFICATION

A. NATURE OF THE PROBLEM

Desertification refers to the process of climate change and human impacts that create desert environments in "drylands"—the arid, semi-arid, or dry sub-humid regions of the world [*see* United Nations Convention to Combat Desertification in Those Countries Experiencing Serious Drought and/or Desertification, Particularly in Africa, June 17, 1994, art. I (a) [HEREINAFTER, Desertification Convention]; Agenda 21, Ch. 12, U.N. Doc. A/CONF. 151/26 (1992)]. Drylands receive less water than forest regions but more than deserts, and are also called "plains" or "grasslands." Climate change may be caused by severe short-term droughts as well as long periods without rainfall. Human impacts arise from the removal of natural vegetation from bioregions, excessive cultivation, the exhaustion of surface water, and the mining of groundwater [4 NEW ENCYCLOPEDIA BRITANNICA 32 (1994)]. Climate change and human impacts destroy the life-supporting quality of drylands and cause erosion, loss of soil fertility, the ability to hold water, salinization of the soil and water, exhaustion of groundwater, and diminution of surface water [Agenda 21 chs. 12.2 &

12.18]. The resulting phenomenon called "desertification" is an advanced stage of land degradation in which the biological potential of the land is destroyed.

Seventy percent of the world's drylands (equal to 25 percent of the total land area of the world) have been affected by desertification. In Africa, Asia, and South America, 70 percent of the agricultural drylands have experienced degradation, and the remaining drylands are threatened. In Kenya, 85 percent of the total landmass exists in degraded condition, with the figure at 40 percent in India and 20 percent in China, respectively. Desertification has also affected 74 percent of North American agricultural drylands and 65 percent in Europe. The impacts are worse in developing nations that have scant resources for rehabilitating degraded land [*see generally* William C. Burns, *The International Convention to Combat Desertification: Drawing a Line in the Sand?*, 16 MICH. J. INT'L L. 831, 845, 848 (1995)].

B. IMPACTS OF DESERTIFICATION

Agriculture on drylands provides more than 20 percent of the world's food supply. The desertification of agricultural drylands reduces soil fertility and lessens crop yields. In Africa, agricultural production has fallen by 25–50 percent, and worldwide the financial cost of lost agricultural production is approximately $43 billion each year. When degraded, land can no longer sustain plant or animal life, and people who depend on the land are forced to migrate to urban areas or to other land. As more marginally productive land is cultivated, or used for grazing, soil degradation advances and once again people must abandon the land. The added stress on urban resources has the potential to create social unrest. In addition to the agricultural, economic, and social impacts, desertification threatens the biodiversity of ecosystems by destroying plants and critical habitat for animals [*see generally*, WORLD RESOURCES INSTITUTE, WORLD RESOURCES 1994–95, A GUIDE TO THE GLOBAL ENVIRONMENT 109–146 (1994) [HEREINAFTER WRI 1995]; *see* Chapter Five, Biodiversity].

C. CAUSES OF DESERTIFICATION

Human activities, driven by population growth, energy needs, and the lack of land have led to over-cultivation: the farming of land beyond its sustainable fertility. Population growth has demanded increased food production and encouraged the farming of marginally productive lands, and the shortening of fallow periods. Over cultivation also arises from economic pressures for revenue-generating cash crops that can be exported. These crops are usually land-intensive, nutrient-depleting and reduce the land area available for food crops. The result of over-cultivation is that drylands, naturally poor in nutrients and organic content, become more susceptible to erosion. Their topsoil is blown or washed away, exposing subsoil that is often infertile and less able to absorb water, thus leading to desertification.

One-half of the world's cattle graze in drylands [WRI 1995, at 296–7]. In developing countries, cattle are raised as a source of food for domestic consumption as well as for export. Overgrazing occurs when land shortages lead to the unsustainable pasturing of livestock. This leads to the loss of vegetation and the replacement of desirable plants such as grasses (which help hold the soil) with shrubs. At the same time, the pulverizing and compacting of soil by cattle hooves leads to soil erosion.

Deforestation exists as another cause of desertification. Forests are cleared in order to provide firewood—an important source of fuel in many developing countries—as well as for crop cultivation and livestock grazing. In developing countries, 90 percent of the population relies exclusively on wood for cooking and heating. The phenomenon of deforestation is most severe in Asia, the Middle East, and Africa, with 90 percent of the forests cleared in Ethiopia and Sudan alone. Often, deforestation acts as a starting point for desertification because destroyed tree and plant roots no longer hold the soil together or provide organic material that fertilizes soil, thereby increasing its water absorbent qualities.

In addition to over-cultivation, irrigation practices that do not properly drain the soil cause the accumulation of salts (salinization) that reduce soil fertility and stunt plant growth. Salinization of irrigated crop land is a serious problem not only in Asia and the Middle East, but also in North America. Salinity of the Colorado River from irrigation practices in the western United States has caused serious land degradation in California and Mexico [*see generally* NEW COURSES FOR THE COLORADO RIVER (Gary D. Weatherford & F. Lee Brown eds., 1986)]. The United States—in order to fulfil its international obligations to Mexico—has built a $260 million desalinization plant, and improved its irrigation practices by lining water canals to reduce salt accumulation (*see* Chapter Twelve, Transboundary Water Pollution).

Some social policies are more responsible for desertification than others. For example, many nations with severe desertification problems have land ownership and tenure systems that do not provide security of tenure for the farmers and ranchers who work the land. Consequently, these groups find no incentives to conserve land or water. Furthermore, some developing nations have encouraged farmers to clear and settle in forests as a means of asserting national sovereignty over native tribes and as a means of appeasing demands for land ownership reform.

D. REMEDIAL OBJECTIVES

Desertification raises questions common to other international environmental problems, and must be addressed within the conceptual framework of sustainable development. In 1992, the United Nations

Conference on Environment and Development ("Earth Summit" or UNCED) adopted Agenda 21, a program for sustainable development, which recommended preventive measures for threatened or slightly degraded drylands and rehabilitative measures for moderately or severely degraded drylands. Recommended activities included improved land- and water-use policies, improved agricultural and ranching technologies, soil and water conservation to restore and sustain productivity, reforestation, protection of special ecological areas, and development of alternative energy sources [Agenda 21 ch. 12]. In 1994, the Desertification Convention, the primary international agreement addressing desertification, was signed by 86 nations. By November 12, 1996, 123 nations had signed the Convention, and it had been ratified by 55 of the signatories.

E. LEGAL RESPONSE

The Desertification Convention, which is expected to come into force in 1997, adopts an innovative "bottom-up" approach to an increasingly destructive environmental problem. The convention defines desertification as "[l]and degradation in arid, semi-arid and dry sub-humid areas, resulting from various factors, including climatic variations and human activities" [art. 1(a)]. In other words, desertification is not—as is often misunderstood—the expansion of existing deserts. The convention places significant emphasis on the human role in creating desertification, identifying causation as a "complex interaction among physical, biological, political, social, cultural and economic factors" [pmbl]. Drought, on the other hand, means the naturally occurring phenomenon brought about by below normal precipitation [art. 1(c)].

The convention seeks to combat desertification and to mitigate the effects of drought, with the goal of promoting sustainable development in affected areas [art. 2(1)]. The emphasis remains on Africa where the problem is seen as most acute, but the Convention contains four Regional Implementation Annexes (RIAs) that also spell out specific provisions for the Northern Mediterranean region, Latin American—the Caribbean, and Asia. Nonetheless, while requiring cooperation and coordination at the sub-regional, regional and international levels, the convention also establishes a strong mandate to involve local communities both in the decision-making and implementation processes. This dedication to a "bottom-up" approach reflects a growing consensus that only a decentralized strategy will work to control environmental degradation, a strategy that includes and rewards local people.

1. COMMITMENTS

(a) Developing Countries

For their part, affected developing country parties must prepare and implement National Action Programmes (NAPs) that seek to meet the objectives of the convention. The purpose of each NAP is to identify the factors causing desertification, as well as practical measures that might ameliorate both desertification and drought [art. 10(1)]. In creating a long-term plan, each developing country must specify the roles of government, local communities and landowners, while also allowing for changing circumstances at the local level [art. 10(2)]. Furthermore, each NAP must provide for participation by Non–Governmental Organizations (NGOs) and "[l]ocal populations, both women and men, particularly resource users, including farmers and pastoralists" at all levels of the decision-making and implementation processes [art. 10(2)(f)]. In the African RIA, the convention notes the necessity of adopting an approach which takes into account the particular conditions of that region, including severe land degradation and poor socio-economic circumstances [art. 3]. In fact, echoing the convention itself at article 4(2)(c), that annex requires African country parties, in accordance with their respective abilities, to "adopt the combating of desertification and/or the mitigation of the effects of drought as a central strategy in their efforts to eradicate poverty" [art. 4(1)(a)].

In addition to the creation of individual NAPs, the convention requires affected country parties to consult and cooperate, as appropriate, in the development of sub-regional and regional action programmes [art. 11]. The African RIA elaborates on these obligations, requiring, among other things, that affected parties establish sub-regional mechanisms both to manage shared natural resources and to deal with transboundary environmental problems

[African RIA art. 11]. At the regional level, the African RIA requires a further action programme that promotes regional cooperation through regular consultations, focusing particularly on capacity-building and the development and exchange of scientific and technological information [art. 13].

At every level, the convention sees the creation of partnership agreements as a means of elaborating and implementing the required action programs [arts. 9(3) & 14]. At the earliest juncture, developing countries should therefore seek the cooperation and involvement of developed countries, intergovernmental organizations and NGOs. In the African RIA these partnership agreements should include both financial and technical assistance, whether attached to national, sub-regional or regional action programmes [art. 18]. In this way the Desertification Convention—again in a "bottom-up" approach that begins at the field level—attempts to create a decentralized system of cooperation and commitment, involving a wide range of prospective donors at the first stages of design.

(b) Developed Countries

The primary obligations of developed country parties remain the transfer of financial resources and technical assistance to developing countries [art. 6]. This means early involvement in partnership agreements, with a focus on addressing the physical, biological *and socio-economic* aspects of the problem [art. 4]. As stated above, fulfillment of these obligations includes strategies for the eradication of poverty in the affected countries [art. 4(2)(c)]. The African RIA further elaborates on these general requirements, while also promoting institutional capacity-building in the areas of administration, science and technology [art. 5].

As with all international environmental regimes, the success of the Desertification Convention rides on tangible contributions from the wealthier parties. Through partnership agreements, this treaty offers a way for developed countries to get involved early, and to monitor the real effectiveness of their donations.

CHAPTER SEVENTEEN

NUCLEAR DAMAGE

A. NATURE OF THE PROBLEM

The military use of nuclear bombs can lead to unparalleled suffering. Civilian deployment of nuclear energy endeavors to turn swords into ploughshares while confronting the risk posed by radiation arising from military and civilian uses. Consequently, this chapter deals with military weapons production, use, and testing—and civilian nuclear energy applications such as power generation, medical uses, and nuclear waste disposal [*see generally,* THE LEAGUE OF WOMEN VOTERS EDUCATION FUND, THE NUCLEAR WASTE PRIMER (1993)].

Radiation is a form of energy consisting of atomic particles and electromagnetic rays that are emitted from radioactive elements, such as uranium and plutonium [DIXY RAY & LOU GUZZO, TRASHING THE PLANET 97 (1990)]. When radiation strikes human tissue, it strips (ionizes) electrons or neutrons of the molecules and atoms and thereby kills or damages human cells. The nature of the harm depends on the type and intensity of the radiation and the part of the body that is exposed. High-level (high intensity) radiation kills cells, and can cause excruciating radiation sickness and death within days or weeks.

In contrast, low-level radiation only damages cells, allowing them to multiply, but the damaged cells may produce cancers and genetic defects years later.

The danger of exposure to radiation arises both from military and civilian uses of nuclear power. While only 2% of the total radiation exposure of an average person living in the United States is attributed to nuclear weapons and power generation (82% is from natural background radiation from the earth and outer space and 16% is from medical uses), the potential exists for catastrophic exposure [The Nuclear Waste Primer 11–12]. In addition to the threat of mass destruction posed by the military use of a nuclear bomb, or a less catastrophic but nonetheless devastating accident in a nuclear power plant, high-level nuclear wastes remain radioactive for thousands of years constituting a major problem.

1.   USE AND TESTING OF NUCLEAR WEAPONS

The devastation caused by the military use of a nuclear bomb arises from: an intensive thermal wave; a blast that causes destructive "shock waves"; initial or "prompt" nuclear radiation; and residual or "delayed" nuclear radiation [see John Harte et al., Toxics A to Z 153–154 (1991); Legality of the Threat or Use of Nuclear Weapons, 1996 I.C.J. No. 95 (July 8)]. Many of the casualties are caused by burns from the thermal wave—a "fireball" of dust and hot gases. Then, as the gases expand, a blast or "shock wave" moves out from the fireball, toppling buildings and causing impact injuries that account for the preponderance of structural damage.

Radiation exposure has two phases. Massive initial or "prompt" nuclear radiation is released during the first minute consisting of particles released by the nuclear reactions that power the weapon, and of X-rays that irradiated air molecules produce almost instantaneously. Prompt radiation is strongest at "ground zero" (the point on the earth's surface immediately below where the bomb explodes) and decreases as the radiation emanates out in a radius around ground zero. Second, radiation released during the first minute ionizes particles of rock, soil, and other materials from the earth's surface that are caught up in the fireball. These ionized materials become "fallout," which is carried for many miles downwind of the explosion, to an area much larger than that exposed to the initial radiation.

Fallout that reaches the ground in the first 24 hours is highly radioactive and can kill. Delayed fallout is often not highly radioactive and may not reach the ground for several years, but still can cause long-term radiation damage. The radioactive particles deposited on the soil from fallout are taken up by plants, which are then consumed by humans or by livestock that provide milk and meat for human consumption. Furthermore, fallout that contaminates surface water may become concentrated in fish and seafood, which might be eaten by humans.

The explosion of numerous powerful nuclear weapons could produce global environmental problems and climatic changes. Edible plants, livestock, and marine food sources could be destroyed or become contaminated, resulting in severe food shortages. Water could be contaminated by radioactivity and by pathogenic bacteria and viruses if sewage treatment and waste disposal facilities are destroyed by the initial explosions. Crop failures may also result from "nuclear winters" caused by the accumulation of soot in the atmosphere from explosion induced fires. Finally, the ozone layer may be damaged by nitrogen oxides released by fires caused by the bomb [see JOHN HARTE ET AL., TOXICS A TO Z 153 (1991)]. As we have seen any damage to the ozone layer will expose the earth to harmful ultraviolet radiation (Chapter Seven, Ozone Depletion).

Since 1945, there have been more than 2,000 nuclear test explosions, primarily underground but also in the atmosphere and underwater. Both the United States and the Soviets conducted nuclear weapons tests in sparsely populated areas within their own borders—as well as without [Stewart L. Udall, *Radiation Nightmare of '50s Guinea Pigs, in* THE ARIZONA REPUBLIC, May 22, 1994, at C1, *available in Westlaw*, File No. 1994 WL 6407671 (noting AEC explosions in Nevada in 1953)]. However, radioactive fallout from above-ground explosions cannot be contained within borders, but rather extends hundreds of miles downwind.

Underground testing also has potentially harmful effects on health and the environment. For example, at the Nevada Test Site, the underground nuclear tests have caused serious radioactive contamination of the groundwater and soil [Danette L. Bloomer, Comment, *Beyond Our Own Backyard: Considering the Legal Implications and Environmental Risks of Importing Spent Nuclear Fuel,* 10 J. ENVTL. L. & LITIG. 157, 184 (1995)]. At French test sites in the South Pacific, underground nuclear testing on atolls has produced fissures in the basalt bases, subsidence, and submarine slides that create fears of a massive release of radioactive debris from further testing and concern about long-term containment of radioactive materials underground [*French Nuclear Testing and the South Pacific Nuclear Free Zone, House Committee on International Relations Subcommittee on Asia and the Pacific* (Nov. 15, 1995) (testimony prepared by Joshua Handler & Thomas W. Clements, Greenpeace), *available in Westlaw,* 1995 WL 12715828]. Water and plankton samples taken downstream from the atolls indicate that radiation may already be leaking.

2. CIVILIAN NUCLEAR ENERGY

The generation of power from nuclear energy amounts to 17% of the electric power generated in the world. In a nuclear power reactor, the chain reaction is controlled to prevent an explosion, using the controlled released of heat to generate power.

The risks created by civilian nuclear power generation arise: a) during the operation of power plants;
b) by accidents; and c) from waste disposal.

The routine operation of nuclear power plants
generates radioactive materials in the form of
stack gases, as well as radioactive liquid effluent.
The International Atomic Energy Agency (IAEA)
has issued standards, regulations, codes of practice, guides and other related instruments dealing
with operational safety. Unfortunately, these are
voluntary not obligatory standards. The continuing
absence of universal standards of safety in the operation of nuclear power plants accentuates the
dangers of accidents.

Unintentional releases of nuclear radiation, such
as occurred at Three Mile Island and Chernobyl,
[see generally SHEPARD BUCHANAN, ET AL., ENVIRONMEN-
TAL COSTS OF ELECTRICITY (1991)] illustrate the perils
of civilian nuclear use. The Chernobyl accident in
the former Soviet Union, in which a meltdown
caused an explosion and massive release of radiation, was the most serious nuclear power reactor
accident ever to occur. Within two months of the
accident, 31 people had died from severe radiation
burns. For the long-term, the United States Department of Energy estimates that the health effects of
the Chernobyl accident on people in the northern
hemisphere will include an additional 28,000 cancer
deaths, 700 additional children born with severe
mental retardation in the next generation, and
1,900 additional children born with genetic disorders.

The meltdown during the Three Mile Island accident in the United States did not result in an explosion, and the amount of radiation released was far less than at Chernobyl. Yet, abnormal radiation was detected 250 miles from the power plant and in Wales, England.

Because reactor design and operation vary with time and among countries, the accuracy of estimating the probability of a serious accident that would release a significant amount of radiation is disputed. However, the Nuclear Regulatory Commission has estimated that the probability of a severe accident at a United States reactor is 1 in 3333 each year.

3. NUCLEAR WASTE

Nuclear wastes are the by-products of nuclear weapons production, nuclear power generation, medical and dental uses, research, and other processes using radioactive elements. By volume, 99% of nuclear waste emits a low level of radiation. Low-level radioactive waste by definition is solid, and has usually been disposed of by packaging in leak-resistant containers and burying in shallow trenches. This poses potential environmental problems if the radioactive contamination leaks from the waste repository. Disposal sites may have hydrological problems—such as erosion, accumulation of water in the trenches, and groundwater movement—that would allow the radiation to contaminate water and food supplies. Contaminated groundwater is the most common pathway for exposure to radiation from nuclear waste. Some low-level waste has also been disposed of at sea by both the United States and the Soviets [Jeffrey L. Canfield, *Soviet and Russian Nuclear Waste Dumping in the Arctic Marine Environment: Legal, Historical, and Political Implications*, 7 GEO. INT'L ENVTL. L. REV. 353 (1994)].

Nuclear weapons production requires plutonium which is made and then extracted from the fuel of military production reactors, leaving large quantities of highly radioactive liquid waste. Nuclear power plant fuel is replaced about once a year and the highly radioactive spent fuel rods are temporarily stored at the power plants to cool down in large ponds of water [*see* JOHN HARTE ET AL., TOXICS A TO Z 162–3 (1991)]. These high-level nuclear wastes will remain radioactive for thousands of years. Two methods of long-term storage of such high-level waste are repositories in deep geologic formations and ocean dumping [*see* RONNIE D. LIPSCHUTZ, RADIOACTIVE WASTE: POLITICS, TECHNOLOGY, AND RISK (1980); *see also* Chapter Nine, Toxic and Hazardous Substances]. With both methods, the concern is the possible effect of radioactive waste leaks and the effects of decay heat on the surrounding environment. Permanent, land-based nuclear storage sites will not be ready in the United States or Russia until after the year 2010.

B. REMEDIAL OBJECTIVES

The destruction caused by nuclear damage was underlined by the recent Advisory Opinion of the

ICJ on the Legality of the Threat or Use of Nuclear Weapons, 1996 I.C.J. No. 95 (July 8) (Legality of Nuclear Weapons case). The court stated: "Nuclear weapons which cannot be contained in either space or time have the potential to destroy all civilization and the entire ecosystem of the planet."

There are many ways of trying to avoid such potential destructions. The most obvious and most difficult is to remove the source of such destructive pollution by banning nuclear weapons all together. In the Legality of Nuclear Weapons case, the I.C.J. appeared to endorse such a view by holding that nations of the world are under a legal obligation to pursue and conclude negotiations with a view to achieving nuclear disarmament. The political problems confronting such a course are formidable. Two merit brief mention. First, nuclear weapons have maintained the peace during the post-Cold War era for over 50 years. Nuclear deterrence and the balance of terror have been the linchpins of Western defense policy. Second, the most powerful nations of the world possess nuclear weapons and may be loathe to give them up.

The cold war and the "balance of terror" based upon nuclear deterrence protected the military use of nuclear weapons, and the environmental devastation they cause, from scrutiny for over half a century. However, the end of the cold war has accelerated a sequence of unfolding conventional (treaty) and judicial developments of great importance. These continuing changes, in the view of many commentators, have transformed the mirage of a nuclear weapons free world into a foreseeable objective. Alternatives to total nuclear disarmament include the non-proliferation of nuclear weapons and the banning of any further nuclear tests. These measures, and even total nuclear disarmament, still leave us with the problem of what to do with the huge quantities of existing nuclear wastes.

In the realm of civilian nuclear energy, an important question is the extent to which preventative and remedial legal responses have been successful. A preventative regime seeks to regulate the construction and operation of nuclear plants in a way that prevents pollution and accidents. It also provides for a system of warning and assistance if accidents do occur. At present the IAEA is not empowered to impose obligatory international safety standards for reactor construction or operations. A remedial regime facilitates the granting of compensation when damages have been caused. The details of how the international community has responded legally are now discussed more fully.

C. LEGAL RESPONSE

As the dangers of nuclear pollution have gradually become more apparent over the years, the international community has struggled to develop rules governing both the civilian and military uses of nuclear energy. In this section of the book, we have first attempted to outline how the international community has addressed the intractable challenge of nuclear weapons, despite formidable political difficulties. We next outline the response of IEL to the dangers of civilian nuclear power generation. Finally, we discuss the regime governing accidents at nuclear installations and the question of liability.

1. USE AND TESTING OF NUCLEAR WEAPONS

(a) Treaty Overlay

The first steps toward nuclear disarmament were taken by the arms control treaties. The United Soviet Socialist Republics—United States: Treaty on the Elimination of Their Intermediate–Range and Shorter–Range Missiles, Dec. 8, 1987, 27 I.L.M. 84 dealt with the reduction of nuclear missiles, while the Strategic Arms Reduction Talks (START) led to the Treaty on the Reduction and Elimination of Strategic Offensive Arms, Nov. 25, 1991, 32 I.L.M. 246 which reduced the awesome nuclear arsenal of the USA and Russia. Second, a cluster of treaties addressed the testing, deployment, possession and use of nuclear weapons in a variety of locales and conditions. The most important of the treaties restricting nuclear testing are the Treaty Banning Nuclear Weapons Tests in the Atmosphere, in Outer Space and Under Water, Aug. 5, 1963, 480 U.N.T.S. 43 (entered into force, Oct. 10, 1963), and the Treaty on Principles Governing the Activities of States in the Exploration and Use of Outer Space, Including the Moon and other Celestial Bodies, Jan. 27, 1967, 6 I.L.M. 386 (entered into force Oct. 10, 1967). Four significant regional treaties confine the deployment of nuclear weapons in Latin America, the South Pacific, South–East Asia and Africa. The Treaty of Tlatelolco for the Prohibition of Nuclear Weapons in Latin America, Feb. 14, 1967, 6 I.L.M. 52 (entered into force Apr. 22, 1968), prohibits the use of nuclear weapons by the contracting parties; while the parties to the Treaty of Rarotonga on the South Pacific Nuclear Free Zone Treaty, Aug. 6, 1985, 24 I.L.M. 1442 (entered into force Dec. 11, 1986), the Organization of African Unity: African Nuclear–Weapon–Free Zone Treaty, June 21–23, 1995, 35 I.L.M. 698, and the South–East Asia Nuclear Free Zone Treaty, Dec. 15, 1995, 35 I.L.M. 635 undertake not to manufacture, acquire or possess any nuclear weapons. These treaties must be read in the context of the Treaty on the Final Settlement with Respect to Germany, Sept. 12, 1990, 29 I.L.M. 1186, and the Treaty on the Non-proliferation of Nuclear Weapons (NPT), July 1, 1968, 7 I.L.M. 809 (entered into force Mar. 5, 1970) which we discuss later.

The contours of a general prohibition on nuclear weapons began to take definite shape with the NPT of 1968. This treaty sought to control nuclear damage by prohibiting "horizontal" proliferation (the spread of nuclear weapons to non-nuclear states in a world of five declared nuclear states) and "vertical" proliferation (the further amassing and development of nuclear weapons by nuclear states). The nuclear states were obligated under article VI "to pursue negotiations in good faith on effective measures relating to cessation of the nuclear arms race at an early date and to nuclear disarmament, and on a treaty on general and complete disarmament under strict and effective international control."

In 1995, the NPT was indefinitely extended by the NPT Review and Extension Conference which endorsed an earlier Security Council resolution [Resolution 988 (1995) of Apr. 11, 1995] that reiterated and re-affirmed the need for "general and complete disarmament" called for by article VI. The Conference did so with a "politically binding" Final Document on Extension of the Treaty on the Non-proliferation of Nuclear Weapons, May 11, 1995, 34 I.L.M. 959 that re-asserted the importance of fulfilling the legal obligation expressed in article VI.

(b) Nuclear Testing

Even at the height of the cold war the nuclear powers recognized the threat to the environment of nuclear explosions, and so negotiated the Treaty Banning Nuclear Weapons Tests in the Atmosphere, in Outer Space and Under Water, which, not surprisingly, forbids all nuclear weapons tests in the atmosphere, outer space and under water [art. I(1)(a)]. The agreement also prohibits any other nuclear explosion, such as an underground explosion, that causes a transboundary exchange of radioactive debris [art. I(1)(b)]. The treaty seeks to end the "contamination of man's environment by radioactive substances," and calls upon the parties to continue negotiations toward the banning of all nuclear testing, including underground explosions

[Pmbl.]. Originally, the treaty was signed by all the nuclear powers except France and China.

Since that date there has been considerable pressure to take the final step toward cessation of all nuclear testing. Of their own accord, the U.S. and the former Soviet Union forged two treaties controlling underground explosions in the 1970s—the Treaty Between the Soviet Union and the United States on the Limitation of Underground Nuclear Weapons Tests, July 3, 1974, 13 I.L.M. 906 and the Treaty on Underground Nuclear Explosions for Peaceful Purposes, May 28, 1976, 15 I.L.M. 891. More recently the General Assembly of the United Nations, responding to increased concern on the part of the non-nuclear nations, called for the development of a Comprehensive Test Ban Treaty (CTBT).

A decisive step in the direction of nuclear disarmament in all its aspects was taken when, pursuant to many years of arduous negotiation, the Comprehensive Nuclear Test Ban Treaty was opened for signature in 1996. The CTBT bans all nuclear testing and thereby effectively prevents the development of new nuclear weapons. It was immediately signed by the five nuclear states: the United States, Russia, China, France and the United Kingdom, and nearly one hundred nations. The treaty must be ratified by the 44 presumptive nuclear powers before it comes into force, and this may present some difficulty because India, one of the 44, has proclaimed that it will not do so.

There is room for optimism for two reasons. First, the overwhelming support enjoyed by the treaty, particularly among the "non-aligned nations," as many developing nations still call themselves, will put pressure on India as a leader of the non-aligned movement. Second, India cites the refusal of the nuclear states to agree to a schedule or time table for total disarmament as the reason for its position. This may change if the nuclear powers become acclimatized to a world without new nuclear weapons, and accustomed to one without any nuclear weapons at all.

(c) Customary Law

i. Nuclear Testing

Until the total phase-out of nuclear testing occurs, the question still exists concerning the customary international law status of such explosions. Given the broad acceptance of the CTBT, coupled with state practice in this area, one can make a strong claim that customary international law forbids the atmospheric, outer space, or under water testing of nuclear weapons. This would appear to be the rule even in the absence of transboundary environmental harm. On the other hand, the status of underground testing remains problematic. Should the testing cause significant environmental damage or a threat of such damage to another state, the well-settled general prohibition against such damage would control. Without transboundary environmental harm, however, and until the CTBT comes into its own, it seems doubtful that underground testing *per se* would violate customary international law.

Though the Nuclear Tests Cases do not resolve the issues surrounding underground nuclear testing, they remain some of the most important cases in international environmental law. And, as they deal first with the issue of atmospheric testing, and in the most recent incarnation consider underground testing, they track the evolution in thinking concerning nuclear weapons testing. More generally, the cases also provide a glimpse into the evolution of international environmental law over a twenty year period. Again, it is not for the resolution of issues that we look to these cases, but for the discussion of important concepts, usually in dissent. The cases also highlight the severe limitations of the World Court—both real and self-inflicted—that continue to hamper the development of international environmental law. For all of these reasons, and to provide a window into the actual functioning of the World Court, we offer an extended analysis of these decisions.

The Nuclear Tests Cases (Round One)

To begin, in 1973 both Australia and New Zealand brought separate, but similar, actions against France in the World Court, complaining of France's imminent atmospheric tests on the Mururoa Atoll in the South Pacific [*see* Nuclear Tests (Australia v. France), 1973 I.C.J. 99 (June 22); 1973 I.C.J. 320 (July 12); 1974 I.C.J. 253 (Dec. 20); 1973 I.C.J. 338 (Aug. 28); 1974 I.C.J. 530 (Dec. 20); Nuclear Tests

(New Zealand v. France), 1973 I.C.J. 135 (June 22); 1973 I.C.J. 341 (Sept. 6); 1973 I.C.J. 324 (July 12) 1974 I.C.J. 457 (Dec. 20); 1974 I.C.J. 535 (Dec. 20)]. From 1967 to 1972 France had conducted atmospheric tests within its own territory there, and appeared about to begin another series of tests in 1973. In its application to the court Australia claimed:

(i) The right of Australia and its people, in common with other States and their peoples, to be free from atmospheric tests by any country is and will be violated;

(ii) The deposit of radio-active fall-out on the territory of Australia and its dispersion in Australia's airspace without Australia's consent:

(a) violates Australia's sovereignty over its territory;

(b) impairs Australia's independent right to determine what acts shall take place within its territory and in particular whether Australia and its people shall be exposed to radiation from artificial sources;

(iii) the interference with ships and aircraft on the high seas and in the super-adjacent airspace, and the pollution of the high seas by radio-active fall-out, constitute infringements of the freedom of the high seas.

Nuclear Tests (Australia v. France), 1973 I.C.J. 99, 103 (June 22).

New Zealand's claim was somewhat different, presenting a *jus cogens* argument and also referring to nuclear testing in general, not just atmospheric nuclear testing. According to New Zealand's application,

(a)[France's action] violates the rights of all members of the international community including New Zealand, that no nuclear tests that give rise to radio-active fall-out be conducted;

(b) it violates the rights of all members of the international community, including New Zealand, to the preservation from unjustified artificial radio-active contamination of the terrestrial, maritime and aerial environment and, in particular, of the environment of the region in which the tests are conducted....

(c) it violates the right of New Zealand that no radio-active material enter [its] territory...., including [its] air space and territorial waters, as a result of nuclear testing;

(d) it violates the right of New Zealand that no radio-active material, having entered [its] territory ..., including [its] air space and territorial waters, as a result of nuclear testing, cause harm, including apprehension, anxiety and concern to the people and government of New Zealand ...;

(e) it violates the right of New Zealand to freedom of the high seas, including freedom of navigation and overflight and the freedom to explore and exploit the resources of the sea and the seabed, without interference or detriment resulting from nuclear testing.

Nuclear Tests (New Zealand v. France), 1974 I.C.J. 457, 512 (Dec. 20).

Though it had previously accepted the compulsory jurisdiction of the court under article 36 of the Statute of the International Court of Justice, France disavowed the court's competence to hear the cases, denied jurisdiction and declined to appear. In spite of France's rejection, the case remained on the court's official list or docket.

Interim Measures

The two petitioners also asked for interim measures, and the court supported these requests in 1973, stating that "no action of any kind [should be] taken which might aggravate or extend the dispute ... in particular, the French Government should avoid nuclear tests causing the deposit of radio-active fall-out" on the respective territories of Australia and New Zealand [Nuclear Tests (Australia v. France), 1973 I.C.J. 99, 106 (June 22); Nuclear Tests (New Zealand v. France), 1973 I.C.J. 135, 142 (June 22)]. France, in turn, ignored the decision and actually conducted two nuclear tests.

Jurisdiction

In 1974 the court then had to decide the question of jurisdiction. As this phase of the World Court proceedings approached, however, the French government suddenly shifted direction—making a number of public declarations to the effect that it would discontinue its atmospheric nuclear tests and would move on to underground tests. Neither Australia nor New Zealand felt assured by these unilateral statements, and both continued to press their respective claims.

In the decision on its competence to hear the cases, the court first had to deal with France's request that the court remove the two cases from its list, based on the fact that France now did not accept the court's jurisdiction. Without elaboration, the court simply stated in both instances that "the present case was not one in which the procedure of summary removal from the list would be appropriate" [Nuclear Tests (Australia v. France), 1974 I.C.J. 253 (Dec. 20); Nuclear Tests (New Zealand v. France), 1974 I.C.J. 457, 460 (Dec. 20)].

In the next step, the court focused on whether a present dispute still existed between France on the one hand, and Australia and New Zealand on the other. On this matter—though France's unilateral promise to stop atmospheric testing was not embraced as sufficient by either applicant—the court decided that France had made a binding commitment. Therefore, with the objective of both applicants presumably met and the "dispute having disappeared," the court dismissed both cases without reaching the merits [Nuclear Tests (Australia v. France), 1974 I.C.J. 253, 271 (Dec. 20); Nuclear Tests (New Zealand v. France), 1974 I.C.J. 457, 475 (Dec. 20)].

The environmental significance of the first round of the Nuclear Tests Cases primarily lies with the granting of interim measures. Though the court did not base its decision on the merits of the Applicants' cases, it did admit that both had established *prima facie* cases of possible harm and that the rights of all parties needed to be preserved for later adjudication. The granting of interim measures thus lends support to the general rule that one country may not inflict transboundary environmental harm on another. On the other hand, the decision on jurisdiction shows how ready the court is to dispose of cases on procedural grounds when faced with controversial substantive issues. Here the court creatively and very narrowly dispensed with a case—following an out-dated formalism—in which it might have made important pronouncements of law.

To its credit, however, the court did provide an opportunity to reopen the cases, stating that "if the basis of this Judgment were to be affected, the Applicant could request an examination of the situation in accordance with the provisions of the statute" [Nuclear Tests (Australia v. France), 1974 I.C.J. 253, 271 ¶ 60 (Dec. 20); Nuclear Tests (New Zealand v. France), 1974 I.C.J. 457, 477 ¶ 63 (Dec. 20)]. It is this opening which leads to round two of the quarrel.

The Nuclear Tests Case(s) (Round Two)

With a new conservative administration firmly in control, France declared its intention to conduct another series of underground tests in the South Pacific beginning in 1995. Outraged by what they perceived as the continued arrogance of France and the renewed threat of environmental harm, the South Pacific countries loudly denounced the action. For its part New Zealand sought to reopen its 1974 case against France, claiming that "the basis of the Judgment had been affected" by the new underground tests proposed by France [Request for an Examination of the Situation in Accordance with Paragraph 63 of the Court's Judgment of 20 December 1974 in the Nuclear Tests (New Zealand v. France) Case, 1995 I.C.J. 288, 298 ¶ 33 (Sept. 22)]. As France no longer accepted the compulsory jurisdiction of the court under article 36 of the I.C.J. Statute, New Zealand could not institute new proceedings but could only hope to gain access through the older case. Australia, as you will remember, had based its original complaint more narrowly on atmospheric testing, and apparently for this reason did not try to reopen its own case. Instead, it later attempted to intervene in New Zealand's proceedings.

In its Application to the court, New Zealand stated:

(i) that the conduct of the proposed nuclear tests will constitute a violation of the rights under international law of New Zealand, as well as of other States; further or in the alternative;

(ii) that is unlawful for France to conduct such nuclear tests before it has undertaken an Environmental Impact Assessment according to accepted international standards. Unless such an assessment establishes that the tests will not give rise, directly or indirectly, to radioactive contamination of the marine environment the rights under international law of New Zealand, as well as the rights of other States, will be violated.

Id. at 290 ¶ 6.

New Zealand asked that the court make a broad interpretation of the words "the basis of the Judgment"—that the phrase should not be restricted to France's atmospheric testing only, but that it referred more generally to the cessation of environmental contamination by nuclear testing [Id. at 293 ¶ 18]. According to New Zealand, as current scientific evidence now showed that the environmental risks of underground nuclear testing were greater than originally thought in 1974, the resumption of such tests would alter the underlying protection afforded by the judgment. Indeed, New Zealand's original Application in 1973 did not even mention atmospheric tests, but instead focused on the right to be free from nuclear damage.

In addition, through its application and oral argument, New Zealand now backed up its complaint with specific advances in international environmental law. (1) It maintained that the duty not to cause transboundary harm—in an early stage of crystallization in 1974—was now a well-settled principle of customary international law. (2) It noted that the principle of inter-generational equity was at stake, that the 20,000 year by-product of nuclear testing invoked a consideration of the rapidly developing principle of inter-generational rights. (3) It claimed that the precautionary principle mandated a shift of the burden of proof to France, and that France should have to conduct an Environmental Impact Assessment before proceeding with its tests. (4) It stated that a number of treaties disallowed the introduction of radioactive wastes into the marine environment, and that France's action violated the high standard afforded this medium [*id.*].

Once again, however, as in the original cases, the court adopted an extremely narrow interpretation of the law. By a vote of twelve to three, the court refused to reopen the case, agreeing with France's argument that the "basis of the Judgment" in the 1974 adjudication had only to do with "atmospheric" testing. As New Zealand knew that France would begin conducting underground tests in 1974, it could not now complain of those tests but only the threatened commencement of atmospheric tests. France, of course, was not proposing atmospheric tests, and New Zealand had no legitimate fears that pertained to the earlier case.

In dissent Judge Weermantry, supported by Judge ad hoc Palmer, devastatingly revealed the unnecessary formalism of the decision, pointing out the dangers of strict construction. Judge Weermantry explained:

> If X should complain to the village elder that Y is threatening him with a sword in a manner caus-

ing reasonable apprehension of an intention to cause grievous harm, and the village elder orders Y to drop his sword, is that order to be construed as an order to refrain from causing bodily harm, whatever the weapon used? If Y thereafter proceeds to harm X with a club, Y would surely not be able to contend that the order issued on him related to the use of a sword and that he did not violate it in any way by using a club. Clearly, a larger reason lies behind the order than the mere prohibition against inflicting harm with a sword. The unexpressed rationale lying behind the order, namely, the desire to protect X from bodily harm, lies at the very heart of the order, if it is to be construed in the light of common sense.

Id. at 334.

Clearly, according to Weermantry, the original decision attempted to protect New Zealand from harm caused by nuclear weapons testing, not just the fall-out from atmospheric tests. If at this juncture progress in scientific knowledge reveals underground testing as causing greater harm that thought in 1974, then a *prima facie* case has been established. The case should then proceed to the merits and the court should engage, rather than bypass, the very important legal issues at hand.

The significance of New Zealand's recent application to the court therefore rests with the opinions of the dissenting judges. In his own dissent Judge Weermantry argues against the narrow formalism of the majority, and shows a willingness to discuss all the important issues brought forward—including transboundary environmental harm, inter-generational equity, the precautionary principle and environmental impact assessment, and protection of the marine environment. Unfortunately, due to the reticence of the present court, a majority decision on these issues of general customary international law must wait another day. And regarding the specific status of underground nuclear testing, in the near future it is unlikely that the court will obtain jurisdiction over a seminal case. More probably, a completed Comprehensive Test Ban Treaty will provide primary guidance in this area.

ii. Use of Nuclear Weapons

The Advisory Opinion the ICJ in the Legality of the Threat of the Use of Nuclear Weapons, 35 I.L.M. 809 (July 8, 1996) forms an important part of the emerging customary law on nuclear weapons. The General Assembly of the United Nations requested the World Court for an Advisory Opinion on the question: Is the threat or use of nuclear weapons in any circumstances permitted under international law? The Court was urged by the United States and other nuclear powers to decline the question. Instead it held, by a wafer-thin majority secured by the double vote of the president, that the threat or use of nuclear weapons would generally be contrary to the rules of international law applicable in armed conflict and in particular the principles and rules of humanitarian law. The Court refrained from ruling unequivocally that the threat or use of nuclear weapons would be illegal under any circumstances. According to the majority, the inadequacy of facts at its disposal precluded the Court from concluding definitively that the threat or use of nuclear weapons would be lawful or unlawful in extreme cases of self defense where the very survival of the state would be at stake.

However, in light of the horrendous threats posed by nuclear weapons, and the growing consensus among the community of nations as evidenced in the treaties referred to above, the Court was of the unanimous opinion that these treaties foreshadowed "a future general prohibition of the use of such weapons" although not presently constituting a prohibition on the use or possession of nuclear weapons [*Id*. at 825 ¶ 62]. Addressing article VI of the NPT, it concluded that: "The legal import of that obligation goes beyond that of a mere obligation of conduct; the obligation involved here is an obligation to achieve a precise result—nuclear disarmament in all its aspects—by adopting a particular course of conduct, namely, the pursuit of negotiations on the matter in good faith" [*Id*. at 830]. This means that nuclear states are under a legal obligation—an "obligation of result"—to bring to a conclusion negotiations leading to nuclear disarmament in all its aspects under strict and effective international control.

Even though the Court did not declare every threat or use of nuclear weapons illegal, it carved out a rule of illegality and confined its exception to cases of extreme self defense where the survival of the state is at stake. Judge Schwebel, the American judge, dissented, arguing that neither law, state practice nor comity supported the conclusion that the use or threat of use of nuclear weapons are generally illegal. On the other hand, Judge Weeramantry reasoned that the decision did not go far enough. He asserted that use or threat of use of nuclear weapons is illegal in any circumstances, and that self defense did not constitute an exception. The implications of this decision are noteworthy. First, it may assail and dismantle the legal foundations of nuclear defense policies premised on first use of nuclear weapons. Second, it confronts the permanent members of the Security Council: United States, England, Russia, France and China, all of whom are nuclear powers, with the illegality of the threat or use of their nuclear weapons except in self defense when their very existence is at stake. Third, it directs all nuclear powers that they must enter into good faith negotiations to achieve total nuclear disarmament. While it is true that the last finding is not as imperative as it may seem because good faith negotiations could go on indefinitely, it appears that the nuclear powers have not taken such a cynical view of their obligations.

2. CIVILIAN NUCLEAR ENERGY

(a) Nuclear Safety

IAEA Standards

Concerning the uses of nuclear energy, three international organizations have primary responsibility. The Nuclear Energy Agency (NEA), created by the OECD, has played a limited role in promoting common safety standards through national legislation in its member countries, but its fundamental function remains that of disseminating information. EURATOM, an EU entity, has developed mostly health-related safety directives that member countries must implement and enforce, but the organization has yet to expand into the area of siting, design and operation. Thus the most significant is the IAEA, created by statute under the auspices of the United Nations in 1956 and supported by nearly all the nations of the world as parties. According to its statute, the IAEA's principal objective is "to accelerate and enlarge the contribution of atomic energy"—though as a secondary function it is required to establish "standards of safety for protection of health and minimization of danger to life and property" [Statute of the International Atomic Energy Agency (IAEA Statute), art.III (A)(6), Oct. 26, 1956, art. II, 276 U.N. T.S. 3 (entered into force July 29, 1957). Thus the IAEA operates with the twin purposes both of fostering the development of nuclear power and controlling its dangers.

Though undertaking the function belatedly, and to its critics at cross-purposes with its development function, the IAEA has gradually assumed the leadership role in health and safety standards. Over the years the agency has generated a broad set of nonbinding rules covering virtually every area of nuclear safety, including the siting, design and operation of nuclear installations. Though in practice many

countries rely on these in setting national requirements, and the IAEA itself remains bound by its
own provisions, the standards legally exist as technical guidelines. Only if by agreement the IAEA
helps establish a particular facility—through the
providing of IAEA materials and expertise—do the
standards as well as follow-up inspections become
binding on that facility. As detailed below, the recent adoption of the 1994 Convention on Nuclear
Safety has raised the profile of the IAEA standards,
but these still remain guidelines rather than obligatory measures.

(b) 1994 Convention on Nuclear Safety

Following the Chernobyl accident in 1986, the
international community—led by the Group of Sev-
en (G–7) economic powers—worked toward the
adoption of a treaty on nuclear safety. As the
preamble states the Convention on Nuclear Safety,
[Sept. 20, 1994, 33 I.L.M. 1514] functions as an
"incentive convention," mandating the creation of
appropriate national standards for civil nuclear installations but not requiring the use of IAEA provisions. Thus, on one hand the convention "entails a
commitment to the application of fundamental safety principles for nuclear installations rather than of
detailed safety standards,"[pmbl. (viii)] and on the
other that "there are internationally formulated
safety guidelines which ... provide guidance on
contemporary means of achieving a high level of
safety" [Id.]. Though many non-nuclear states desired more stringent and specific standards, the

requirements of the convention remain largely hortatory, with the parties simply charged with taking "appropriate steps" at the national level. The hope is that "appropriate" national standards will follow IAEA or other international standards, fostering an improved level of nuclear safety throughout the world.

Under the convention, each party must install "a legislative and regulatory framework to govern the safety of nuclear installations" [art. 7]. The convention actually only covers power plants, and does not deal with nuclear fast breeder reactors or any aspect of the nuclear fuel cycle, most notably radioactive waste. In addition to the establishment of national safety standards, each party must develop a competent regulatory authority which, unlike the IAEA itself, does not engage in the promotion of nuclear energy [art.8]. As to general areas of action, each nation must take "appropriate steps" to ensure emergency preparedness [art.16], assessment and verification of safety [art.14], quality assurance [art.13] and radiation protection [art.15]. More specifically, concerning the safety of installations, each party must develop "appropriate" standards and procedures regarding siting [art.17], design and construction [art.18], and operation [art.19].

Regarding existing nuclear plants the convention is more strict. Each party must make "all reasonably practicable improvements" of existing nuclear installations and, if upgrading cannot be undertaken, should close the nuclear installation "as soon as practically possible" [art.6]. In considering the timing of any necessary shut-down, the party may weigh "the whole energy context and possible alternatives as well as the social, environmental and economic impact" [art.6].

The IAEA acts as the secretariat of the convention, though as such it has little independent power. Instead, the convention again relies on national implementation and oversight, requiring parties to submit compliance reports to the contracting parties at review meetings [arts. & 20]. At these meetings each party may discuss and seek clarification of another party's report, but no official dispute resolution machinery exists by which to challenge that report's content [art.29]. Following the same logic, neither the IAEA nor any other institution created by the convention possesses formal enforcement powers [art.20].

(c) The 1986 IAEA Convention on Early Notification of a Nuclear Accident (Notification Convention)

Another treaty prompted by the Chernobyl accident, the Notification Convention, Sept. 26, 1986, 25 I.L.M. 1369 (entered into force Oct. 27, 1986) attempts to prevent delay by parties in reporting accidents to its neighbors. Presently in force and signed by nearly all the nuclear capable nations, the Notification Convention covers any civilian accident in which the "release of radioactive material occurs or is likely to occur and which has resulted or may result in an international transboundary release that could be of radiological safety significance for another State" [art.1]. In short the treaty encompasses present as well as probable nuclear accidents, if these cause significant or potentially significant transboundary harm. Unfortunately, a major shortcoming of the convention exists in the broad discretion given to parties in interpreting the word "significance." In another important limitation, the treaty does not mandate notification regarding accidents at military facilities. This problem has since been ameliorated by the declaration of the five nuclear states that they will extend the convention's provisions to these incidents.

Faced with such a nuclear accident, a party must "forthwith notify" either the IAEA or the potentially "physically" affected states as to the nature, time and location of the accident [art. 2(a)]. Furthermore, the party must promptly provide any information that might minimize the radiological effects of the accident, such as the possible cause, general release characteristics and any results of environmental monitoring [art.2(1) & 5]. A party also must "promptly" respond to any request for consultations by an affected state, when such consultations would seek to minimize the radiological consequences inside the latter's territory [art. 6].

(d) The 1986 IAEA Convention on Assistance in the Case of a Nuclear Accident or Radiological Emergency (Assistance Convention)

Complementing the Notification Convention, the Assistance Convention, Sept. 26, 1986, 25 I.L.M. 1377 (entered into force Sept.26, 1987) creates a framework of cooperation that strives to facilitate aid among countries in the event of a nuclear accident. The treaty situates the IAEA as the conduit of such assistance, but also encourages other bilateral or multilateral arrangements [art.1]. Though nothing in the convention forces a party to request assistance, upon doing so it must "specify the scope and type of assistance required and, where practicable, provide the assisting party with such information as may be necessary for that party to determine the extent to which it is able to meet the request" [art.2(2)]. In turn, the providing party must promptly respond concerning the availability, scope and terms of any assistance [art.2(3)]. For its part, the IAEA proactively collects and distributes information as to each party's available experts, equipment and material in the event of a nuclear accident and, if requested, assists parties in the preparation of emergency plans and the development of personnel training and radiation monitoring programs [art.5(1)]. The convention also provides for immunity from legal proceedings for the assisting party and its agents, though any party may at the time of accepting the convention declare itself not bound by these specific provisions [*see* arts. (8,10)]. In short, the convention seeks to expedite voluntary assistance by other nations, removing administrative and legal roadblocks.

(e) Liability

i. *State Responsibility*

The legal fallout from Chernobyl has arguably undermined the strength of the customary law rule prohibiting states from causing transboundary environmental harm. In the specific area of liability for nuclear accidents, the necessary doctrinal component of state practice appears lacking as no aggrieved state brought a formal claim against the former Soviet Union (though several reserved the right to do so). The result obviously questions whether states are legally responsible for this type of nuclear harm under customary international law. Simply put, if in the face of widespread damage no claims were filed and no compensation volunteered or awarded, then how can liability for nuclear accidents exist under international law?

The fact that states declined to press claims does not mean that they believed the claims legally unwarranted. It is perfectly feasible that states declined to prefer claims for fear of establishing precedents that could be used against them. The states harmed by Chernobyl fallout were themselves nuclear states and may have decided it was in their self interest not to create a legal weapon that might be used against them. Moreover, in the particular case of Chernobyl the harmed states may only have decided that the costs of pursuing compensation outweighed the benefits—especially given the inability to pay on the part of the former Soviet Union.

In fact, evidence of a liability regime applicable to radioactive contamination is supplied by another case. In 1979 Canada pressed a claim against the USSR for damages caused by a nuclear-powered satellite that broke up over its territory. Canada made its claims both under general principles of international law and the 1972 Convention on International Liability for Damage Caused by Space Objects (1972 Space Objects Convention), Mar. 29, 1972, 961 U.N.T.S. 187 (entered into force Sept.1, 1972). This time the USSR agreed to pay Canada US $3 million as compensation. As the legal basis for liability remained unnamed in the concluding document, the result permits an argument in favor of applying both custom and the 1972 Space Objects Convention. More recently, by resolution on Dec.14, 1992 the U.N. General Assembly adopted Principles Relevant to the Use of Nuclear Power Sources in Outer Space, which again provides for state responsibility for damage caused by outer space operations utilizing nuclear power [Principle 8].

Furthermore, the general rule against transboundary environmental harm—first provided in the Trail Smelter Arbitration case, (United States v. Canada), 3 R.I.A.A. 1938 (1949)—continues to find universal support in international environmental treaties and declarations. Therefore, to carve out an exception to the rule for nuclear accidents seems premature, as nations have consistently embraced the rule in such important documents as the Rio Declaration on Environment and Development, and in major international treaties such as the Biological Diversity Convention and Climate Change Convention.

As for the standard of liability, this question also obviously remains unresolved. On the one hand, some scholars argue for strict or absolute liability because nuclear energy is an ultra-hazardous activity. The 1972 Space Objects Convention, for example, makes the launching state "absolutely liable to pay compensation for damage caused by its space object on the surface of the earth or to aircraft in flight" [art. II]. Similarly, in the civil liability conventions described below the standard is one of strict liability.

Others have argued for a due diligence standard regarding nuclear accidents, in which liability would arise for a state in whose territory an accident occurred only if the state acted negligently in the development, application and monitoring of appropriate safety standards. Adherents of this view look to Chernobyl as an incident *not* causing a breach of due diligence, pointing out that the plant in question was built according to national standards set by the Soviet Union. Though these standards may not rise to the level of the plants built in the West, so the argument goes, this does not necessarily mean that the Soviet Union acted negligently.

Striving for coherence in the aftermath of Chernobyl, the IAEA created a Standing Committee on Nuclear Liability, which in attempting to revise the Vienna Convention on Civil Liability for Nuclear Damage (1963 Vienna Convention), May 21, 1963, 7 I.L.M. 727 (entered into force Nov. 12, 1977) continues to discuss the issue of state responsibility. However, with a number of nuclear powers rejecting the notion, it now appears unlikely that any form of state responsibility for nuclear accidents will make its way into that treaty. On the other hand, the 1994 Convention on Nuclear Safety asserts in the preamble that responsibility for nuclear safety rests with the state having jurisdiction over a particular nuclear installation. This is to be contrasted with article 9 of the same convention, which holds that prime responsibility lies with the operator of an installation. The result is a double-tiered program of responsibility under this treaty, with the state's duty one of regulation and monitoring, and the operator's one of stringent compliance.

ii. Civil Liability

With no global regime in place for state responsibility, the international community long ago developed two separate conventions on civil liability for nuclear damage—two conventions now outmoded and in the slow process of revision. The two conventions share a number of characteristics, including strict liability for the operator, compulsory insurance and a monetary limit on compensation for damage. In considering these one should keep in mind that the former U.S.S.R. was not a party to either convention, and so neither could be invoked in the case of Chernobyl. One should also be aware of the existence of another treaty—the Convention on the Liability of Operators of Nuclear Ships, May 25, 1962, 57 A.J.I.L. 268 (entered into force July 15, 1975)—which creates similar obligations but, because it has limited acceptance and scope, is not discussed further.

The 1960 Paris Convention on Third Party Liability in the Field of Nuclear Energy (1960 Paris Convention)

Created under the auspices of the OECD, the 1960 Paris Convention, July 29, 1960, 956 U.N.T.S. 264 strives to unify civil liability rules for nuclear damage in Western Europe. The treaty has nearly all western nuclear nations in the region as parties—including France, Germany and the United Kingdom. The convention channels all liability to the operator of the nuclear installation for "damage to or loss of life of any person" and "damage to or loss of any property" [art. 2]. Whether this includes environmental damage remains unclear. The treaty does cover transport of nuclear substances, for which the operator in charge remains liable and not the carrier [art. 4]. If an incident occurs, the operator's liability is strict rather than absolute, though the convention actually only exempts responsibility in the few cases of armed conflict, hostilities, civil war, insurrection or grave natural disasters of an exceptional character [art. 9].

To pay for any liability, each operator must carry insurance in the amount specified under the convention [art. 10]. The liability remains limited—an important feature of this convention—to 15 million Special Drawing Rights (SDR) as defined by the International Monetary Fund [art. 7] (At 1996 values one unit of SDR approximately equals one U.S. dollar ($1)). In fact, under the 1960 convention a party may even set the liability limit as low as 5 million units of account. As the parties quickly perceived, however, a maximum of 15 million SDR would not cover an accident of any magnitude, and so they adopted the 1963 Brussels Convention Supplementary to the 1960 Convention on Third Party Liability in the Field of Nuclear Energy (Brussels Convention), Jan. 31, 1963, 2 I.L.M. 685.

This convention, which has been updated by later protocol, leaves the operator's liability at the same level and establishes a supplementary system of public funding [art. 3]. Thus, in the event of an accident in its territory, a party must provide up to an additional 170 million SDR to compensate worthy claimants. Furthermore, should the damage exceed that amount, the other parties to the convention would provide up to 125 million SDR according to a formula based on thermal power and GNP [art. 12]. On the other hand, if the damage results from fault by the operator, the party in whose territory the installation exists may pass legislation allowing both itself and other contracting parties recourse against that operator [art. 5(b)].

In general, jurisdiction lies with the courts of the party in whose territory the nuclear incident occurred [art. 13(a)], and final judgments must be honored and enforced by all the contracting parties [art. 13(d)]. Moreover, though a state may actually be the installation operator in many cases, no party may invoke jurisdictional immunities to avoid actions [art. 13(e)].

The 1983 IAEA Vienna Convention on Civil Liability for Nuclear Damage (1963 Vienna Convention)

The 1963 Vienna Convention, May 21, 1963, 1063 U.N.T.S. 265 closely resembles the 1960 Paris Convention, and presently remains the subject of negotiations to modernize its provisions. As such, it has the potential to emerge as the global convention on civil liability for nuclear damage, but at the moment counts only a small number of parties—none of whom possess significant nuclear industries.

As with the Paris Convention, the Vienna Convention covers damage to persons and property but makes no mention of environmental damage—though it has been pointed out that the latter does allow national courts expansive interpretive power in providing for "nuclear damage" [art. I(k)(ii); PHILLIPE SANDS, I PRINCIPLES OF INTERNATIONAL ENVIRONMENTAL LAW: FRAMEWORKS, STANDARDS AND IMPLEMENTATION 655 (1994)] Similarly following the 1960 Paris Convention, the operator's liability is strict with comparable exceptions [art. v]. Again jurisdiction generally lies with the installation state, and final judgments must be honored and enforced by other contracting parties.

Unlike the OECD regime, however, the 1963 Vienna convention contains no supplemental funding by the parties themselves. Instead, the convention limits liability for the operator to $5 million dollars (U.S.). Obviously, without a dramatic increase in this amount, or without additional public funds, the Vienna Convention would prove woefully inadequate in compensating real victims. Thus for the treaty to become the global instrument on civil liability that the IAEA envisions, the future parties clearly must address this weakness.

Meanwhile, in the 1988 Joint Protocol Relating to the Application of the Vienna Convention and the Paris Convention, Sept. 21, 1988, 42 Nuclear Law Bulletin 56 (entered into force Apr. 27, 1992) parties to both conventions agreed to bring together the functional elements of the two treaties. Under the protocol, which is now in force, the convention ratified by the installation state governs liability for damage incurred by a state-party to the other convention [arts. II & IV]. In addition, each convention applies to each incident to the exclusion of the other [art. III]. Though offering a more unified approach, the protocol only points out the necessity of completing negotiations for a new Vienna Convention— a global convention that would uniformly deal with civil liability for nuclear damage.

CHAPTER EIGHTEEN

THE FUTURE OF IEL

We have learned how an expanding IEL patrols a increasingly interconnected and interdependent world, in which practitioners and judges, at all levels of national law, are coming alive to its impact and import. Furthermore, it is firmly ensconced in the law school curriculum, and has become the subject of burgeoning scholarly attention.

What of the future? We offer a mottled yet cautiously optimistic picture of IEL based on a realistic, albeit subjective assessment of its successes and failures, that leads to an incremental and pragmatic view of possible future developments. This chapter does not venture to reconceptualize the subject in conformity with our own hopes and aspirations, or to offer an utopian blue print for future action. Instead, we use the Rio Declaration on Environment and Development, June 13, 1992, 31 I.L.M. 874 (hereinafter Rio Declaration) as our baseline to focus on a few selected areas of substantive law, concepts, and institutions. These subjects, possessed of varying degrees of promise and uncertainty, have been chosen because of their potential importance for the future development of IEL.

A. SUBSTANTIVE IEL

Sustainable development, though proclaimed as the foundational norm of IEL, is possessed of a chimerical character, and needs to be honed, refined and more clearly defined. Despite the Rio Declaration's profuse professions of sustainable development, we have noted the retreat from environmental protection embodied in some of its principles (*see*, Chapter One, Introduction). In fact it has been argued by some commentators that the Rio Declaration institutionalized a preeminent right to economic development that enfeebled and attenuated the imperative of sustainable development. [Marc Pallemaerts, *International Environmental law in the Age of Sustainable Development: A Critical Assessment of the UNCED Process*, 15 J. L. & COM. 623, 630–635 (1996)].

It is necessary, therefore, to point to other developments of IEL that countervail any such moves, and to recognize that the attempted retreat at Rio is offset by other advances that block attempts to make sustainable development synonymous with economic development. Two key principles—prevention of transboundary harm, and conservation—form a bulwark against any such thrust. The resilience and dynamism of these two principles help maintain the parity of status between environmental protection and development within the framework of sustainable development.

The prohibition on transboundary pollution, codified by Principle 21 of Stockholm, is now entrenched in numerous provisions of pre-Rio treaties and declarations, and has received such strong support through the practice and *opinio juris* of states that it has become a principle of customary international law [*see* Chapter Two, Sources of IEL]. The attempt in the Rio Declaration to undermine the illegality of transboundary pollution by emphasizing the suzerainty of developmental policies, fails to overcome the overwhelming body of law that mirrors Principle 21 of Stockholm, and defines it as an environmental wrong.

Furthermore, principle 21 of Stockholm, and not principle 2 of Rio, is reaffirmed in article 3 of the Biodiversity Convention—a post Rio treaty. The significance of this fact is that an instrument of hard law (the Biodiversity Convention) is normatively superior to the non-legal Rio Declaration. The Biodiversity Convention's prohibition on transboundary pollution makes no exceptions for transboundary pollution arising from developmental policies.

The principle of conservation confirms the equality of environmental protection, not its subordination to development, within the dynamic of sustainable development. We have seen how the Biodiversity Convention has sought to strike this balance (*see* Chapter Five, Biodiversity). Moreover, post Rio developments such as the 1995 Agreement for the Implementation of the Provisions of UNCLOS of 10 Dec.1982, relating to the Conservation and Management of Straddling Fish Stocks and Highly Migratory Fish Stocks (Straddling and Highly Migratory Fish Stocks Agreement or

SHMFSA), have reiterated the importance of conservation.

Furthermore, it is necessary to reinforce the importance of conservation by moving toward a World Forestry Convention—something that was repudiated at Rio. Such a Forestry Convention should protect old forests, particularly tropical forests, that are home to up to 50% of the plant and insect biological diversity of the world. Though an earlier Administration rejected any attempts to bring United State's old growth forests under the protective umbrella of a World Forestry Convention, the Clinton Administration appears ready to do so. Using the new United States policy as a bargaining chip for a larger international commitment toward preserving biodiversity, it is necessary that the world be presented with a plan to save its tropical forests, and conserve the gene banks of the planet.

B.   OTHER PRINCIPLES

At the same time, embryonic principles of soft law should be developed either into widely accepted legislative treaties, or into customary IEL. This would transform them from being aspirational and hortatory norms into legal obligations. The principles in question include the polluter pays principle articulated for example in Principle 16 of Rio; the preventive and precautionary principles of good neighborliness and cooperation embodied in article 130r, para. 2, of the Treaty of European Union, Feb.7, 1992, 31 I.L.M.247, 285, hereinafter Maastricht Treaty, and later restated by Principle 15 of Rio; and the principle of common but differentiated responsibility found in Principle 7 of Rio, and article 4 of the Climate Change Convention.

These principles have been institutionalized and incorporated in different, and sometimes widely accepted, treaty regimes and conference declarations. They are, however, highly qualified in the Rio Declaration and can evolve into customary IEL when more broadly embraced and acted upon by nonparties (practice), who do so believing that these principles are law (opinio juris).

C. TRADE AND ENVIRONMENTAL PROTECTION

While trade as an instrument of economic growth is another component of sustainable development, the clash of environmental and trade norms has assumed an importance that warrants separate treatment. The reliance on free trade to achieve economic growth—a foundational premise of post-World War II international development strategies—appears to have been strongly endorsed in the Rio Declaration. Articles 4, 11 and 12 lean toward interpreting sustainable development as economic development. Principle 12, for example, is strongly supportive of "an open international economic system that would lend itself to economic growth and sustainable development...." It goes on to state that "unilateral actions to deal with environmental challenges outside the jurisdiction of the importing country should be avoided...."

The General Agreement on Tariffs and Trade, [Oct. 30, 1947, 61 Stat. A–3, 55 U.N.T.S. 187] [hereinafter GATT 1947], institutionalized the universality of free trade, while the World Trade Organization (WTO) establishes an international organization to implement it [General Agreement on Tariffs and Trade, Final Act Embodying the Results of the Uruguay Round of Multinational Trade Negotiations, Apr. 15, 1994, LEGAL INSTRUMENTS— RESULTS OF THE URUGUAY ROUND vol. 1, 33 I.L.M. 1125] [hereinafter WTO]. Together, GATT and WTO (GATT/WTO) are perceived by its advocates as semi-constitutional treaties aimed at eliminating interference and intrusion in international trade.

The tension between free trade and environmental protection is an important aspect of this dispute between economic growth and environmental protection, and requires resolution within the conceptual framework of sustainable development. The future of IEL will be critically affected by how this conflict is settled. The extent of the clash between principles of free trade and those of environmental protection was illustrated by an assertion made by the GATT Secretariat in an important and often cited GATT report of 1992 [GATT Secretariat, *Trade and the Environment*, Doc.1529, at 18 (1992)]. The report focused on three important environmental conventions—1) the Montreal Protocol, 2) CITES, and 3) the Basel Convention—asserting that the use of trade restrictions to achieve the treaties' environmental goals was contrary to GATT/WTO. The WTO will prove to be far more formidable an advocate of free trade than the GATT secretariat, and its existence and active presence accentuates the reality that international free trade and environmental protection are competing paradigms.

Amidst such a clash of paradigms and goals, what determines their ascendancy and primacy within a horizontal and consensual international legal order will remain subject to conjecture and will depend upon an undetermined combination of the strength of the legal obligations, the effectiveness and authority of the implementing institutions and bureaucracies, the motivation and leadership of "hegemon" or dominant states, and the character of the legal forum. In some cases, institutional strength and a favorable legal forum can prove critical. The institutions and legal forums of IEL have been fragmented and lack a world environment organization with the institutional authority, financial backing, and legal and political status of the WTO. The onus of implementing environmental laws embodied in numerous environmental treaties by nation states has received only marginal support, encouragement, and supervision from functional regional and international environmental institutions, which do not possess the jurisdictional authority or the supervisory implementing powers of WTO.

As GATT panels were under the older GATT regime, the new stronger Dispute Settlement Body (DSB) under the WTO remains the sole legal forum for resolving many disputes between environmental protection and free trade. The substantive law applied by GATT is trade law—which holds as a fundamental premise that environmental policy be treated as irrelevant unless embodied in covered agreements under GATT/WTO. What is painfully striking is that IEL issues are being litigated in GATT/WTO forums where the substantive law, and the judges who interpret it, either ignore or are antagonistic toward international environmental protection. Their mission is to liberalize free trade by eliminating controls and restrictions; it is not to advance international environmental protection which is based upon controls and restrictions. It is not necessary for IEL to be forced into the procrustean bed of trade law. A significant number of the issues now litigated in GATT tribunals could be canvassed before a more friendly jurisdiction in which IEL is honored and upheld, not diminished or enfeebled. UNCLOS possesses the substantive law, jurisdiction, and adjudicatory authority necessary for this purpose.

It is essential to the future of IEL that clashes between international environmental protection and free trade be resolved in a forum more impartial and less overtly biased than the DSB of the WTO. The dispute settlement procedures of UNCLOS are eminently qualified to take on this task. While UNCLOS does not create a world oceanic organization, its dispute resolution provisions arguably are strong and binding. The fact that an UNCLOS tribunal possesses parallel jurisdiction means, for example, that the jurisdiction of an UNCLOS as opposed to a GATT/WTO tribunal could be invoked to settle disputes involving environmental actions sanctioned by UNCLOS that may be contrary to the GATT/WTO.

Within key areas of potential conflict, both the substantive international environmental obligations, as well as the dispute settlement procedures of UNCLOS can prevail over GATT. The substantive environmental provisions of UNCLOS do in fact countervail the trade provisions of GATT, while its dispute settlement procedures offer a competing legal forum for vindicating international environmental protection. [*See generally* Lakshman Guruswamy, *Environment and Trade: Competing Paradigms in International Law*, in FESTSCHRIFT TO JUDGE WEERAMANTRY, (Anthony Anghie ed., forthcoming 1997)].

D. THE COMMON LAW OF HUMANKIND

National environmental laws govern environmental problems within nation states. A review of the environmental laws of various nations that make up the international community reveals the extent to which environmental problems—whether arising from air and water pollution, land use or exploitation—are omnipresent. Uniformities of biophysical reactions are part of nature's writ that runs ubiquitously and universally, and the laws of nature can give rise to identical biophysical reactions. If, for example, the receiving medium is the same, discharges of wastes or residuals, whether in Los Angeles, Liverpool, Dusseldorf or Auckland lead to pollution. Common biophysical reactions take place regardless of where in the world the environment is abused. If the necessary conditions exist, sulphur dioxide and nitrogen oxide will react and result in acidic deposition in the Ruhr, Northern England, or in the Raquette, New York. Polychlorinated biphenyls (PCBs) act to cause cancers in West Virginia in the same way as they do in Newcastle upon Tyne, UK, or Colombo, Sri Lanka.

In responding to these common problems, nation states have often arrived at common regulatory patterns of control. Time does not permit any systematic exploration of the compass of comparative environmental law, but we know from the examples of acid rain and PCBs that, when faced with this common problem, nation states hardly ever deny their deleterious effects or decide to ignore them. The actions nations take, of course, are dependent upon their state of economic development and national priorities. While recognizing the evil of pollution, nations may be economically unable to take action to remedy these evils whether in the form of technological, emission, or ambient standards placed on industry or with other restrictions placed on the consumers or society at large. This denotes that there is a near universal recognition of the damage caused by pollution and a resolve to address this problem. Such action may, therefore, be postponed while states remain cognizant of what is required, and may even solicit international assistance to do so.

National boundaries do not, however, constitute biophysical or chemical boundaries, and pollution sometimes migrates from one state to another causing transboundary legal problems that fall within the province of international, not national law. The customary IEL principle prohibiting a state from using its property so as to injure that of another responds to this phenomena, reflects the climate of world opinion, and symbolizes the confluence of national and international law. It is restated in numerous declarations and treaties founded upon a universal appreciation of the need to control damage caused by pollution. These articulations recognize a principle, rooted as much in national law as in international comity, that has become part of the common law of humankind.

Hersch Lauterpacht authenticated the extent to which international law is molded by domestic sources, analogies, and experience [See HERSCH LAUTERPACHT, PRIVATE LAW SOURCES AND ANALOGIES OF INTERNATIONAL LAW (1970)]. He also demonstrated how article 38 of the Statute of the International Court of Justice directs the ICJ to apply the "general principles of law recognized by civilized nations" [Id. at 69]. By "general principles" he referred to principles of law expressing rules "of uniform application in all or in the main systems of private jurisprudence" [Id]. While Lauterpacht applied his reasoning to private law analogies, the principle underlying his thesis, on a parity of reasoning, is equally applicable to domestic public and regulatory law analogies. The general principles of environmental law universally recognized by States enables us clearly to see that the formidable body of IEL dealing both with global and non-global problems is itself part of the greater universal rubric of the common law of humankind—a system of law that the international community and judicial tribunals are obliged to recognize and embrace.

In this context, a fecund recommendation of Agenda 21 is worthy of exploration. It urges that NGOs be given the opportunity of vindicating treaty rights in national forums [¶ ¶ 27.10 & 27.13]. In addition, principle 13 of the Rio Declaration provides that "[s]tates shall develop national law regarding liability and compensation for the victims of pollution and other environmental damage...." These expressions of international consensus underscore the importance of giving: 1) national courts jurisdiction; and 2) individual plaintiffs access and standing in national courts to pursue environmental rights and duties created by treaty. We have seen that such remedies are unusual and effectively remain confined to the subjects of nuclear and oil pollution.

Some commentators view the Rio Declaration's emphasis on adjudication by national courts, based on civil liability as distinct from international state liability, as illustrative of "inertia" that has deflected the development of the latter (PHILIPPE SANDS, PRINCIPALS OF INTERNATIONAL ENVIRONMENTAL LAW 630 1995). While we have noted the lack of progress at Rio, it seems that on this occasion national liability may be a functional and practical way to develop the concept of liability for environmental harm. We have already reviewed the shortcomings of international judicial remedies, and are confronted with having to deal with the stubborn political fact that in the absence of strained political relationships, states do not generally take each other to court. Whether based on self-interest arising from the mutual vulnerability of a state to actions by others, or a desire not to offend friendly states, the crop of cases has been meager.

On the other hand, environmental litigation in national courts is proliferating and it makes sense to use national courts to advance international remedies. The ILC, in the *Draft Articles on the Law of the Non-navigational Uses of International Watercourses* (ILC Draft Articles), U.N. GOAR, 46th Sess., Supp. No. 10 at 161, U.N. Doc. A/46/10, *available in Westlaw*, 1991 WL 568515 (1991), recognizes the importance of national remedies in a curiously named article on "Non-discrimination" [art. 32]. Article 32 prohibits states from discriminating on the basis of nationality or residence in granting judicial remedies to any natural or juridical person who has suffered appreciable harm. Although this principle has not been accepted by states either by enacting national legislation *en mass,* or agreeing to an international treaty, the fact that it has received some acceptance in the Rio Declaration and Agenda 21 is evidence of an evolving "soft" law. As we have seen, the Nordic Convention establishes this principle and it is to be hoped that it could be built upon through implementing mechanisms of other treaties.

E. THE ACTORS IN IEL

It is almost obvious that IEL needs to develop innovative means of overcoming the deficiencies of a sovereignty-based system of international governance. Global environmental problems have to be solved within a consensual legal system of sovereign states who alone are empowered to make legal and political decisions about them. Legal or economic theories support the plain fact that nation states act in their own best interests and not that of the global community. While they might act to save the global commons where their own self-interest is affected, their actions are premised on individual, not community needs. Not surprisingly, there are many situations in which the cries for legal measures to arrest or avert environmental perils are left unanswered.

Despite attempts to re-conceptualize international legal society along different lines, there is little evidence to support a fundamental change of the present sovereignty-based legal system. The suggestions for reform we propose accept that sovereignty will remain the basis of decision-making, and are of an incremental and functional nature premised on what appears possible. Even so, it is perfectly feasible for the present sovereignty based system to give better status and delegate more functions to NGOs.

As we have seen, NGOs are a fact of international life and they have long played an active role in IEL [see Appendix]. As such, it does not take a big leap to institutionalize them as actors entitled to contribute in the law-making and implementing processes. This has already been done by the International Labor Organization (ILO) [*see* Appendix] and it is achievable for the various international organizations to take measures to accord NGOs a similar status in their deliberations. There will, of course, be some problems concerning selection and accountability, but these are not insurmountable obstacles, and could be resolved along the same lines as the ILO. We have also already seen how that the Commission on Sustainable Development (CSD) entertains reports from NGOs. Since such a move was based on consensus, it is well within reach to hope that other organizations created by treaty will do likewise. In addition, Agenda 21 envisions a greater role for NGOs and calls on the UN system to give them increased administrative and financial support. [¶ 27.12] It further calls on the UN system to enhance the contribution of NGOs to decision-making, implementation and evaluation of its projects. [¶ 27.9 (a)]. The infusion of people power into the law-making and implementing process will help to reduce the "democratic deficit" in international law-making and implementation.

APPENDIX

A. COMMISSION ON SUSTAINABLE DEVELOPMENT

The Commission on Sustainable Development (CSD) is a functional commission of the UN Economic and Social Council (UNESCO). It was established in 1993 by the UNESCO at the request of the UN General Assembly. The CSD facilitates and reviews the progress of commitments made under the final documents of the Earth Summit. To serve this purpose, the CSD promotes a dialogue between governments and seeks to build partnerships and facilitate projects that further sustainable development. Many important conferences and meetings are held each month in New York City which seek to bring governmental officials together to work towards implementing protection for biological diversity, reducing global warming and managing and conserving the world's forests. The CSD also provides written policy guidance on implementing the Earth Summit's principle documents.

The CSD has 53 members who are elected for three year terms of office by the UNESCO from UN member countries. States that are not represented, UN organizations, accredited inter-governmental and non-governmental organizations can observe CSD sessions when they meet each year for two to

three weeks. To learn more about the CSD, see
http://www.un.org.dpcsd/did/csdback.htm.

B. EARTH COUNCIL

The Earth Council is an NGO that was formed as
a direct result of the "Earth Summit" or the "United Nations Conference on Environment and Development" (UNCED) held in Rio de Janeiro, Brazil in
1992. The Earth Council provides advice on environmentally sound, conservation-oriented approaches to sustainable development, and promotes
public awareness of environmental and conservation issues. Membership includes interested scientists, non-governmental organizations, and individuals. The organization is working on an Earth
Charter that will designate principles for guiding
and accelerating sustainable development; it will
"operationalize sustainability." The Earth Council's
headquarters are in San Jose, Costa Rica. For more
information visit http://www.ecouncil.ac.cr/.

C. THE EUROPEAN UNION

The European Union (EU), presently consisting
of 15 European member states, was first conceived
as the European Coal and Steel Community by the
Treaty of Paris in 1951, and became the European
Economic Community (EEC) pursuant to the Trea-
ty of Rome of 1957. In 1986, the Single European
Act (SEA) changed the EEC into the European
Community (EC), and its present incarnation, the
European Union (EU), is the result of the Maas-
tricht Treaty of European Union of 1993 [*see* PHI-

LIPPE SANDS & RICHARD TARASOFSKY, DOCUMENTS IN EUROPEAN COMMUNITY ENVIRONMENTAL LAW 3 & 5 (1995)]. The Treaty of Rome did not confer express or explicit power to make environmental laws upon the EC. Despite this fact, commencing in 1973 the EEC made environmental laws dealing with a variety of problems traversing air, aquatic, and terrestrial pollution, in addition to the protection of natural resources. It did so primarily on the legal basis— subsequently approved by the European Court of Justice—that such environmental laws removed non-trade barriers and harmonized trading conditions. The EC was given express power to legislate on environmental matters by the SEA, and this was reinforced by the Maastricht Treaty.

The law-making, enforcing, and judging powers of the EU are without parallel in other international organizations. The Commission and Council, with the advice of the Parliament, are empowered to make environmental laws (Regulations and Directives) within all areas of the EU's activities. To date, there are Directives and Regulations on a whole range of environmental issues, including air and water pollution issues, waste disposal and management, nuclear waste, and the protection of biodiversity. The Commission supervises the enforcement of these laws, and can bring a defaulting Member State before the compulsory jurisdiction of the European Court of Justice. In 1990, the EU established an European Environmental Agency that provides scientific and technical support to the EU and its Member States.

The EU is an unique international polity with an ambiguous legal character. It possesses a constitutional structure that approximates more closely to a non-unitary confederation than to an international organization. To the extent that it is created by treaty and derives its legal status under international law, it can be treated—at least functionally—as a new legal order or organization within international law. To learn more about the European Union, visit http://europa.eu.int/.

D. GLOBAL ENVIRONMENTAL FACILITY

The Global Environmental Facility (GEF) is a funding institution jointly created by the World Bank, the United Nations Environment Program (UNEP) and the United Nations Development Program (UNDP). It was formed in 1990, initially with $1.2 billion to be used to fund environmental protection efforts. The GEF is designed to aid developing countries with four primary environmental issues: 1) climate change, 2) stratospheric ozone depletion, 3) loss of biological diversity, and 4) pollution of international waters.

The Biodiversity and Climate Change Conventions designate the GEF as their financial mechanism [Biodiversity art. 39; Climate Change art. 11]. Pursuant to the restructuring agreed to in Agenda 21, the GEF was partially reinvented in order to enhance the methods of governance and guarantee a more balanced and equitable division of resources between the interests of developing and donor (developed) countries [Agenda 21 ch. 33.14 (a)(ii)]. To summarize the restructured GEF, the entity now has both a Council and an independent Secretariat. The Council employs a voting method known as "the double-weighted majority," in which affirmative decisions require a 60 percent majority of the total number of participants as well as a 60 percent majority of the total contributions. UNEP monitors GEF projects to ensure they have been brought into conformity with other international environmental agreements and projects, while the UNDP provides the GEF with expertise on institution building and personnel training. Because of the GEF's broad and important environmental goals, and the careful attention given to it by the Earth Summit and other environmental organizations, the GEF has been reshaped to play an important role in future efforts to protect the environment.

Administratively, the GEF Secretariat is located in the World Bank which also oversees the disbursement of GEF funds. The GEF maintains a WWW site at: http://www.worldbank.org/html/gef/gef.html.

E. GREENPEACE

In 1971, Greenpeace developed out of a Canadian citizens committee that was named "Don't Make a Wave." The organization was renamed and redirected with the purpose of "creating a green and peaceful world." Greenpeace, by its own definition, is only concerned with protecting the environment. It seeks to influence the use of the seas by "bearing witness" and by drawing attention to what it perceives to be abuses of the environment.

Greenpeace exploits, and the boats that carried Greenpeace members have become legend. The first Greenpeace action was undertaken by 12 crew who sailed a small boat into a United States atomic test site off the Alaskan coast. In the 1970s Greenpeace's first ship, the Rainbow Warrior carried out actions in the South Pacific that helped to focus world-wide attention on atmospheric bomb testing. In the 1990s the ship the Mv Greenpeace protested the use of the Antarctic as a testing ground for Trident missiles. It was rammed and nearly sunk by the United States Navy. In the 1990s the Mv Greenpeace monitored environmental damage in the Arabian Gulf during the Gulf War, and lead a campaign to designate a whaling sanctuary in the Southern Atlantic.

Today, Greenpeace maintains a network of 43 offices in 30 countries; it is headquartered in Amsterdam. It is privately funded, with 5 million contributors in 130 countries. Its staff exceeds 1300 persons. To learn more about Greenpeace, "surf" over to http://www.greenpeace.org/.

F. INTERNATIONAL ATOMIC ENERGY AGENCY

The International Atomic Energy Agency (IAEA) was established by the Statute of the International Atomic Energy Agency Oct. 26, 1956, 276 U.N.T.S. 3 (entered into force July 29, 1957). It is the product of a compromise following the failure of a United States proposal for an international body to manage and supervise all civilian nuclear operations. It is an independent intergovernmental organization that has close associations with the UN but has not been given specialized agency status. It is comprised of 113 members states, that meet annually, and a Board of Governors of 35 member states including 10 of those most advanced in atomic energy technology,

According to its Statute, its main purpose is to encourage the research, development and application of atomic energy for peaceful purposes, and to ensure through safeguards that nuclear materials are not used for military purposes [art. III (1) & (5)]. It was also required "where appropriate" to establish health and safety standards [art. III (6)]. The Chernobyl accident transformed this marginal safety mandate into a central mission, though the standards do not have the force of law, and States are not obliged to comply with them.

Despite their non-legal character, IAEA standards, regulations, codes of practice and guides cover all aspects of radiation protection and radioactive waste disposal, and are widely followed. Under the Treaty of the Non Proliferation of Nuclear Weapons, July 1, 1968, 7 I.L.M. 809 (entered into force Mar. 5, 1970) (*see* Chapter Seventeen), which was extended indefinitely in 1995, non-proliferation safeguards are made obligatory through bilateral agreements with the IAEA, and periodic compulsory inspections by the Agency are also mandated. In the result, the IAEA has assumed the role of an important international environmental organization.

G. INTERNATIONAL COURT OF JUSTICE

The International Court of Justice (ICJ) hears disputes between nation-states that have accepted its jurisdiction and provides advisory opinions to international organizations authorized to request them [*see* 48 Y.B.U.N. 1518 (1994)]. The ICJ, located in The Hague, Netherlands, was established by the Charter of the United Nations, June 26, 1945, 1 U.N.T.S. xvi (entered into force Oct. 24, 1945) and the Statute of the International Court of Justice, June 26, 1945, 59 Stat. 1031 (entered into force Oct. 24, 1945).

The ICJ consists of 15 judges who each are appointed for 9 year terms that can be renewed. Sixty states have accepted the compulsory jurisdiction of the ICJ (often with reservations) and 20 international organizations have the authority to request advisory opinions on legal questions that arise in the scope of their activities. However, the UN General Assembly and the Security Council can request an advisory opinion from the ICJ on any legal question. In July 1993, the ICJ established a seven member Chamber for Environmental Matters to aid in the formulation of an international environmental jurisprudence. But the ICJ's impact on international environmental law begins much earlier in cases [*see* Chapter Two, Sources], and it continues to play a significant role in the development of IEL [*see* Chapter Seventeen]. Though reticent at times to flex its power, the ICJ has provided authoritative restatements on many aspects of international law that have an important bearing on environmental matters. To learn more about the ICJ, visit http://www.un.org/Overview/Organs/icj.html.

H.   INTERNATIONAL LABOR ORGANIZATION

The International Labor Organization (ILO), located in Geneva Switzerland, was established in 1919 as an independent international body associated with the League of Nations. Currently, the ILO is a UN intergovernmental organization. The ILO promotes social justice and works to improve labor conditions and living standards. Substantively, the ILO's work has focused on nuclear hazards, carcinogenic substances, construction safety, and occupational health services. In a consortium with the World Health Organization and the United Nations Environment Programme, the ILO established an intergovernmental forum on chemical safety at the 1994 Stockholm International Convention on Chemical Safety. Additionally, the ILO was one of six intergovernmental organizations that finalized and adopted International Basic Safety Standards for Protection Against Ionizing Radiation.

An outstanding feature of the ILO is its tripartite character, consisting of government, employers, and employees. Each member state is represented in the ILO by a delegation made up of two members from government, one from the employers and one from the employees. Delegates vote independently, and a resolution requires a two-thirds majority.

One of the principle achievements of the ILO is its conventions (treaties) dealing with a variety of safeguards, which member states are obliged to implement. The ILO requires such compliance with a unique supervisory system, annual reports, and a complaint system granting any member the right to complain about non-observance of any ILO convention.

I. INTERNATIONAL LAW COMMISSION

The International Law Commission (ILC), comprised of eminent jurists from various countries, was created by the UN General Assembly in 1947 to help the progressive development and codification of international law. It currently has thirty-four members, each representing a different country. "Progressive development" is defined as "the preparation of draft conventions on subjects which have not yet been regulated by international law or ... not yet been sufficiently developed in the practice of states" (art.15). The ILC's first priority is acting upon requests by the General Assembly for legal work. In reality, this rarely takes place. The ILC customarily initiates draft articles which are sent to Member States, who are then requested to make comments. This preparatory work meets the definition of "progressive development," and is intended to lead to codification and the eventual formation of customary international law. The ILC is involved in various projects traversing IEL. These projects include the Draft Articles of the Law on the Non-Navigational Uses of International Watercourses, the Draft Articles on State Responsibility, the Draft Articles on International Liability, and its current project on International Liability for Injurious Con-

sequences Arising out of Acts Not Prohibited by
International Law. The International Law Commission does not presently maintain a WWW site, however, see http://www.un.org/ for information.

J. INTERNATIONAL MARITIME
ORGANIZATION

The International Maritime Organization (IMO) was established by the United Nations Maritime Conference in March, 1948. In May, 1982, the IMO adopted its current name. The IMO fosters international cooperation and exchange of information on technical matters among member states affecting international merchant shipping, encourages the general adoption of maritime safety standards, and works to prevent and control maritime pollution. The IMO makes recommendations upon issues presented to it by member states and convenes international conferences on other matters within its competence.

The IMO worked towards the recent prohibition on the dumping of low level radioactive substances at sea, which was adopted by amendment to the 1972 London Dumping Convention that also bans the dumping or incineration of industrial wastes at sea. The IMO has also been involved in strengthening the requirements of the International Convention for the Prevention of Pollution from Ships, 1973/1978 (MARPOL). In 1994, the IMO (with $5.5 Million from the Global Environment Facility and the World Bank) began the Wider Caribbean Initiative for Ship–Generated Waste in an effort to reduce vessel pollution in the Caribbean.

The IMO has aided in the establishment of major IEL conventions designed to protect the environment, including the Convention on Safety of Life at Sea 1974; the International Regulations for Preventing Collisions at Sea 1972; Standards of Training, Certification, and Watchkeeping 1978; Prevention of Pollution from Ships 1973–1978; the Establishment of an International Fund for Compensation for Oil Pollution Damage 1969; and, the International Convention on Oil Pollution Preparedness, Response, and Cooperation 1990.

The IMO consists of an Assembly, a Council, a Maritime Safety Committee, a Secretariat, and small subsidiary bodies, created to address specific issues, such as the Legal Committee or the Facilitation Committee. Currently, the organization has 153 members, and its headquarters are in Geneva, Switzerland. For more information regarding the IMO please see: http://www.navcen.usca.mil/marcomms/imo/imo.htm.

K. ORGANIZATION OF AMERICAN STATES

The Organization of American States (OAS) is an intergovernmental organization whose origin dates back to 1890, beginning with a series of conferences called the International Union of American Republics, a conference that met for commercial purposes. The OAS charter was signed in Bogota in 1948 and entered into force in 1951. The charter has since been amended many times, most recently in 1996.

The OAS has a history of promoting environmental awareness, dating back to 1938 with the Convention on Nature Protection and Wildlife Preservation in the Western Hemisphere, and most recently in the creation of an Inter–American System of Nature Conservation.

The OAS strengthens the peace and security of the Western Hemisphere and OAS member states, seeks the solution of political, juridical and economical issues, and promotes economic, social and cultural development.

The OAS meets annually and has 35 member states. Cuba's present government has been excluded from participation since 1962, but remains a member as a national entity. For more information on the OAS, see http://www.oas.org/.

L. ORGANISATION FOR ECONOMIC CO-OPERATION AND DEVELOPMENT

The Organisation for Economic Co-operation and Development (OECD) was established as the Organisation for European Economic Co-operation (OEEC) on April 16, 1948 to administer United States aid granted under the Marshall Plan and the Economic Co-operation Administration. In 1960—after Europe had attained economic recovery—the OPEC was transformed into the OECD. Attempts to strengthen the organizational structure of OECD to create a stronger institution have not been successful; it lacks supra-national legal powers which results in Members acting merely on a voluntary basis.

Article 2 of the OECD constitution requires it "to promote the efficient use of the [member] resources." Under this mandate, the OECD fosters sustainable economic growth and economic development, contributes to sound economic expansion and the expansion of world trade on a multilateral, non-discriminatory basis. The OECD began addressing environmental concerns in 1970 with the creation of the Environment Committee which is affiliated with the OECD's Executive Committee. The Committee evaluates the impact of international exchanges on the environment. The OECD was the first organization to legally define pollution. And in 1972, OECD was among the first to develop the influential "polluter-pays principle."

The OECD's Headquarters are in Paris. It is comprised of 24 Members including the European states, Canada, the United States and Japan. The administration of the OECD includes of a Council, an Executive Committee, a secretariat and various committees. Membership in the OECD is open to any government. For further information on the OECD see http://www.oecd.org/

M. SOUTH PACIFIC REGIONAL ENVIRONMENT PROGRAMME

The South Pacific Regional Environment Programme (SPREP) was founded jointly by UNEP and the South Pacific Commission in 1982. Originally under the auspices of the Regional Seas Programme, it is now an autonomous organization promoting the environmental protection of the region. It helps countries form environmental policies, educates the general population about environmental issues and conducts tests and experiments on pollution, as well as protected area management. The South Pacific Regional Environment Program does not maintain a WWW site.

N. UNITED NATIONS

The United Nations (UN) has a membership of 185 States. Article 7 of the UN Charter creates seven "principal organs": 1) the General Assembly; 2) the Security Council; 3) the Economic Council; 4) the Social Council; 5) the Trusteeship Council; 6) the International Court of Justice; and 7) the Secretariat. It also maintains fourteen specialized agencies: the International Labour Organization (ILO), the Food and Agriculture Organization of the UN (FAO), the UN Educational, Scientific and Cultural Organization (UNESCO), the World Health Organization (WHO); the World Bank, the International Monetary Fund (IMF), the International Civil Aviation Organization (ICAO), the Universal Postal Union (UPU), the International Meteorological Organization (WMO), the International Maritime Organization (IMO), the World Intellectual Property Organization (WIPO), the International Fund for Agricultural Development (IFAD), and the UN Industrial Development Organization (UNIDO). Two other important agencies are affiliated with the United Nations that cooperate with it and its various organs, but are structured as independent organizations—the International Atomic Energy Agency (IAEA) and the World Trade Organization (WTO). The UN has no specialized agency committed to the protection of the international environment, although many specialized agencies carry out functions that impact upon the environment adversely as well as beneficially. The United Nations Environment Program, though not a specialized agency, has played a vital role. The UN has also supported major environmental conferences including Stockholm in 1972, and Rio in 1992. The UN maintains an extensive WWW site at: http://www.un.org/.

O. UNITED NATIONS CONFERENCE ON TRADE AND DEVELOPMENT

The United Nations Conference on Trade and Development (UNCTAD) was created by the UN General Assembly as a one-time conference, but was later established as a permanent organ. The UNCTAD encourages international trade to stimulate economic growth and development. It also formulates procedures and policies on international trade, and makes proposals to place those procedures and policies into effect. In 1992 UNCTAD adopted "A New Partnership for Development," a program that seeks to foster economic development and environmental protection through "proper management of natural resources with a view to achieving sustainable development."

The UNCTAD has 188 member countries, drawn from the United Nations or its specialized agencies, and the International Atomic Energy Agency. To learn more about the UNCTAD take your computer for a visit to http://www.unicc.org/unctad/.

P. UNITED NATIONS DEVELOPMENT PROGRAM

The United Nations Development Program (UNDP) was formed by the UN General Assembly in 1965 from the UN Expanded Program of Technical Assistance and the UN Special Fund. UNDP's environmental efforts have primarily filled the role of strengthening existing programs and institutions. For example, UNDP played a major role in the development of the GEF. As its listed goals, UNDP works to advance human development and to serve as a consultative resource in efforts to eliminate poverty, regenerate the environment, create jobs, and advance the role of women. UNDP also helps developing countries increase the efficient use of human and natural resources. It could emerge as an important agency for advancing sustainable development in the future. The UNDP maintains a WWW site at http://www.undp.org/.

Q. UNITED NATIONS EDUCATIONAL, SCIENTIFIC, AND CULTURAL ORGANIZATION

Founded in 1946, the United Nations Educational, Scientific, and Cultural Organization (UNESCO)—a subsidiary organization of the UN—advances peace through the promotion of education, science, and culture. UNESCO has played an important role in IEL in that it has attempted to influence public opinion in environmental matters. For example, UNESCO initiated the Man and Biosphere Program in 1970 and the Intergovernmental Oceanographic Commission in 1960. It also aided in the formulation of and acts as a secretariat for the Ramsar Convention 1971 and the World Heritage Convention 1972. In addition, UNESCO works to eliminate illiteracy through worldwide elementary education programs. It also safeguards world culture, books, and art, encouraging member countries to cooperate and provide access to their intellectual and cultural enterprises.

UNESCO maintains a General Conference, an Executive Board and a Secretariat. It has 183 members, and its main office is located in Paris, France. To learn more about UNESCO, see its web site at http://www.unesco.org/.

R. UNITED NATIONS ENVIRONMENT PROGRAM

The United Nations Environment Program (UNEP) was founded in 1972 as a result of recommendations made at the Stockholm Conference on the Human Environment. It may be seen as the "environmental conscience" of the UN. UNEP coordinates solutions of different countries and agencies to environmental problems, addressing on a global scale such issues as ecology, sustainable development, methods of connecting development with environmental problems, and environmental management. UNEP seeks partnerships with other UN agencies, private businesses, non-governmental organizations, scientists, and all others who might have something to contribute to environmental solutions. One of UNEP's major functions is the maintenance of information systems. The Global Environmental Monitoring System (GEMS) is a worldwide effort to keep track of changes in the terrestrial ecosystem. The Global Resource Information Database (GRID) is a global network that maintains information referenced by the Global Environmental Outlook (GEO), which has produced the State of the Environment Report since 1994. Environment and Natural Resource Information Networking (ENRIN) coordinates local institutions, creating regional and national state-of-the-environment reports which keep those regions updated on important environmental changes.

UNEP has helped to formulate programs and treaties. For instance, UNEP was involved in the Regional Seas Programme, encompassing more than thirty environmental agreements, the Zambezi Agreement and Action Plan, the Vienna Convention on Ozone, Montreal Protocol, the Basel Convention, and the Biodiversity Convention. Moreover, the UNEP provides supportive functions as well as Secretariat functions in many of these treaties.

UNEP's Headquarters are maintained in Nairobi, Kenya. Policies are directed by its Governing Council, whose 58 members are elected to four year terms by the UN General Assembly. UNEP highlights its current activities at http://www.unep.no/.

S.   UNITED NATIONS INSTITUTE FOR TRAINING AND RESEARCH

The United Nations Institute For Training And Research (UNITAR) was established in 1965 as an independent organization maintained within the UN. Primarily, it trains UN officials, diplomats, officials of developing countries and staff of the specialized agencies within the UN. UNITAR publishes papers on such international topics as multilateral cooperation in regional development, women's roles in decision making, disaster preparedness and the elimination of racism. UNITAR plays a vital role in the formulation of IEL in that it adopts training programs and initiates research programs that foster environmental issues. The UNITAR maintains a WWW site—in French—at http://antares.mpl.orstom.fr/unitar/.

T.   WORLD BANK

The World Bank began with the formation of the International Bank for Reconstruction and Development (IBRD) at the United Nations Monetary and Financial Conference held at Bretton Woods in 1944. The Bank's original purpose was the rebuilding of post-WWII Europe. Today, the Bank provides funds and expertise for the improvement of developing nations. The World Bank is a group composed of five organizations: 1) the International Bank for Reconstruction and Development (IBRD—established in 1944), 2) the International Development Association (IDA—established in 1960), 3) the International Finance Corporation (IFC—established in 1956), 4) the Multilateral Investment Guarantee Agency (MIGA—established in 1988), and 5) the International Centre for Settlement of Investment Disputes (ICSID—established in 1966). In the 1980's, the World Bank responded to environmental concerns by creating an Environment Department and Operational Directives that addressed involuntary resettlement, indigenous people, the involvement of non-governmental organizations, and environmental assessments. Moreover, it operates the Tropical Forest Action Plan with the World Resources Institute, and the Global Environmental Facility (GEF), which assists developing countries in offsetting costs incurred from adopting environmental measures. To learn more about the World Bank, visit http://www.worldbank.org/.

U. WORLD CONSERVATION UNION

The World Conservation Union (IUCN), founded in 1948, is a non-governmental organization whose broad capabilities include the development of conservation strategies. The IUCN seeks "to influence, encourage and assist societies throughout the world to conserve the integrity and diversity of nature and to ensure that any use of natural resources is equitable and ecologically sustainable." The IUCN has 865 members which include both governments and non-governmental organizations. Although it has played an important role in the formulation of IEL jurisprudence, its resolutions are non-binding. It has helped formulate a Convention on Preservation of Biological Diversity, The 1972 World Heritage

Convention, the 1973 Convention on Trade in Endangered Species, The 1971 Convention on Wetlands of International Importance, and the 1979 Convention on Conservation of Migratory Species of Wild Animals. To learn more about the IUCN, log on to http://www.iucn.org/.

V. WORLD HEALTH ORGANIZATION

The World Health Organization (WHO), formed in 1948, is affiliated with the Economic and Social Council of the United Nations. The WHO is a directing and coordinating authority on health issues, establishing international collaboration while assisting governments as they strengthen health services and promote medical research and training. WHO's objective since 1977 has been "health for all by the year 2000."

WHO's environmentally related activities stem from the 1992 Earth Summit's declaration that countries should implement development in a sustainable fashion. Since then, the WHO assisted a number of countries in incorporating health and environmental concerns in their development plans. In 1994 the WHO created "Africa 2000" in an effort to universally provide water and sanitation services on the continent. Together with the UNEP, WHO maintains air quality monitoring devices in more than 60 countries, and the WHO has also contributed to the study of the ozone layer and climate change. In 1993, the WHO requested the ICJ to issue an advisory opinion on the Legality of the Threat or Use of Nuclear Weapons.

WHO is given authority to promote conventions on the international health issues, often in consort with other organizations. One hundred eighty-nine governments are members. Located in Geneva, Switzerland, the WHO has a full-time staff of more than 4,000 people from more than 100 nations, and a billion dollar per year budget. To learn more about the WHO, make a virtual stop at http://www.who.ch/.

W. WORLD METEOROLOGICAL ORGANIZATION

The World Meteorological Organization (WMO), which came into existence in 1950, became a specialized member of the UN in the same year. The WMO establishes international networks that work together to monitor the atmosphere and standardize measurements and statistics. The WMO has a number of programs, including the World Climate Programme (WCP). As part of the WCP, the WMO and the United Nations Environment Programme (UNEP) established the Intergovernmental Panel on Climate Change (IPCC) in 1988, which has become the platform for leading authorities on the climate change issue. WMO is developing the World Hydrological Cycle Observation System (WHYCOS) which will work towards the reduction of desertification and tempering the effects of drought.

The WMO has 184 state members and is comprised of an Executive Council, a Congress and a Secretariat, employing a full time staff of about 300 people from 50 different countries. To learn more about the WMO, visit http://www.wmo.ch/.

X. WORLD TRADE ORGANIZATION

The World Trade Organization (WTO) is a permanent institution, established in 1995 as a result of the Uruguay Round trade negotiations and the Marrakesh Declaration. It is a centralized international agency for promoting free trade. The WTO is at once a platform for international trade relations, a provider of framework trade legislation, an overseer of trade policies and a forum for the resolution of trade disputes. In a tentative and hesitant attempt to incorporate an environmental dimension in its policies, a WTO General Council Committee on trade and the environment reported to the WTO ministerial conference at Singapore in December of 1996. Potentially, 152 countries could join the WTO. To learn more about the WTO, see http://www.wto.org/.

Y. WORLD WILDLIFE FUND

The World Wildlife Fund (WWF) is a non-governmental, public and charitable organization that was established by a group of scientists and public relations experts, and was closely aligned with the World Conservation Union (IUCN). Originally, the WWF was a fund, established through charitable fund raising, that donated money to conservation efforts throughout the world. Today, WWF is an organization that also works directly with government and business to focus attention on key environmental issues like energy conservation, climate change, habitat destruction, and education. The WWF's mission is "to reverse the destruction of the Earth's natural environment and build a future in which humans can live in harmony with nature." To learn more about the WWF, go to http://www.wwf.org/.

INDEX

References are to Pages

437

ANTARCTICA

APPLICATION OF INTERNATIONAL LAW

ATMOSPHERE

AUSTRALIA

†